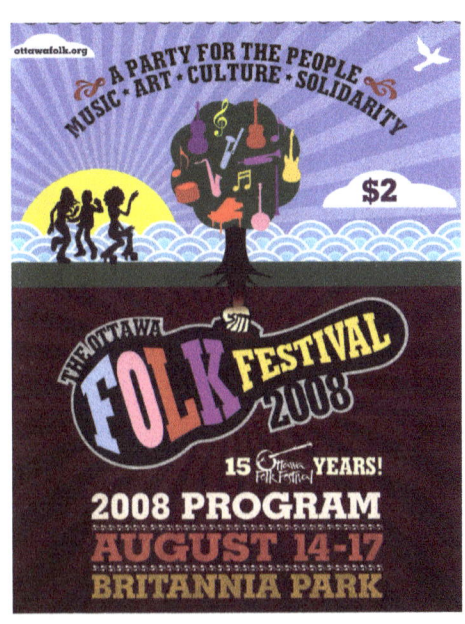

A History of the Ottawa Folk Festival (1994–2012)

Text copyright © 2018 Joyce MacPhee

Images copyright The Ottawa Folk Festival (now CityFolk) and their respective photographers

Third printing February 2019 – Minor corrections

Designed and published by Jake Morrison, With Flare Press
Ottawa, Ontario, Canada
www.withflare.ca – Jake@withflare.ca

ISBN: 978-0-9959213-1-3

The OttawaFolkHistory.org website was set up to support *A History of the Ottawa Folk Festival (1994–2012)* and to provide a home for those interested in the history of folk music in Ottawa. This book can be ordered on the website and the index is available there as a free downloadable PDF.

Drop in and say hi!

All Rights Reserved. This book cannot be reproduced, in whole or in part, nor transmitted in any form or by any means, electronic or mechanical, including xerography, photocopying, recording, nor stored in a computer system or retrieval system, without written permission from the author, Joyce MacPhee.

Tous droits réservés. Ce livre ne peut être reproduit, en tout ou en partie, ni transmis sous aucune forme ou par quelque moyen électronique ou mécanique que ce soit, y compris la xérographie, la photocopie, ou l'enregistrement, ni être stocké dans un système informatique ou de recherche documentaire, sans l'autorisation écrite de l'auteur, Joyce MacPhee

Thanks to Thom Fountain for his generous support of this book.

A History of the Ottawa Folk Festival
(1994–2012)

by Joyce MacPhee

Dedicated to the memory of Chopper McKinnon

Contents

Introduction i
Foreword
   Max Wallace v
   Chris White vii
   Jake Morrison ix
Ottawa Folk Festival Timeline xi
Year 1 – 1994 1
Year 2 – 1995 5
Year 3 – 1996 9
Year 4 – 1997 13
Year 5 – 1998 19
Year 6 – 1999 25
Year 7 – 2000 31
Year 8 – 2001 39
Year 9 – 2002 47
Year 10 – 2003 55
Year 11 – 2004 63
Year 12 – 2005 71
Year 13 – 2006 79
Year 14 – 2007 87
Year 15 – 2008 95
Year 16 – 2009 105
Year 17 – 2010 117
Year 18 – 2011 125
Year 19 – 2012 135
Volunteer Crew Pictures – 2008, 2009 149
Index
The index is available either as a separate volume or as a free PDF on the OttawaFolk.org website. It includes three categories: Ottawa Folk, Artists and Workshops.

Introduction

The **Ottawa Folk Festival** has been a spectacular success from its inception in 1994 through its evolution as **CityFolk Festival** beginning in 2015. The twenty-fifth anniversary of the Ottawa Folk Festival was celebrated at **CityFolk Festival** in fine style in September 2018 with several activities, and an impressive display of photos, videos and original artwork in the historic Aberdeen Pavilion at Lansdowne Park.

A **Folk Fest Founders' Forum** held on September 16 was moderated by music journalist **Joe Reilly** and featured key members of the original organizing committee. On hand were co-founders **Max Wallace** and **Chris White**, as well as **Joyce MacPhee**, **Pam Marjerrison**, **Gene Swimmer**, **CityFolk** executive director **Mark Monahan** and a special guest, longtime Ottawa Folk Festival co-emcee **Karen Flanagan McCarthy**. The forum members discussed the many challenges of organizing the festival, the camaraderie of the organizers and volunteers, the magical quality of the festival, and its family friendly aspects and community focus. The role played by the pillars of the Ottawa folk community, CKCU-FM folk music show *Canadian Spaces*, the **Ottawa Folklore Centre** and **Rasputin's Folk Café** was recognized. Moving or amusing anecdotes were told throughout the forum. Max Wallace was particularly adamant in explaining that without the enthusiasm and support of **Chopper McKinnon**, founder and host of *Canadian Spaces*, the festival would not have seen the light of day.

This history of the **Ottawa Folk Festival** from 1994 to 2012 is one of the twenty-fifth anniversary

CKCU Ottawa Folk Festival co-founders Max Wallace and Chris White.

projects. It was not originally intended to be in book format and consists of write-ups created each year following the festival. The chapter for each year stands as it was written and the primary enhancement is a selection of evocative photos pared down from more than 20,000 shots taken over the years by the volunteer photographers.

The **Ottawa Folk Festival** was established to showcase Canada's folk traditions through music, dance, storytelling and crafts. It grew from a vision to "one of the premier North American events of its kind", according to Allan Wigney of *X Press*. Ottawa is home to many festivals. Our festival was known for its relaxed atmosphere, enthusiastic grassroots following and loyal volunteer contingent. What a great way it was to enjoy some of the best folk music offered in the country!

The festival was initially called the **CKCU Ottawa Folk Festival** and was founded by **Max Wallace** and **Chris White**. Wallace, who was then the station manager of community radio station CKCU-FM, teamed up with White, a performing songwriter. They were joined by an enthusiastic organizing committee and an army of volunteers who helped to turn their vision into reality. The festival was launched with an enchanting day of entertainment on **Victoria Island** in 1994, where an advance ticket could be had for six bucks. The next year the festival moved to **Britannia Park**, where it flourished in this beautiful natural setting. In 1997, the festival became a not-for-profit, charitable organization, but kept "CKCU" as part of its logo until 2006.

Following a difficult financial year in 2010, the Ottawa Folk Festival came under the management of **Ottawa Bluesfest** with Executive Producer **Mark Monahan**. The festival relocated to **Hogs Back Park** in 2011 and attendance grew considerably. Thanks to the continuing generous support of **sponsors, granters, partners, donors, dedicated staff and volunteers**, the Ottawa Folk Festival operated year-round as a vibrant cultural and community organization until 2014.

In 2015 the Ottawa Folk Festival was rebranded as **CityFolk Festival** and relocated to historic **Lansdowne Park**, home of the former **Central Canada Exhibition** from 1888 to 2010. In its fourth year, **CityFolk Festival** is thriving and has introduced many innovations including **Marvest**, free concerts held in local bars and restaurants that bring the community together to enjoy music.

The inspiration for the Ottawa Folk Festival dates back many years. In 1960, the iconic coffee house **Le Hibou** opened its doors and until 1975 showcased many folk legends, including Canadians Joni Mitchell and Bruce Cockburn, and Americans John Prine and Kris Kristofferson. In 1976, the **Ottawa Folklore Centre** opened as a folk music emporium and served the community as a combination retail store and musical educational centre for 38 years. The **Festival for the Folks,** a major Canadian music festival, was launched the same year and ran until 1979.

After the Festival for the Folks ended, Ottawa continued to be a major centre for folk music. *Canadian Spaces*, the longest-running folk show on Canadian community radio, was launched in 1980 by the late **Chopper McKinnon**, who was host till his death in 2013. The show still thrives with host **Chris White** at the sound board. In 1981, **Rasputin's**, one of Canada's finest folk venues, opened its doors. After operating for 27 years, sadly the club closed in 2008 following a fire and owner **Dean Verger** retired from the restaurant business. Fortunately, **Spirit of Rasputin's** formed the next year. This volunteer organization presents myriad folk concerts and events each year in the community.

The **Ottawa Folklore Centre**, founded by Arthur McGregor and his wife the late Terry Penner, closed in 2015 due to financial problems after 38 years of operation. It is greatly missed by customers, musicians, music students and others in the folk community. However other initiatives including the **Grassroots Festival**, which was launched in 2015, are continuing to celebrate Canadian folk music and contribute to the local community.

Many people were involved in bringing the festival to fruition and helping it thrive over the years. **Max Wallace** dreamed up the idea for the Ottawa Folk Festival and had a talent for inspiring a team that made it all happen. We called him our "fearless leader" and he led us into the festival years. Max was greatly missed when he left Ottawa in 1995 to pursue writing opportunities. It is not surprising that he has enjoyed considerable success as an internationally known author!

Chris White has played many essential roles in the Ottawa Folk Festival. Not only was he a co-founder of the festival along with Max Wallace, he was artistic director from 1994 to 2009. Chris, who is known for his enthusiasm and support of all things musical, is the ultimate community event organizer. His organizational abilities were put to good use for the celebration of the twenty-fifth anniversary of the folk festival at CityFolk this year, where he spearheaded numerous activities including a multi-media display, a master class with veteran folk singer Janis Ian and off-site concerts. Chris is also an incredible singer-songwriter on topics both humorous and profound, with music that appeals to both children and adults, and leads several local choirs.

The Ottawa Folk Festival would probably not have survived without the capable leadership of **Gene Swimmer**, who was a member of the original organizing committee and executive director from 1996 to 2006. Under Gene's wise management the festival weathered early financial crises and came into its own at Britannia Park. "I think we have the best quality of life of any festival," said Gene in the *Ottawa Citizen* in 2002. "We don't want to be the biggest festival, we want to be a good middle-sized festival." Kudos also to Gene's wife **Carol Silcoff**, an invaluable volunteer who worked diligently behind the scenes as a fundraiser and grant writer.

Pam Marjerrison and her husband **Alan Marjerrison** made exceptional contributions to the Ottawa Folk Festival and are one of many families that worked together over the years to make the event viable.

While Alan masterminded the schedule for volunteer drivers during the festival, Pam supported the festival in several ways. A member of the original organizing committee, she served as vice-president and later president of the board of the Ottawa Folk Festival. She also took on tasks including writing press releases and promotional information, proofreading the festival programs, and assembling photo boards.

One of Pam's most important projects was helping to organize the Ottawa Folk Festival materials to be deposited in the City of Ottawa Archives, which was a gargantuan task.

Artist **Roberta Huebener** created many images that publicized the festival, including the famous banjo logo that graced many signs, posters, banners and volunteer pins. Another exceptional contributor to the Ottawa Folk Festival was musician and artist **Arthur II**, who facilitated the creation of several participatory murals, and encouraged everyone to have as much fun as humanly possible while taking part.

A special thanks goes to **Pam Marjerrison** and **Chris White**, who carried out many careful reviews of this history over the years. A big thank you to **Jake Morrison**, who spent a great deal of effort in making the photos available in digital format over the years and is the publisher of this book.

Finally, I would like to acknowledge some of the

performers, volunteers and contributors who have passed away since the festival began in 1994. The following people are remembered fondly: **Daisy DeBolt**, **Dario Domingues**, **Willie Dunn**, **Beth Ferguson**, **Levon Helm**, **Ron Hynes**, **Penny Lang**, **Kate McGarrigle**, **Chopper McKinnon**, **Stuart McLean**, **Larry "the Bird" Mootham**, **Odetta**, **Richard Patterson**, **Colleen Peterson**, **Terry Penner** and **Jesse Winchester**.

Like the festival itself, this history was a labour of love. I was so thrilled with the festival I wrote an account each year, beginning with year one, never knowing each year if it would continue. The book recounts the festival's roots and highlights. Luckily, I had help over the years from many people who offered information or support. **Rachel Hauraney** assisted with the write-up for 2010, and **Lynn Haggarty** wrote the synopsis for 2011. In 2012, dedicated note takers included **Corinne Baumgarten**, **Elizabeth De Castro**, **Roberta Della Picca** and **Mary McHale**.

Read on to get a taste of the Ottawa Folk Festival's flavour and relive some of its most wonderful moments. Feel free to submit any comments about this book to the **OttawaFolkhistory.com** website and share your own memories and photos.

See you at the next **CityFolk Festival**!

Joyce MacPhee

Local artist Maryl Morris created this watercolour of the main stage while attending an early CKCU Ottawa Folk Festival performance at Britannia Park.

Local artist Maryl Morris created this mixed media artwork portraying Valdy at the CKCU Ottawa Folk Festival in either 1994 or 1997.

Rising from the Ashes

by Max Wallace

The Ottawa Folk Festival was almost over before it began. It was 1993 and I was the Station Manager of CKCU-FM. A year earlier, I had started the Ottawa International Busker Festival in response to the City of Ottawa's crackdown on street performers. The festival – which attracted 135,000 people to Sparks Street Mall over Civic Holiday weekend – had just wrapped up its second edition and enjoyed a healthy financial surplus. Still on a festival high (or perhaps another type), I happened to be listening to *Canadian Spaces* – the station's most popular program – and wondered why Ottawa didn't have its own folk festival. We now had an infrastructure in place, a massive pool of volunteers, credibility in the folk community, and the ability to secure cultural funding. How hard could it be to start our own?

So with the idealism and naiveté of youth (I still had all my hair), I paid a visit to the old Ottawa Folklore Centre to consult the elder statesman of the local folk scene, Arthur McGregor, expecting him to embrace the idea with his seal of approval. Instead, he told me a harrowing tale.

Less than 15 years earlier, Ottawa had hosted a renowned folk festival, the Festival for the Folks, which by 1979 had emerged as one of the country's greatest showcases for Canadian folk music, including legends such as Stan Rogers, Liona Boyd and the McGarrigle Sisters. That year, however, a Carleton University bar manager absconded with the entire gate receipts. (He was later arrested in Texas by the FBI for gun running, but that's another story.) According to Arthur, nobody got paid. Not the talent, not the suppliers. "Nobody's going to want to have anything to do with another folk festival," Arthur warned. Dispirited, I vowed then and there to abandon the whole hare-brained scheme.

Not long afterwards, I was working on a Saturday while Chopper McKinnon was on air hosting *Canadian Spaces*. I wandered into the studio to chat with him and happened to mention the idea of a folk festival along with Arthur's dire warning. To my surprise, he immediately embraced the idea wholeheartedly. At the time, Chopper happened to be working at the CBC as a music programmer. Days later, he marched me to the studios of their afternoon drive show, "All in a Day", where we went on air to talk about CKCU's new folk festival. Somehow, it had already become a fait accompli. When the host asked Chopper what the festival might look like, he said he could picture an eclectic line-up featuring the likes of Murray McLauchlan and (the great Ottawa indie punk band) Furnaceface.

A day later, I received a call from a fellow named Chris White, who had heard us on the CBC. Chris was the organizer of a local song-writing group and had extensive contacts in the local music community. I suggested we meet at Carleton's graduate pub, Mike's Place, to discuss the idea. That afternoon over Strongbows, Chris and I discussed our common vision for a festival and it was immediately clear we were on the same page. We knew that long-established Canadian folk festivals such as Mariposa and Edmonton had run into continuous financial disasters and racked up huge deficits by relying on headliners. Those festivals, it seemed, were always one rainy weekend away from bankruptcy. We vowed instead to create an event that promoted local and Canadian talent and drew crowds with a family-friendly vibe rather than big name acts. And because CKCU was backing the risky enterprise, I was determined to use the same formula that I had employed for the successful Ottawa Busker Festival. Through a combination of funding grants and advance ticket sales, the fest would ideally break even before the first person passed through the gates.

Chris sent word through his networks and I wrote a short piece in CKCU's magazine, *Trans-FM,* that we were starting a folk festival launching in the summer of 1994. Before long, we had assembled a team and had also secured support from Arthur McGregor who was now convinced that we could pull it together after all. With a seemingly impossible deadline, we met each week at the late lamented Rasputin's – the wonderful folk café run by Dean Verger, carrying on the legacy of his mother Helen, the godmother of the Ottawa folk scene.

Twenty-five years later, I have unforgettable memories of the festival itself that still bring tears to my eyes from the two years that I served as Executive Director before I moved back to Montreal to make films. When Valdy sang "Rain Rain Go Away" and the sun finally came out over Victoria Island on August 28, 1994 (banishing the ulcer that had formed in my gut when I saw the weather forecast that morning), it was a moment that would presage a truly magical event. But for me, the indelible memory forever imprinted in my mind is those months eating Dean's pasta and home fries while bringing the festival to life with the greatest group of people I have ever had the privilege to work with.

The rest is history.

November 2018

Max Wallace is a New York Times-bestselling author and Gemini-nominated documentary filmmaker whose book Muhammad Ali's Greatest Fight, *about Ali's battle with the US government over the Vietnam War, was turned into a Hollywood movie directed by Oscar-winning filmmaker Stephen Frears. His book* In the Name of Humanity: The Secret Deal to End the Holocaust, *was shortlisted for the RBC Taylor Prize for best work of literary non-fiction and won the 2018 Canadian Jewish Literary Award.*

Co-founder Max Wallace was presented with this beautiful photograph taken by Alan Marjerrison of the first CKCU Ottawa Folk Festival at a celebration to honour him before he left Ottawa to pursue other opportunities in Montreal.

Looking Wa-a-ay Back...

by Chris White

Composed – with thanks – on unceded traditional Algonquin territory

First of all, thank you *so* much to Jake Morrison and Joyce MacPhee for the amazing skill, energy and dedication they have put into creating this amazing testament to the fascinating phenomenon known as the Ottawa Folk Festival! Thanks also to the other photographers, writers, proofreaders, pre-purchasers and well-wishers who have made this book possible. I would also like to reiterate Max Wallace's statement that the core reason for the festival's creation was the large, loyal contingent of "Space Cadets" who loved the *Canadian Spaces* folk radio show Chopper McKinnon founded in 1980. Let us all raise a favourite hot or cold brown drink to Chopper...!

Looking back over the past 25 years (hey, how did that happen?), I am awestruck by the many incredible and beautiful things we all accomplished together over the years. My primary feeling at this point is one of immense *gratitude* to everyone who worked together to make those things possible! To the many fine, fun, fabulous people I have met along the way – thank you, one and all, for being who you are and for lending your time and talents to the cause – it has been a magnificent team effort right from the start!

From its humble beginnings as a one-day experiment in 1994 – an experiment that, as Max notes in his article, was possibly rescued from rain by the magic of Valdy's singing (!) – the Ottawa Folk Festival has had a major impact on countless volunteers, performers, audiences and community partners.

My model for folk festival programming was based on the brilliant work of the late Estelle Klein who programmed the Mariposa Folk Festival between 1964 and 1980. I still remember lining up at the Toronto Ferry Terminal waiting to make the journey – literally and symbolically – across the water to the magical world of Mariposa, where I was transfixed and transformed by the many marvels on multiple daytime stages and activity areas. One of Estelle's specialties was putting musicians from vastly different musical, cultural and geographical backgrounds on stage together – with unique and astounding results. She also created numerous opportunities for attendees to learn new skills and to participate in arts activities of various types. Another highlight of her programming approach was her early and ongoing focus on Indigenous traditions and art forms.

Imagine my surprise some years later when the opportunity materialized for me to help create and program a folk festival located on the shores of the beautiful and sacred Ottawa River in a gorgeous park featuring magnificent trees, hills, sunsets, moon and stars... oh my!

Over time, my experience with the festival taught me that environments can be designed in a way that will increase the probability that magic, serendipity and synchronicity will occur ... as anyone who attended the festival during the day can attest! I also learned over time how deeply satisfying it is for people to *build* something as part of a group workshop, whether it be a paper crane, a ukulele, a dance floor, a weekend choir or an entire festival. It turns out that when we build things together, the experience also builds *us* as individuals and as a community.

As we all worked together to evolve the festival over the years, we developed more and more ways for festival goers of all ages and abilities to play an active role, by doing things like rehearsing and performing with a festival choir, learning to play an instrument, painting on a mural, building a ukulele, making an origami crane, dancing on a sprung floor in an inspiring dance tent... and much more!

Another important area of increasing focus for us was finding ways to make the experience of volunteers as satisfying and enriching as possible, in recognition of the fact that the volunteers are the heart, the soul and the future of the festival.

I'm proud of the early leadership we showed as an organization in demonstrating environmental responsibility, respecting Aboriginal rights and traditions, developing "win-win-win" community partnerships, and finding ways to increase accessibility in all senses of the word.

One of my favourite folk festival memories was sitting in a tipi at Britannia Park with the late Algonquin elder, Grandfather William Commanda. We were facing the main stage where Tony D was playing a wonderful solo set in the middle of the afternoon. The uplifting "folkfest vibe" was in the air everywhere. Buffy Sainte-Marie was heading to the festival to meet with Grandfather Commanda and members of a youth group from the Odawa Native Friendship Centre. It was one of those moments where everything was perfectly aligned, and life's wonder and beauty were fully evident – yay!

As we look back now at the extensive, impressive, ongoing results of those first small steps we took years ago, it seems clear that we should never underestimate the potential impact of our actions, no matter how humble they might appear at first. As we reflect on how many fabulous things resulted from a small group of community-minded music lovers following their dream, here's a suggestion: Let's start now to plant some seeds for new projects and events that will grow and flourish over the *next* 25 years! Please get in touch if you have suggestions or would like to get involved in any way! In the meantime, to paraphrase Chopper, I'm chris@folkzone.ca ... and I love you!

Chris
November 2018

"Getting to a world of peace and justice will involve millions of smiles as we recognize and treasure our diversity, our different paths, our different values." – Pete Seeger

Picture this...
by Jake Morrison

Going through the old materials I see the creativity that blossomed in all areas of the festival including graphic design, programming, site construction, sign-making, volunteer engagement, stage design and lighting – to name a few – and (especially dear to my heart) photography.

In 1994 and 1995 **Joyce MacPhee** was the primary photographer for the event and other volunteers such as **Alan Marjerrison** also contributed some excellent shots. **Jim Martin** coordinated a crew of four in 1996. Over the years some people joined and some left. By 2012 the crew had grown with the festival to 10.

I have made some effort to get the names of all the photographers involved. **Tim Ladd**, crew leader from 1997-2004, and **Shaun Weatherup**, crew leader from 2005-2008, have helped quite a lot. I joined the crew in 2008 and then joined **Dave Haggarty** as coleader from 2009-2011. In 2012 **Kate Morgan** joined me as co-leader. I have a pretty good handle on who the photographers were in those years but, in the end, I have had to be satisfied with what I know is a partial list for the earlier years. If you don't see yourself named below please get in touch as there may be a second edition and corrections will be made! For the years 1994-2012, in alphabetical order, the photographers I have found were:

≈ Sandy Anweiler ≈ Brian Arscott ≈ Robin Chu ≈ Peter Coffman ≈
≈ Jim Commins ≈ Heather Dawe ≈ Paul Dickie ≈ Kristi Dyck ≈ Jamie Fleck ≈
≈ Thom Fountain ≈ Graham Grant ≈ Michele Grignon ≈ Dave Haggarty ≈
≈ David Harvey ≈ Cari Hauraney ≈ Sarah Hautcoeur ≈ Suzy Juneau ≈
≈ Mark Knight ≈ Tim Ladd ≈ Joyce MacPhee ≈ Steve Malone ≈
≈ Jim Martin ≈ Kate Morgan ≈ Jake Morrison ≈ Mark Prest ≈
≈ Graham Sibthorpe ≈ Julie Stern ≈ Edie Tomaso ≈ Sebastian Traczyk ≈
≈ Nick Wadden ≈ Shaun Weatherup ≈ Andrea Wickham ≈ Lisa Wong ≈
≈ Michele Wozny ≈ Ming Wu ≈ Mike Young ≈

Finally I want to thank the people who have helped so much in the last two months: Shaun, Tim, Pam, Alan, Chris and, especially Joyce. The helpfulness and enthusiasm has brought back a strong whiff of the magic of the volunteer folk festival!

Thanks for the journey!

Jake Morrison
November 2018

Various Photography Crew members – always looking.

Ottawa Folk Festival Timeline

Year 1 – 1994
- First CKCU-FM Ottawa Folk Festival is held on **Victoria Island**.
- Festival is cofounded by Executive Director **Max Wallace** and Artistic Director **Chris White**. One-day volunteer-driven festival is a success despite weather challenges.
- Five daytime stages, one evening stage sets pattern.
- Support came from **CKCU-FM, Ottawa Folklore Centre, Rasputin's Folk Café, Rogers Television, Nortel** and dedicated organizing committee members.
- Concert series is launched in the fall thanks to a partnership with the **National Library of Canada** (now **Library and Archives Canada**).

Year 2 – 1995
- Festival moves to **Britannia Park** and extends to two days (Saturday and Sunday). The first **Helen Verger Award** is presented.
- First festival auditions are held at **Rasputin's**.
- **Festival of the Friends Program** is launched.

Year 3 – 1996
- **Gene Swimmer** assumes role of Festival Director.
- Festival expands to three days (Friday, Saturday and Sunday).
- Financial crisis at CKCU-FM leads to festival severing formal ties with the radio station; without any income reserves, the prospect of a summer festival is very much in doubt.
- In early December, much-needed funds are raised from two sold-out **Arlo Guthrie** benefit concerts and accompanying silent auctions (organized by **Carol Silcoff**).
- Festival website created by **Alrick Huebener**.

Year 4 – 1997
- Festival registers as a non-profit corporation and applies for charitable status. Festival banjo logo is created by **Roberta Huebener**.
- Thanks to additional concert revenues and government grants, the festival goes ahead.
- **Bruce Cockburn** has successful homecoming; he performs solo and in a reunion with **The Children**. First **Festival Weekend Choir** is led by **Andy Rush**.

Year 5 – 1998
- After hours concerts begin at **Luxor Hotel**.
- Radio and television broadcasts are made from the festival.
- *FolkBits* e-mail bulletin is launched by **Brian Silcoff** on November 26.

Year 6 – 1999
- First year of sponsored stages names.

Year 7 – 2000
- Acts from every province and territory are featured.

Year 8 – 2001
- NAC/Fourth Stage partnership launches second concert series. Festival has its first sold-out night with **John Prine**.
- Last year of **Nortel** sponsorship.

Year 9 – 2002
- First year of **CUPE** sponsorship/partnership.
- Green initiatives including reusable plates are introduced.
- **CUPE EnviroTent** is created and presents workshops.

Year 10 – 2003
- Festival celebrates tenth anniversary and expands to four days (Thursday is added).

Year 11 – 2004
- Emphasis is on youth acts including the **Weakerthans, Feist** and

Broken Social Scene.
- **Galaxie Rising Stars Award** and **One Fret Less Award** are introduced.
- Videocassette released for sale titled **"Inspiration"** featuring performers from the 10th anniversary of the festival (produced by **Chris White** in conjunction with **Rogers Television**) and **"Ten Years of Uninterrupted Folk"**, a documentary celebrating the tenth anniversary of the festival (written, produced and directed by **Joyce MacPhee** in conjunction with Rogers Television).

Year 12 – 2005
- Rolling Stones concert leads to change of festival dates to third week in August. Emphasis is on youth acts, including the **Weakerthans** and **Feist**.

Year 13 – 2006
- **Ottawa Folklore Centre** cofounder **Arthur McGregor** receives **Helen Verger Award**. **Rasputin's Folk Café** celebrates 25th anniversary. Thursday night programming held in downtown venues.

Year 14 – 2007
- **Tamara Kater** joins festival as Executive Director.
- Major site redesign reduces vehicular traffic and puts volunteers and artisans at centre of site. More green initiatives and connections to community organizations are created.
- **Arthur II** heads participatory mural project.
- **GCTC Acoustic Waves** series is revived to great acclaim.

Year 15 – 2008
- Fifteenth anniversary of festival.
- Paid staff includes Executive Director, Artistic Director, and Volunteer and Outreach Manager. New governance approach and strategic plan are adopted; board of directors is expanded.
- New larger office increases efficiency.
- More educational and outreach initiatives begin.
- Festival receives nomination for **Best Festival** at **2008 International Folk Alliance Conference**. Dance tent is a hit!

Year 16 – 2009
- **Tatiana Nemchin** joins as Director of Planning and Operations. Artistic Director **Chris White** resigns in October 2009.
- **Festival Green Team** and partners create the first plastic water bottle-free festival.

Year 17 – 2010
- **Dylan Griffith** signs on as Festival Director. Programming focused on community involvement and sustainability. Last festival is held at beautiful **Britannia Park**.

Year 18 – 2011
- Ottawa Folk Festival comes under the supervision and artistic guidance of **Mark Monahan**, Bluesfest Executive Producer.
- New General Manager (**Mark Morrison**) is brought on board, with continuity provided through core staff members (sponsorship manager **Ana Miura**, volunteer manager **Emily Addison** and office manager **Crystal Kirkpatrick**).
- Venue changes to **Hogs Back Park** with a four-day format.
- **Free section** of festival features workshops and interactive sessions.

Year 19 – 2012
- Ottawa Folk Festival enjoyed continued success at new location and under new management. Festival moves to early September timeslot with a five-day format.

- Attendance doubles to between 25,000 and 30,000.
- Free section of festival flourishes with 4,000 to 5,000 visitors.
- Last festival appearance of long-time emcee and supporter **Chopper McKinnon**, who passed away in 2013.

Sources: Roberta Huebener and Joyce MacPhee

Year 1 – 1994
The Festival Is Launched

In 1994, after CKCU-FM Station Manager **Max Wallace** wrote a brief article in the program guide *Trans FM* about the possibility of starting up the CKCU-FM Ottawa Folk Festival, he was delighted with the response. Many eager volunteers came forward to offer their services. Wallace worked closely with Chris White and a strong volunteer contingent to bring the project to fruition. After 10 months of preparation, the first annual CKCU Ottawa Folk Festival was held on **Victoria Island**. This idyllic setting nestled between Ottawa and Hull proved to be the perfect spot for a small festival. The one-day event ran from noon to midnight on August 28, 1994 and included afternoon theme stages and evening concerts. The festival has maintained this basic format.

Festival framed by the ruins of the Carbide Building on Victoria Island.

The historic Victoria Island site provided an intimate performance space in a natural setting, and offered panoramic views of the Ottawa River, the Parliament Buildings, and other National Capital Area landmarks. The hospitality, storytelling and craft areas were housed in the picturesque ruins of the historic **Carbide Building**.

If the verdant island setting was idyllic, the lineup was equally impressive for a modest event operating on a shoestring budget. In the weeks leading up to the festival, an enormous amount of excitement and publicity was generated by the media when it was announced that **David Wiffen** would appear. Although the morning of the festival dawned grey, windy and rainy, the clouds parted and the evening main stage performances commenced beneath the canopy of a cloudless sky. **Valdy**, **David Wiffen**, **Lynn Miles**, **Ian Tamblyn**, **Dario Domingues**, **The Bird Sisters**, **Penny Lang** and **Seventh Fire** performed on the main stage.

View of Parliament Hill from the Discovery Stage.

Festival goers were greeted at the entrance gate by the African-inspired drumming of **Kebba Jobateh** and his drumming circle. The afternoon workshops proved popular, taking place simultaneously on five stages offering the audience a wide variety of musical styles and themes to choose from. Over a hundred musicians appeared throughout the day.

The main stage opened with **Arthur McGregor**, the owner of the **Ottawa Folklore Centre** and a generous founding sponsor. He performed a beautiful acoustic version of "O Canada" to start things off in style. Arthur opened the festival with an acoustic version of the national anthem from each year until 2013. Although Arthur usually performed the anthem on acoustic guitar in a ragtime style, he played it on the mandolin one year (in 2006 or 2007).

Front: Tony Turner and Jennifer Noxon. Back: Christine Graves, Beth Ferguson and Lee Hayes.

Local artists at the festival included **Alex Sinclair**, **Willie Dunn**, **Alex Houghton**, **Nathan Curry**, **Sneezy Waters**, **Guy Del Villano**, **Andrea Karam**, **Malaika** and **Bob Stark**. The workshops included the themes of First Nations, bluegrass, blues, protest, humour, acoustic guitar, international, women's voices and vocal harmonies.

Two popular showcases celebrating the area's traditional folk heritage included the **Ottawa Valley Fiddling and Stepdancing Stage** and a lively **Ceilidh** (Celtic jamboree). **Gina Gilchrist**, daughter of legendary stepdance champion Donnie Gilchrist, appeared with some of her stepdance students. Ottawa Valley musicians, including veteran fiddler **Wilf Gillis** accompanied the dancers. A lively ceilidh hosted by **Ian Robb** of **Friends of Fiddlers' Green** and **Finest Kind** followed. They were joined by a number of local musicians performing Celtic and Celtic-inspired material.

Alex Houghton and Ian Tamblyn

For pure nostalgia, it was hard to beat the three tribute stages: the **Stan Rogers Stage**, the **Le Hibou Stage** and the **Woodstock Stage**. **Ian Robb** hosted more than a dozen local musicians who performed their favourite Stan Rogers songs. The popular **Le Hibou Stage** featured artists who had appeared at the legendary Ottawa club such as **Valdy**, **David Wiffen**, **Sandy Crawley** and **Bonnie Bradley**. When the **Woodstock Stage** was halted by a sudden downpour, **Valdy** led the audience in an impromptu rendition of "Rain, Rain Go Away" with the desired positive results.

Talented but not yet seasoned musicians had the opportunity to appear on the **Discovery Stage**. **Acoustic Moon**, a group of high school students, were among the youngest performers. **Writer's Bloc**, a local songwriting group, also held a session on this stage.

Malaika on the Tree Stage: Lee Hayes, Neema Mugala, Beth Ferguson and Stella Haybukai.

The evening concert featured a triumphant return to the stage by **David Wiffen**, who was greeted by a thunderous standing ovation. The excitement continued with an energetic and polished set by **Valdy**, who proved he had not forgotten his Ottawa hometown roots.

Valdy performing on a daytime stage.

Valdy was presented with a **Lifetime Achievement Award** in recognition of his valuable contributions to Canadian folk music. This award was designed by **Arthur McGregor**, co-owner of the **Ottawa Folklore Centre**. It was constructed from a 1940s handmade guitar by master builder **Edward Dick**. The evening wound down with a singalong around the bonfire, where fire juggler **Tawney Ross** gave a mesmerizing performance.

Volunteers at a CKCU
Ottawa Folk Festival benefit concert.

The main stage emcees, **Chopper McKinnon** and **Karen Flanagan McCarthy**, played an important role in the festival. The two enjoy a special chemistry onstage and their repartee is an important part of the main stage shows. Chopper provides the English introductions while Karen provides both French and English commentary.

Chopper McKinnon modeling the festival t-shirt and clowning for the camera.

Chopper McKinnon has been a vital force on the Ottawa music scene since the 1970s. His many accomplishments include hosting *Canadian Spaces*, the longest running folk show on Canadian community radio. *Canadian Spaces* first took to the airwaves of CKCU-FM in 1980 and has attracted a loyal following of "Space Cadets". Chopper also hosts the **CKCU Ottawa Folk Festival Benefit Concert Series** and the **Acoustic Waves** concert series.

Karen Flanagan McCarthy is a freelance writer and broadcaster whose work has been heard on CBC Radio programs including *Morningside, Gabereau, Between the Covers*, and *All in a Day*. She appears frequently as an emcee at local music and charitable events.

Year 2 – 1995
The CKCU Ottawa Folk Festival Finds a New Home

Buoyed by the initial success of the CKCU Ottawa Folk Festival in 1994, the festival organizers decided to expand to a two-day format. Out of respect for the native occupation of Victoria Island by Algonquin Indians, the festival was moved to a new location. The natural choice was **Britannia Park**, a beautiful west-end site on the Ottawa River. Britannia Park was also the site of the **Festival for the Folks** from 1977 to 1979. **Chopper McKinnon** and **Karen Flanagan McCarthy** returned to host the main stage throughout the festival.

Ottawa's fine folk tradition was celebrated with music, dance and storytelling. There was plenty to celebrate. Fifteenth anniversary theme stages paid tribute to two Ottawa institutions: ***Canadian Spaces***, the longest-running Canadian folk music program on community radio; and the folk club **Rasputin's**. The **Le Hibou Déjà Vu** workshop tipped the hat to Canada's longest running coffeehouse and featured several prominent artists who performed there.

Kids cavorting with a parachute.

Colleen Peterson and Murray McLauchlan onstage.

Sunshine sparkling like a million diamonds on the water in Britannia Bay, a warm summer rain, a glowing pastel sunset, and a meteor crossing a dark Ontario sky. All of these natural elements helped to create an enchanting atmosphere at the **second annual CKCU Ottawa Folk Festival** held **August 26 to 27, 1995**. The festival exceeded all expectations with double the attendance of the previous year, and garnered rave reviews from critics and the community alike. "If a festival can be measured in moments of music magic, the second annual CKCU Ottawa Folk Festival was a resounding success," enthused **Lynn Saxberg** of the *Ottawa Citizen*.

Arthur McGregor, owner of the **Ottawa Folklore Centre**, opened the main stage with a wonderful acoustic guitar interpretation of "O Canada".

Ottawa Valley fiddling, stepdancing and singing were showcased during three sessions, including a tribute to the late **Mac Beattie**. The **Ottawa Songwriters** session hosted talented local performers, as did the songwriting group **Writer's Bloc**. On both days, Ottawa storytellers wove magical tales for their attentive audiences. The **Ottawa Citizen Family Area** kept kids busy all weekend long with a variety of daytime activities, crafts, costumes and entertainment, including face painting and great performers.

Young juggler.

The afternoon stages featured **Celtic**, **country**, **bluegrass**, **gospel** and **world music**. There were also afternoon sessions highlighting **instrumental music**, as well as sessions exploring the **potential of the human voice** and our **connections to the natural world**. A wonderful blend of familiar and new musicians performed 30-minute sets on the **Showcase Stage**. The lineup for the acoustic guitar theme stage was hard to beat: **Don Ross**, **Stephen Fearing**, **Alex Houghton**, **Lynn Miles** and **Alan Marsden**.

Alex Houghton

Audience participation was an important element of the festival. Kids clapped and sang along with **Eric Nagler** at a Saturday afternoon concert, while families sashayed around the hall during a traditional contra dance on Sunday afternoon. **The Arrogant Worms** were successful in getting adults and children alike to imitate a chomping alligator, with hysterical results.

Hundreds of stargazers were on hand Sunday afternoon to witness the **Swingin' on a Star** stage. **Murray McLauchlan** performed along with other stellar artists who had appeared on his national CBC Radio show from 1989 to 1994 including **Colleen Peterson, Lynn Miles** and **David Wiffen**. The sweethearts of the festival proved to be **Malaika**, a four-woman acoustic harmony group that specializes in acapella music performed in several different languages.

As if by cue, a meteor streaked across the sky during a passionate encore by guitarist **Don Ross**.

Willie P. Bennett

The most poignant moment of the festival was when **Murray McLauchlan** was presented with the first **Helen Verger Award** for his contributions to Canadian folk music. The award was instituted to honour the memory of the late **Helen Verger**, co-owner of Rasputin's coffeehouse, mother of **Dean Verger**, and a friend to many in the Ottawa folk community. Helen's generosity and love of music embodies the spirit of the CKCU Ottawa Folk Festival, and the award is a fitting tribute to a woman who did much to foster the local folk scene.

Finally, the crowd bid adieu to CKCU Ottawa Folk Festival Director **Max Wallace**, who left his job as station manager at CKCU-FM to pursue writing opportunities in Montreal. The baton was passed into the capable hands of **Gene Swimmer**, an avid folk fan and a professor in the School of Public Administration at Carleton University.

The 1995 CKCU Ottawa Folk Festival had celebrations of the three pillars of folk music in Ottawa

Dean Verger, owner of Rasputin's Folk Café, with a cake in honour of its 15th anniversary.

Cake celebrating the 15th anniversary of the CKCU folk music program *Canadian Spaces*.

Arthur McGregor celebrates the twentieth year of the Ottawa Folklore Centre.

Year 3 – 1996

A Three-Day Festival at Britannia!

In 1996, the CKCU Ottawa Folk Festival flourished under the direction of **Gene Swimmer** and artistic director **Chris White**. The festival made another natural progression, and expanded to three days of folk at **Britannia Park (August 23 to 25)**. It continued to offer an eclectic range of performers and styles. The main stage performers included **Quartette**, **Bert Jansch**, **Lynn Miles**, **Moxy Früvous**, **Thomas Handy Trio**, **Laura Smith**, **Lennie Gallant**, **Danielle Martineau and Rockabayou**, and **Malaika**. The year also marked the 20th anniversary of the **Ottawa Folklore Centre**. **The Helen Verger Award** was jointly presented to **Colleen Peterson** and **Sylvia Tyson** for their valuable contributions to Canadian folk music. **Chopper McKinnon** and **Karen Flanagan McCarthy** returned to host the main stage throughout the festival.

Karen Flanagan McCarthy enjoying a laugh with Chopper McKinnon.

Benefit Concert Series

The 1995/1996 **Benefit Concert Series** held at the National Library of Canada featured the following performers.
- Dec. 16: **Don Ross** (with special guests Finest Kind)
- Feb. 24: **Imaginary Heaven** (with special guest Karen Leslie Hall)
- April 6: **Connie Kaldor** (with special guest Night Sun)
- May 4: **Colleen Peterson** and **Willie P. Bennett** (double bill)

Friday, August 23

Ottawa Folklore Centre owner **Arthur McGregor** started things off on the main stage with his acoustic guitar ragtime version of our national anthem. The Friday evening main stage opened with **Les Hardis Moussaillons**, an eclectic group of French-language performers with diverse influences: "rock, punk, flamenco and Latino thrown in a blender at high speed". Montreal's first lady of folk, **Penny Lang**, next graced the stage, followed by the exotic Latin American rhythms of **Miguel Fenton**. Songstress extraordinaire **Lynn Miles** performed to an appreciative crowd. Then the wild and wacky group **Moxy Früvous** exploded onto the stage. The evening of folk under the stars ended with the swirling sounds of **Orealis**, a Montreal-based Celtic band.

Ottawa performer Lynn Miles.

Saturday, August 24

The Saturday daytime entertainment was packed with talent. On the main stage you could choose from a country session hosted by **Lonesome Paul**, a bluegrass session hosted by **Ron Moores**, or a king-size performance of the **Purple Dragon Puppet Troupe**. For many, the highlight was the **Ottawa Folklore Centre Tribute**, celebrating the centre's 20th anniversary. Participants included **Alex Houghton**, **Lynn Miles**, **Ian Robb**, **James Stephens** and **Bob Stark**.

Down by the water on the **Point Stage**, you could enjoy children's entertainment with **June and Kathy**; a **Nortel Showcase** with the **Miguel Fenton Band**; a world-beat session hosted by **Dario Domingues**; and an **Ottawa Folklore Centre** session on how to play the harmonica.

In the cool confines of the **Inside Stage**, the audience sampled a guitar session with **Alan Marsden**, **Alex Houghton**, **Bert Jansch** and **Allan Gorman**. A session on toe-tappin' tunes hosted by **Marion Linton** set the atmosphere for the participatory dance sessions that followed. **Catherine Burns** hosted a contra dance with musical accompaniment provided by **The Old Sod Band**. **Danielle Martineau** hosted the lively **Dansez!** session with **Rockabayou**.

Jennifer Cayley signing with Malaika.

The **Red Stage** was a showcase for singer-songwriters. The **All in the Family** session was hosted by the **Bovine Sisters** and included members of six families. The fabulous **Laura Smith** and **George Antoniak** were featured in a **Nortel Showcase**, while the **Heart and Soul** session hosted by **Beth Ferguson** featured **Bert Jansch** and **Penny Lang**. The session **See What I Say** featured the music and stories of **Malaika**, **Jennifer Cayley**, and **Ruth and Brian Bowen**. **Deborah Herr** provided beautiful sign language interpretation combined with dance.

The **Green Stage** packed a lot of entertainment into one afternoon. The **Le Hibou Revisited** session was one of the most popular of the weekend. Host **Richard Patterson** welcomed **Sylvia Tyson**, **Colleen Peterson**, **Penny Lang** and **Bob Stark** for an hour of recalling the glory days of the legendary Ottawa coffeehouse, **Le Hibou**. The **Generation F** session showcased a younger generation of folk artists. **Bob Stark** hosted the **Writers are a Strange Breed** session, exploring the art of songwriting. Two showcases featured **Doug Reansbury** and **Orealis**.

Singer-songwriter Willie Dunn.

Diversity was the theme on Saturday evening. The main stage opened with native singer-songwriter **Willie Dunn**, and continued with the bluegrass-fusion quartet **The Emory Lester Set**. **Malaika**, a four-woman acapella group that performs music

Song circle with Bob Stark, Bill Hawkins and Penny Lang.

from around the world, was followed by the **Thomas Handy Trio**. The trio combines a heady combination of jazz and East Indian rhythms to create music with an hypnotic effect. Up next was **Quartette**, a four-woman group that featured the considerable talents of **Colleen Peterson**, **Sylvia Tyson**, **Cindy Church** and **Caitlin Hanford**. Sadly, it would be one of Colleen Peterson's last performances. She passed away barely six weeks later. British guitar legend **Bert Jansch** and the energetic **Danielle Martineau and Rockabayou** rounded out the eclectic evening.

Chopper McKinnon presenting the Helen Verger Award to Sylvia Tyson and Colleen Peterson.

Sunday, August 25

What better time to enjoy some gospel music than on Sunday morning? Host **Andrea Karam** introduced **John Steele**; **Michelle Sweeney**, a woman with a wonderfully powerful voice; and the many members of **Voices of Praise**, an Ottawa gospel ensemble. Other early birds were treated to devotional music from the **Ottawa Shape Note Chorus**, in a session hosted by **Shelley Posen**.

Traditions old and new could be found on the daytime main stage on Sunday. A **ceilidh** hosted by **Ian Robb** boasted the likes of **Ann Downey**, **Shelley Posen**, **Janet Munson**, **James Stephens**, **Wilf Gillis** and **Dan Schryer**. Meanwhile, the **New Traditions** session hosted by **Ann Downey** featured **Jimmy George**, **The Toasted Westerns** and **Night Sun**. **Stepdance Heaven** was the title of a toe-tappin' session featuring the **Ottawa Valley Dancers**. The **Ottawa Citizen Family Concert** featured **The Dinosaur Show with Kirk & Magoo**.

Kids participating at the craft table.

The children's entertainment continued at the **Point Stage** with concerts by **Magoo** and **Tom Plant**. The session **Music from the Isles** and a session on how to play the pennywhistle reflected a traditional theme. The session **In the Groove**, hosted by **Suzie Vinnick**, explored the art of grooving. **Cabin Fever**, one of the winners of the festival's **Last Chance Saloon** competition, strutted their stuff out at the **Point Stage**.

For those who took refuge in the air-conditioned comfort of the **Inside Stage**, there was plenty to see and do. A lively square dance was hosted by

Fred Weihs, with musical accompaniment by **Paddies on the Tundra**. The **Words and Music** session hosted by **Alrick Huebener** featured **SugarBeat**, **thom barker** and **Aaron Zaadich**. More words and music were examined in the **Songs from the Heart** session featuring **Jody Benjamin**, **Lucie Blue Tremblay**, **Laura Smith** and **Lee Hayes**. Nortel showcases presented performances by **Night Sun**, and **Gerry Griffin & Dario Domingues**.

The **Red Stage** was in danger of bursting into flames during the **Fiddles on Fire** session featuring the talents of **Oliver Schroer**, **Janet Munson**, **Michael Ball**, **Pierre Schryer** and **Nathan Curry**. One of the highlights of the day was the **Maritime Stories & Songs** session hosted by **Shelley Posen** and showcasing the talents of **Lennie Gallant**, **Kevin Head** and **Tom Lips**. More stories were shared during the **Ottawa Valley Stories & Songs** session hosted by **Gail Gavan**. Performers included **Cal Cummings**, **Gord McAlpine**, **Tri-Lys**, **Le Grand Portage** and **Donna Stewart**. The daytime sessions ended with a Nortel showcase hosted by **Neema Mugala** featuring the **Sifa Choir**.

The **Green Stage** presented a session on blues music hosted by **Larry "The Bird" Mootham** and featuring **Rick Fines**, **Suzie Vinnick**, **Guy Del Villano** and **Vince Halfhide**. Festival goers could also listen to **Spirit Voices**, a session hosted by **Cliff Thomas**. **Willie Dunn**, **Stephen Augustine** and **Mary Carpenter** performed music and told stories that reflected their heritage. **Brenna Rivier** hosted a session called **Songs of Freedom**, with participants **Lennie Gallant**, **Lucie Blue Tremblay** and **Willie Dunn**. Two showcases presented the talents of **Steafan Hannigan** and **Jimmy George**.

The Sunday evening main stage opened with the fabulous sounds of the **Folk Festival Children's Choir**. Celtic-inspired ensemble **Jimmy George** appeared next, followed by local favourites **Finest Kind**. This traditionally based trio consists of **Ian Robb**, **Shelley Posen** and **Ann Downey**. French-Canadian singer-songwriter **Lucie Blue Tremblay** performed a bilingual set. She was followed by **Suzie Vinnick** and **Rick Fines**. This duo combines the vocal talents of blues singer Suzie Vinnick with the guitar stylings of Rick Fines. The evening wound down with two superb East Coast performers: **Laura Smith** and **Lennie Gallant**. **Laura Smith** has been described simply as an actress who performs her own songs. **Lennie Gallant** is a native of P.E.I. who lives in Halifax. His music combines lyrics reflecting the struggles and dreams of real people with Acadian and Celtic influenced music.

Laura Smith on the main stage.

Organizing committee and staff of the 1996 festival.

Year 4 – 1997
Welcome Home Bruce!

The fourth CKCU Ottawa Folk Festival, held from **August 22 to 24** at **Britannia Park**, was a hit. Bruce Cockburn returned to his hometown, much to the delight of the record crowds that gathered for his dynamic performances. Cockburn appeared at a main stage evening concert on the opening night of the festival. The next day he participated in the reunion of the famous sixties Ottawa group, **The Children**. The festival main stage lineup was particularly strong: **Lawrence Gowan**, **Shari Ulrich**, **Robert Paquette**, **The Arrogant Worms**, **Alpha Yaya Diallo**, **Melanie Doane**, **Tamarack**, **Cindy Church** and **Rebecca Campbell**. **Chopper McKinnon** and **Karen Flanagan McCarthy** returned to host the main stage throughout the festival.

Ottawa native Bruce Cockburn, winner of the 1997 Helen Verger Award.

The year 1997 also marked the 20th anniversary of the first folk festival to be held at **Britannia Park**. The **Festival for the Folks** was held there from 1977 to 1979. Perhaps the most poignant moment of the 1997 festival was a special ceremony in memory of the late **Colleen Peterson**, which was attended by some of her closest friends and many fans.

Festival Director **Gene Swimmer**, Artistic Director **Chris White** and the organizing committee worked harder than ever to put on the 1997 festival. The funding from major sponsor CKCU ended due to the community radio station's financial problems.

Benefit Concert Series
A tremendously successful **Benefit Concert Series** made the festival possible. The 1996/1997 benefit concert series included the following concerts held at the National Library of Canada.
 Nov. 16: **Pamela Morgan**
 Dec. 7, 8: **Arlo Guthrie**
 March 6: **Laura Smith**
 April 10: **Soweto Singers**
 April 19: **Penny Lang**, **Georgette Fry**
 May 30: **Moxy Früvous**

The festival held its first **Silent Auction** during the intermission of the **Arlo Guthrie** concerts on Dec. 7 and 8. Thanks to **Carol Silcoff** and a team of volunteers, and the many generous donations from local artisans and businesses, the event was a huge success.

The **Regional Municipality of Ottawa-Carleton**, the **Ontario Arts Council**, **Nortel**, the *Ottawa Citizen*, **Phase 2**, **Air Nova**, **CS CO-OP**, **Hershey**, the **SOCAN Foundation**, the **Luxor Hotel** and the **Glebe Loeb** also provided vital support to the festival.

Friday, August 22
There was a sense of eager anticipation in the air when the festival opened on Friday night, as the audience awaited the appearance of **Bruce Cockburn**. **Arthur McGregor**, longtime sponsor and owner of the **Ottawa Folklore Centre** played a wonderful acoustic guitar version of our national anthem to open the festival. Performers including the female group **Travelling with Jane**, the popular **Robert Paquette**, the zany **Arrogant Worms**, the fiery African-inspired **Alpha Yaya Diallo**, and another Ottawa native, singer **Rebecca Campbell**. Cockburn's polished and dynamic

set was greeted with enormous enthusiasm by an appreciative hometown crowd. Although an international star in his own right, Cockburn made it clear he was enjoying a return to his roots. He was presented with the keys to the **City of Ottawa**, as well as the **Helen Verger Award** for his valuable contributions to Canadian folk music.

Saturday, August 23

The daytime entertainment on Saturday featured a potpourri of styles and subjects. Quite a buzz was generated by **The Children** and **Le Hibou** workshop hosted by **Richard Patterson**. The musical group of hopefuls that first banded together in 1965 included many who would make considerable contributions to the Canadian cultural scene: **Bruce Cockburn**, **David Wiffen**, **Richard Patterson**, **Sandy Crawley**, **Sneezy Waters**, **Neville Wells** and **Chris Anderson**. **The Children** often appeared at legendary folk venue **Le Hibou**.

The Children, a famous sixties Ottawa group included Bruce Cockburn, David Wiffin, Sandy Crawley, Sneezy Waters, Bill Hawkins and Richard Patterson (hidden).

Sessions focusing on the themes of passion and the lives of girls and women took place on the **Green Stage**. **Guitars are Us** was the amusing title for a session that showcased the many styles of this versatile instrument that is so prevalent in folk and roots music.

Participatory sessions abounded. The **Ottawa Folklore Centre** hosted a series of sessions encouraging people to sing along, or to play the slide guitar or harmonica. **Debbie McWatty Reid** hosted a session on how to **stepdance**, while **Kate McKay** encouraged everyone to **dance**, **dance**, **dance**. A **country dance** was presented by **Lonesome Paul and the Valley Ramblers** with **Jody Benjamin**. An enthusiastic group took part

The festival choir with choirmaster Andy Rush.

in the **Ottawa Folklore Centre Weekend Choir Practice**, hosted by **Andy Rush**.

Kids on the Nortel Stage celebrating the rhythms of Africa.

The **Ottawa Citizen Family Area** was just the place to see juggling, magic shows, "kidsongs" with **Tom Plant** and stories with **Dean Verger**. Kids also ventured to the **Inside Stage** for a **Valdy for Kids** session.

The **Nortel Stage** featured a session highlighting the rhythms of Africa and a live version of the CKCU traditional country, western and bluegrass music show *The Back 40*; **Alex Sinclair** hosted an **Acoustic Waves** session featuring performers who had appeared in the longstanding folk/roots concert series. The **Red Stage** showcased double bills by **Robert Paquette** and **Lizanne Evely**; and **Shari Ulrich** and **Mélisse Lafrance**; while **Cindy Church** appeared solo. The **Green Stage** offered double bills with **Bill Bourne and Bill Huggins**; **Joe Hall and Barb Matticacci**, as well as **Alpha Yaya Diallo** in concert. At the **Point Stage** you could go around the world in 30 minutes with **George Sapounidis**!

Singer-songwriter Melanie Doane is a multi-instrumentalist who plays the fiddle.

The evening main stage performances opened with **Guy Davis**, an acoustic blues revivalist. Singer-songwriter and instrumentalist **Melanie Doane** was followed by a band she once belonged to: **Tamarack** of Guelph, Ont. The group is well known for its traditional arrangements that tell tales of the history of Canada. **Meryn Cadell** provided her own unique spin on contemporary life through music and the spoken word. The Montreal-based band **Zekuhl** had the crowd hopping with an eclectic set of African and Latin rhythms.

Sunday, August 24

Some skeptics doubted that **Lawrence Gowan** could make the transition from arena rocker to folk festival headliner. Gowan proved that he could, and delivered his piano-based music with panache and style to spare. The former rock star illustrated that good music begins and ends with the story and song.

David Wiffen performing on the main stage.

Sunday was another gorgeous day at the festival. The afternoon exemplified Gary Cristall's idea of a good festival lineup: "a program with so much music you want to see, you do not know where to go". The **Nortel Stage** featured a live broadcast of the CKCU Celtic music program, *Music From the Glen*; stories and songs with **Dean Verger**; and **Meryn Cadell** in concert. **Fiddle Fever** featured fiddlers aplenty, while the session **It Was 20 Years**

Arthur McGregor leads a participatory workshop encouraging people to sing along.

Ago Today showcased **Ian Tamblyn**, **Shari Ulrich**, **David Wiffen** and others who had appeared at the **Festival for the Folks** at Britannia Park two decades earlier!

The **Inside Stage** was the location of a lively square dance with **Paddies on the Tundra**; and double bills featuring **Pamela Morgan** and the **Last Chance Saloon** competition winners the **Mudpouts**; and **Lawrence Gowan** and **Meg Lunney**. Kids were delighted with concerts designed with them in mind presented by **James Gordon** and **Del Fuego**. Those who camped out in front of the **Red Stage** were treated to double bills with **Linda Morrison** and **Jennifer Noxon**; **Gaston Bernard** and **Kagiso Mpala**; and a bluesy triple bill with **Paul Fenton**, **Vince Halfhide** and **Guy Davis**. Fans of the spoken word were entertained by members of **SugarBeat**, along with **Alex Mortimer**, **Justin Haynes**, **Sandra Nicholls** and **Kagiso Mpala**. On the **Green Stage**, **CBC Radio** recorded a live-to-tape broadcast of the acoustic/roots music show *Heartland Live*, hosted by **Bill Stunt**. The **Green Stage** also showcased the talents of the worldbeat acoustic band **Raintree**; **Generation F** performers **Shoshona Kish**, **Lizanne Evely**, **Raven Kanatakta** and **Rob Commins**; **Melanie Doane** and **The Toasted Westerns**. The session **Play Me a Rock & Roll Song** featured **Valdy**, **Lawrence Gowan** and **Lizanne Evely**.

Raven Kanatakta of Digging Roots.

At the **Point Stage**, way down by the water, you could take in performances by wind instrumentalist **Robbie Anderman**, or sample the acoustic blues of **Larry "The Bird" Mootham**, **Vince Halfhide**, **Linda Morrison**, **Paul Fenton** and **Guy Davis**. The **Family Area** showcased awesome feats by **Tawney Ross**; "kidsongs" with **Linda Morrison** and **Russell Levia**; and stories with **Dean Verger**. **Doctor Magic** provided what you would expect, and **Del Fuego** appeared unplugged.

The media team was led by Denis Labossière.

Robbie Anderman plays a pipe in front of a memorial tree planted in honour of Colleen Peterson who passed away in 1996.

The **Ottawa Folklore Centre Weekend Choir** kicked off the evening main stage performances. A flurry of fiddling next ensued with renowned instrumentalists **Calvin Vollrath**, **Trent Brunner** and **April Verch**. The dynamic **Shari Ulrich** performed next, followed by the bluegrass stylings of **Steel Rail**. Ottawa favourite **Ian Tamblyn** appeared with his usual assortment of musical gems. The evening ended with a heartfelt performance by Newfoundlander **Pamela Morgan** and perennial festival performer **Valdy.**

Year 5 – 1998
The Year of the Double Rainbow

A record crowd of approximately 12,000 attended the 1998 CKCU Ottawa Folk Festival, held **August 28-30** at **Britannia Park**. Despite intermittent downpours, rainbows appeared more than once in the festival skies, much to the delight of the participants. One of the festival highlights was a performance by folk veteran **Arlo Guthrie**, who played to an enthusiastic crowd on Sunday evening. **Ferron** received a warm response when she was awarded with the **Helen Verger Award**. The crowds were also dazzled by artists such as Americans **Martin Sexton** and **Vance Gilbert**. **Chopper McKinnon** and **Karen Flanagan McCarthy** returned to host the main stage throughout the festival.

1998 Ottawa Folk Festival birthday cake.

The highest number of performers to date participated in this year's festival, showcasing a wide spectrum of styles. Traditional roots music was represented by acclaimed artists such as **David Essig**; **Bourque, Bernard et Lepage**; **Gail Gavan** and **Cindy Thompson**. Exciting musical hybrids such as the African-inspired ensembles **Cheza** and the **Sifa Choir**, the French/Cajun performer **Danielle Martineau**, blues crooner **Georgette Fry**, and the unique Celtic/klezmer/blues-influenced band, **Night Sun**, kept the crowd dancing.

Canadian festival veterans **Roy Forbes**, **Connie Kaldor**, **Moxy Früvous**, **Fred Eaglesmith**, the **Wyrd Sisters** and **Holmes Hooke** rounded out the evening's lineup.

Aerial view of the main stage.

Friday, August 28

"If anyone wondered about the future of acoustic and folk-style music they only needed to take in last night's opening set of concerts at the Ottawa Folk Festival to see that there's a bevy of new artists already taking up the torch," reported Rick Overall in the *Ottawa Sun*. The fun began on Friday evening on the **Nortel Stage** in traditional festival fashion, with **Ottawa Folklore Centre** owner **Arthur McGregor** performing an instrumental guitar version of "O Canada". Eclectic singer-songwriter **Christine Graves** was followed by **Oh Susanna**, a Vancouver native who puts a new spin on traditional North American country music. The wonderful and witty **Vance Gilbert** wowed the crowd with his awesome vocal style and accomplished guitar playing. Many considered his dynamic performance one of the most memorable at the festival. The **Mike Plume Band** delivered a spirited plugged-in set that reflected the band's alternative and country roots.

Following intermission, crowd-pleasers **Moxy**

Früvous had the crowd in stitches during their lively performance featuring their recent hits. The mood shifted to the gentle acoustic sounds of Seattle-based **Erin Corday**. **Fred Eaglesmith** was accompanied by his stellar band including **Willie P. Bennett** and **Washboard Hank**. The evening ended on a high note with an infectious and highly danceable set by the irrepressible band **Night Sun** featuring husband and wife **Chris Coleman** and **Ellen Hamilton**.

Tom Leighton and Mark Haines (Haines and Leighton) featured on a workshop stage.

The **1997-98 Ottawa Folk Festival Benefit Concerts** featured an eclectic cross-section of talent. The successful series included the following concerts:

- November 9, 1997: **The Wyrd Sisters** and **Malaika** (double bill), Bronson Centre
- December 6, 1997: **Lawrence Gowan** (opening act **SugarBeat**), National Library of Canada
- December 13, 1997: **Ian Tamblyn** (CD release concert), National Library of Canada
- January 18, 1998: **Dar Williams** (opening act Jennifer Noxon), Great Canadian Theatre Company
- February 21, 1998: Hot Music for a Cold Night (Winterlude event featuring a double bill with **Georgette Fry** and **Rawlins Cross**), Congress Centre
- March 20, 1998: **Connie Kaldor** (opening act **Beth Ferguson**), National Library of Canada
- April 17, 1998: **Lennie Gallant** (opening act **Terry Tufts**), Canadian Museum of Nature
- May 29, 1998: **Stephen Fearing** (opening act **Mélisse Lafrance**), Canadian Museum of Nature

Extraordinary storyteller Holmes Hooke spinning a yarn.

Saturday, August 29

There was plenty of daytime entertainment at this year's festival, giving festival goers many opportunities to enjoy intimate performances. The **Nortel Stage** kicked off the afternoon with **The Old Sod**, music from Great Britain and France, featuring **Finest Kind**, **Erin Cassidy**, **Bobby Watt**, **Aengus Finnan**, and **Bourque, Bernard et Lepage**. **Christmas in August**, hosted by Shelley Posen, was a collection of the songs you would expect as interpreted by **Finest Kind**, **Roy Forbes**, **Mark Haines**, **Tom Leighton** and **Jan Andrews**. **Moxy Früvous** took to the stage next for a lively 45-minute concert. The **Saskatoon Moon** session featured a double bill with Canadian folkies **Connie Kaldor** and **Roy Forbes**.

Richard Knechtel hosted the **Songs from the Heart** session on the **Red Stage**. The participants, all SOCAN award winners, included **Jennifer Noxon**, **Ellen Hamilton**, **Glen Reid**, **Michaela Foster Marsh** and **Holmes Hooke**. Legendary guitar player **David Essig** hosted the **I Love My Guitar** session with **Brandon Scott**, **Rick Fines**, **Andy Sheppard** and **Shelley Jennings**. Talented Irish flute player **Erin Cassidy** performed tunes from her album *The Wind at Play*. **Lizzie Shanks** and **Brandon Scott** were joined by a few musical friends during the **Besharah in Concert** session. The **On the Fiddle** session showcased a diverse lineup of talent: **Gaston Bernard**, **Jami Sieber**, **Mark Haines**, **Gary Weinger** and **Peter Jellard**. **Tom Leighton** hosted the **My Main Squeeze** session, a rollicking roundup of accordionists **Danielle Martineau**, **Bonnie Dawson** and **Benoit Bourque**, and concertina player **Ian Robb**.

by **Sherry Shute** and showcasing **Ferron**, **Vance Gilbert**, **Bobby Watt** and **Deborah Herr-Allen**. A 30-minute concert with **Night Sun** followed. **Dance with Akpokli** gave the audience an opportunity to sway to the rhythms of traditional drum music from Ghana. **Gloria May Eshkibok** hosted the **Personal Politics** session, a one-hour presentation of issues-oriented music with **Bob Stark**, **Moxy Früvous** and **Nishtu**.

Some kids took a break from crafts to bounce.

Vance Gilbert wowing the crowd.

The **Green Stage** opened the afternoon with **It's Only Rock & Roll**, hosted by **Roy Forbes** and featuring **Terry Tufts**, **Sherry Shute**, **David Essig** and **Fred Guignion**. Local singer-songwriter **Charlie Sohmer** was up next with a 30-minute concert. The struggle against adversity was the theme in the **Breaking Through** session hosted

At the **Point Stage**, near the Ottawa River, **Arthur McGregor** hosted a **Singalong Folk Jam** with plenty of audience participation. Animator **Erin Cassidy** hosted the **Learn to Play the Pennywhistle** workshop. **Just For Laughs** featured the lighthearted music of **Richard Knechtel**, **Vance Gilbert**, **Steve Fruitman** and **Robert Atyeo** and was hosted by **Ann Downey**. **Vance Gilbert** in concert featured one of North America's most exciting folk performers.

In the cool confines of the air-conditioned **Inside Stage**, the **Black Sheep Salute** was hosted by **Paul Symes**, the owner of the **Wakefield, Quebec** club. **Mike Plume**, **Christine Graves**, **Oh Susanna** and **Kwasi Dunyo** were the featured performers. A double bill followed with artists **Terry Tufts** and **Erin Corday**. Host **Nancy Ziebarth** joined forces with **Cindy Thompson** and **Bourque, Bernard et Lepage** for the **Learn to Stepdance** workshop. The second double bill of the day showcased the talents of **Ana Coutinho** and **Lindy**. The day ended with a dance featuring the music of the **Mike Plume Band**.

The popular **Family Area** was a whirlwind of activity. Animator **Judy Halla** got things underway with **Aerobics for Kids**. Three separate **Kindermusik** sessions were animated by **Claudia Mack**, **Kathy Ruggiero** and **Monica Wolfe**, who explored rhythms for the very young. **Cindy Thompson** was on hand to teach the **Stepdancing for Kids** session. The **Dickie Bird for Kids** session featured **Richard Knechtel**, an entertaining and versatile folkie. **Crafts for Kids**, led by crafter **Janet Whittam**, gave family members a chance to make decorations.

The evening performances on the **Nortel Networks Stage** kicked off with premier Ottawa Valley fiddler-stepdancer **Cindy Thompson** The 25-member **Sifa Choir** was in the midst of performing when the skies darkened and the rain poured down in torrents, sending the audience running for cover. The storm abated within 20 minutes and the Sifa Choir returned to the stage, gamely performing without microphones. Their music lifted the spirits of the festival goers, who were delighted when the sun came out and a double rainbow appeared in the sky above the stage.

Connie Kaldor was a fan favourite at the Ottawa Folk Festival.

Veteran folk festival performer **Roy Forbes** appeared in concert. Montreal singer-songwriter **Danielle Martineau** performed with the **Stephen Barry Blues Band** in a set that combined French-Canadian roots music, zydeco and reggae.

Saskatchewan native **Connie Kaldor** performed her lyrical and humorous songs about life on the prairies.

Following intermission, **The Unceded Band** featuring **Gloria May Eshkibok**, **Miche Hill** and **Sherry Shute** performed with their usual passion and playfulness. The band gets its name from one of the largest unceded Aboriginal territories in the world. **Martin Sexton** wowed the evening crowd with his evocative vocal style and original material. **Ferron** mesmerized everyone with her powerfully poetic self-penned songs. Much of her material was so well known that the audience sang along. After her performance Ferron was presented with the **Helen Verger Award**. **Georgette Fry** ably demonstrated why she she had been given *Jazz Report Magazine's* Blues Artist of the Year award when she delivered a rousing closing set.

Singer-songwriter Ferron was a deserving recipient of the Helen Verger Award.

Sunday, August 30

Sunday morning and afternoon offered plenty of folk fun at **Britannia Park**. On the **Nortel Stage**, the day opened with **Aengus Finnan** in concert. **Canadian Spaces Live**, hosted by **Chopper McKinnon**, showcased the talents of Space Cadets **David Essig**, **Bob Stark**, **Lonesome Paul** and

Crow's Feet. A double bill followed featuring **Martin Sexton** and **The Wyrd Sisters**. The **Courriers** in concert featured the legendary Ottawa folk group of the 1960s. **Arlo Guthrie** and **Connie Kaldor** were the dynamic duo who appeared in the **Together Again for the First Time** session. **Heartland Live**, hosted by **Bill Stunt**, recorded the performances by **Robert Atyeo**, **Ana Coutinho**, **Crow's Feet** and **Charlie Sohmer**, which were later broadcast on Bill's CBC Radio show.

First up on the **Red Stage** was the session **Now That's a Stretch** with **Ray Bonneville**, **Mark Haines**, **Tom Leighton** and **Deborah Herr-Allen** and was hosted by **Lindy**. **Tall Tales and Strange Songs** followed, featuring host **Holmes Hooke** and performers **Robert Atyeo**, **Bobby Watt** and **Larry "The Bird" Mootham**. **Ron Moores** hosted the **That Good Old Time Music** session with traditional songs by **Lonesome Paul**, **Gail Gavan**, and **Bourque, Bernard et Lepage**. A double bill with singer-songwriters **Glen Reid** and **Gord Johnston** followed. **The Great Outdoors** session hosted by **Jan Andrews** was a truly Canadian experience with **Blackflies**, **Holmes Hooke**, **The Wyrd Sisters** and **Glen Reid**. **Alan Weekes** hosted a rousing session of **American Acoustic**, honouring the CKCU-FM folk show of the same name. Musicians included **Martin Sexton**, **Ann Downey**, **Vance Gilbert** and **Erin Corday**.

The **Unceded Band** set the pace with a concert on the **Green Stage**. This trio expresses in song the plight of indigenous peoples and other social issues. A little gospel music does a soul good on a Sunday morning. **Neema Mugala** hosted the **Glory, Glory** session, featuring songs of joyous celebration from the **Sifa Choir**, **May Lebrun**, **Gord Johnson**, **Mark Haines** and **Tom Leighton**. Montreal musician **Elana Harte** showed off her infectious rhythms and sparkling vocals in a 30-minute concert. The audience had the privilege of an intimate concert with **Ferron**. **Lee Hayes** was host of **For the Love of Music** session, an international collection of songs presented by **Malaika**, **Vance Gilbert**, **Robert Atyeo**, **Crow's Feet**, and **Bourque, Bernard et Lepage**. The closing session was **Dance with Dam'Deride**, featuring the Montreal women's choir directed by **Danielle Martineau**.

Shelley Posen led the workshop titled **Learn to Sing with Shape Notes** on the beautiful **Point Stage**. **Larry "The Bird" Mootham** and **Southside Steve** led the **Learn to Play the Harmonica** workshop. **Vince Halfhide** followed suit with **Learn to Play the Slide Guitar**, and was assisted by two masters of the form: **David Essig** and **Rick Fines**. Host **Georgette Fry** was accompanied by **Ray Bonneville**, **Martin Sexton**, **Larry "The Bird" Mootham** and **The Mighty Popo** in the **Acoustic Blues** session.

Larry "The Bird" Mootham and Southside Steve (Steve Marriner) onstage during the Learn to Play Harmonica workshop.

The air-conditioned **Inside Stage** was a cool setting for the opening double bill with **Rick Fines** and **Andy Sheppard**. Rasputin's owner **Dean Verger** hosted the **Special Blend** session, which featured **Elana Harte**, **Lindy** and **Andy Sheppard**. World music was the theme of **See and Hear the World** with **Cheza**, **Gypsy Jive**, **Mel M'Rabet**, **Kebba Jobateh**, **The Mighty Popo**, **Ras Kagiso Mpala** and host **Stella Haybukhai**. **Erin Corday** was the host of the **I Still Love My Guitar**, a roundup of several styles as demonstrated by **Terry Tufts**, **Mel M'Rabet**, **Ray Bonneville** and **Richard Knechtel**.

Dancing was definitely encouraged during the **Dance with Gypsy Jive** session. The dancing continued with **Dance with Cheza**, a session driven by African rhythms.

In the **Family Area**, **Danielle Martineau** hosted **Accordion Tales**, a roundup of styles of this sometimes misunderstood instrument. **Judy Halla** led the **Aerobics for Kids**. The **Baobab Young Performers** showcased the talents of a drum and dance society whose members range in age from 12 to 17. The group's teacher, **Kathy Armstrong**, was on hand to show off her students. The **Crafts for Kids** workshops were hosted by **Heather Boyd** (jewellery) and **Ted Kordner** (drawing). The day ended with **Dean Verger for Kids**, where "Uncle Dean" told tales for the entire family.

The evening entertainment on the **Nortel Stage** began with a lively set from **Blackflies**, a Cajun group that hails from Ontario. The **Ottawa Folklore Centre Weekend Choir**, directed by **Andy Rush**, promised to make the sun come peeking from behind the clouds and managed to accomplish this feat. This group had practiced throughout the weekend, and performed with panache. Popular Ottawa Valley singer **Gail Gavan** had a lively response from the audience, which welcomed her traditional songs and stories. Guitar wizard **David Essig** knew he was on the right track when he played "Sunrise II", the theme song for *Canadian Spaces*. This song was the best received in his polished set. **Bourque, Bernard et Lepage** had fun singing and dancing their way into the hearts of the crowd. One audience-pleasing number saw Bourque stepdance and shave a volunteer from the audience.

After the intermission, **The Wyrd Sisters**, a Winnipeg-based trio performed their eclectic brand of music. The much-anticipated set by **Arlo Guthrie** delighted the audience, who were thrilled to hear their favourite songs from the author of "Alice's Restaurant". The festival presented Arlo with an original painting by **Roberta Huebener**, as a thank you for the role he played in helping to save the festival, which nearly foundered in its third year. In 1996, Arlo performed in two sold-out benefit concerts that helped raise enough funds to put on the 1997 festival. The amazing African-inspired rhythms of **Cheza** were featured as the last act of the evening and brought to a close the fifth annual CKCU Ottawa Folk Festival at Britannia Park.

Year 6 – 1999

CKCU Ottawa Folk Festival Reaches a New High

Best ever festival! That was the consensus of performers and festival goers alike for the 1999 CKCU Ottawa Folk Festival, held from **August 27 to 29** at **Britannia Park**. The record-breaking crowds were treated to blue skies, warm summer weather and an impressive lineup. The festival attained a high level of professionalism evidenced by superb performances, and excellent lighting and sound. Several musicians including **Jane Siberry**, **Ian Tamblyn**, **Lucy Kaplansky** and **Lynn Miles** lavished praise for the festival. A particularly warm response was extended to **Chopper McKinnon**, who accepted the **Helen Verger Award**. **Chopper** and **Karen Flanagan McCarthy** returned to host the main stage throughout the festival.

"The performers were ecstatic about this year's festival," said festival organizer **Pam Marjerrison**. The festival crowds were equally ecstatic and turned out in record numbers. Attendance was high for the daytime performances, Marjerrison was happy to point out. "This is what we've always wanted. The daytime performances are as important as the evening ones."

Daytime sessions held in **Lakeside Gardens** were particularly well attended. The hilarious **Laugh It Up** session featuring **Trout Fishing in America**, **Vance Gilbert** and **Jane Siberry** was standing room only. Festival staff had to turn people away from the **Burgundy**, **Bailey's and Bourbon** workshop with **Laura Smith**, **Georgette Fry** and **Margo Timmins**, as the hall was filled to capacity.

The CKCU Ottawa Folk Festival is now being held up as a model for organizers of other festivals. On the Labour Day weekend, *Ottawa Sun* reporter Ian Nathanson stated in a review of another local music festival: "If you want advice on how to *properly* organize a festival, check with the people behind the Folk Festival and the Ottawa Chamber Music Festival."

A record number of performers from south of the border appeared. American acoustic music was well represented by **Karen Savoca**, **Trout Fishing in America**, **Annie Gallup**, **Cry Cry Cry (Dar Williams**, **Lucy Kaplansky** and **Richard Shindell)**, **Vance Gilbert**, **Bill Morrissey** and **Chuck Brodsky**.

Festival patron peruses program.

Jane Siberry making her magic.

Some magical moments included **Jane Siberry** performing an improvisational version of "The Water is Wide" with cellist **Jorane Peltier** on Saturday evening. Those who gathered for a **Tom Wilson** showcase on Sunday afternoon were treated to a one-hour performance from the supergroup **Blackie and the Rodeo Kings**. Finally, Inuit performer **Lucie Idlout** proved that popular music can take on serious social issues and still rock.

Benefit Concert Series

The festival was the culmination of a busy year of concerts under the festival banner. The annual CKCU Ottawa Folk Festival Benefit Concert Series featured the following performers:

- November 28: **Nancy White** and **The Toasted Westerns**, First Unitarian Congregation
- February 6: **Fred Eaglesmith** and **Ray Bonneville**, Barrymore's
- February 27: **Martin Sexton**, Bronson Centre
- March 20: **Don Ross** and **Besharah**, First Unitarian Congregation
- April 17: **The Arrogant Worms** and **Holmes Hooke**, First Unitarian Congregation
- May 28: **Christine Lavin** and **Tom Lips**, First Unitarian Congregation
- May 29: **Dar Williams** and **Tammy Raybould**, Glebe Collegiate

A **special photo exhibit** opened on Monday, August 23, at the **National Press Club** at 150 Wellington Street featuring photography of the folk festival by **Nix Wadden**, **Jim Commins** and **Dave Haggerty**. **Mike McCormick**, a member of the wacky and wonderful **The Arrogant Worms** entertained those who turned out for the event.

The **festival preview concerts** began on Sunday, August 22, when **Trace Elements** performed at the Chapters store in Kanata. A series of **free lunchtime concerts** held at the **World Exchange Plaza** began on Tuesday, August 24, with a double bill featuring **Ian Tamblyn**, along with **Andrea Karam** and **Fred Guignion**. On August 25, **Wendy DeMos** and the African-influenced rhythms of **Mel M'Rabet** were showcased. **The Unceded Band** and **Laura Smith** performed on August 25.

Several **late-evening concerts** were held at the **Luxor Hotel** from August 26-28. These popular concerts featured the likes of **Laura Smith**, **Richard Wood** and **Trout Fishing in America**.

The CKCU Ottawa Folk Festival is grateful for the generosity of its sponsors: Nortel Networks, Ottawa Folklore Centre, the Luxor Hotel, *Ottawa Citizen*, Rogers Community TV, Phase 2, CBC Radio One, Bell Mobility, Ontario Arts Council, Loeb, Ginn, CKCU, US Airways, VIA Rail Canada, Michael Davies Plymouth Chrysler Ltd., Steve's Music Store, Pepsi, CS Co-op, Alexander Keith's India Pale Ale, Chez 106, National Library of Canada, Mexicali Rosa's, Nutshell Music, Chapters, Regional Municipality of Ottawa-Carleton, The Ottawa Food Bank, *X Press*, Canada NewsWire and Human Resources Development Canada.

Friday, August 27

On Friday, August 27, **Blackie and the Rodeo Kings** (**Stephen Fearing**, **Colin Linden** and **Tom Wilson**) performed a lunchtime concert outside the HMV store on Sparks Street.

Friday evening opened in traditional festival manner with **Arthur McGregor**, owner of the **Ottawa Folklore Centre** performing a charming acoustic guitar version of our national anthem. First up was Ottawa singer-songwriter **Jennifer Noxon**, who entertained the crowd with her original compositions. **The Angstones** were next with an energetic set including the local favourite,

Blackie and the Rodeo Kings perform at the World Exchange Plaza.

"Bytown It's My Town". The musical surprise of the evening was **Karen Savoca**, a dynamic conga-playing singer-songwriter from Syracuse, New York. **Njacko Backo** presented African-inspired music. **Jorane Peltier**, a young Québécois cellist with a dramatic vocal style, dazzled the crowd with her imaginative original compositions. P.E.I. fiddling sensation **Richard Wood** gave a high-energy performance that was received with much appreciation.

The audience enthusiastically received **Lynn Miles**, whose set included music from her latest CD, *Night in a Strange Town*, and some new material inspired by her life south of the border. **Blackie and the Rodeo Kings**, a supergroup of performers **Stephen Fearing**, **Tom Wilson** and **Colin Linden**, delivered a powerful set that brought the evening to a rollicking close.

Traditional Inuit throat singers.

Saturday, August 28

Saturday afternoon had so much to offer that many festival goers expressed frustration that they could not see it all! These well-attended afternoon sessions were held on six stages, a record number for the festival.

The **Nortel Networks Stage** was the setting for the **Living Traditions** workshop hosted by **Ian Robb** and including **Finest Kind**, **Kebba Jobateh**, **Matapat**, **Eve Goldberg** and **Alain Chatry**. **Ron Moores** hosted **Back 40 Live** featuring the **Cowboy Junkies**, **Sarah Harmer**, **Big Gravel** and **Sherwood Lumsden**. The session was aired live on CKCU-FM for the popular program *The Back 40*, which features traditional country, bluegrass and old-time music. **Bill Stunt** of CBC Radio was also on hand to host **Heartland Live**, **Part I** featuring **Terry Tufts**, **Fireweed**, **Tom Wilson** and **Katherine Wheatley**. This performance was recorded for later broadcast on the CBC Radio program *Heartland*, which features music from Ontario. Separate concerts were performed by **Ray Bonneville** and **Stephen Fearing**. The afternoon sessions wound down on a comical note, with **Njacko Backo** and **Trout Fishing in America**.

On the **Ottawa Folklore Centre Stage**, the entertainment began with **Alain Lauzon** in concert. Ottawa Folklore Centre owner **Arthur McGregor** hosted a rousing **Singalong Folk Jam**. **Terry Eagan**, a folk enthusiast from Waltham, Massachusetts, hosted the **Boston Connection** featuring **Annie Gallup** and **Bill Morrissey** from south of the border, and Canadian performers **Beth Ferguson** and **Rick Fines**. **Benoit Bourque** and **Alain Chatry** held a session titled **Learn to Play the Spoons**. A double bill featuring **Katherine Wheatley** and **Jorane Peltier**, two distinctly different performers from Ontario and Quebec, ended the daytime performances.

The **Phase 2 Stage** opened with Ottawa performer **Wendy DeMos** in concert. **East Meets West** was the theme of the next session, hosted by **Kurt Walther** and featuring **Victor Nesrallah**, **The Angstones** and **Njacko Backo**. The poetic and beautiful **Laura Smith** next graced the stage. **Paul Symes**, owner of the **Black Sheep Inn**, hosted some acts that had performed at the popular Wakefield, Quebec club: **The Grievous Angels**, **Sarah Harmer**, **Stephen Fearing** and **Jennifer Noxon**. A double bill was provided by **Richard Wood** and **John Prince and A Piece of the Rock** in concert. There was fiddling aplenty at the cleverly named **Fiddle Heads** session hosted by **Marion Linton**, with **Richard Wood, Gaston Bernard, Greg Brown** and **Peter Jellard**. The audience was delighted when a half-hour session with **Tom Wilson** turned into a one-hour session of **Blackie and the Rodeo Kings**. **Stephen Fearing** and **Colin Linden** were welcome additions!

The entertainment on the **US Airways Stage** began with two local women in concert: **Brenna Rivier** and **Sally Robinson**. A session titled **L'Amour** was lovingly hosted by **Benoit Bourque** and showcased **Jorane Peltier, Wendy DeMos** and **Luann Kowalek**. The funky **Stringed Things** session included **Mel M'Rabet, Ruth Bowen, Rick Fielding** and **George Sapounidis**, and was hosted by **Ann Downey**. **Vance Gilbert** hosted the **American Acoustic I** session with **Bill Morrissey, Annie Gallup** and **Karen Savoca**. The **Edge of Folk** session included **Tom Wilson, Lucie Idlout** and **Martina Sorbara** and was hosted by **Stephanie Guzman**. **Ian Tamblyn** was an apt choice as the host of a **Back to Nature** session featuring the talents of **Jane Siberry** and **Bill Morrissey**.

The **Rogers Stage** inside **Lakeside Gardens** opened with the comically named **It's a Dobro, Bro** with **Rick Fines, Doug Cox** and **Vince Halfhide**. **Guitars Galore**, hosted by **Alex Houghton**, sizzled with the likes of **Terry Tufts, Stephen Fearing** and **Alan Marsden**. **Rasputin's** owner **Dean Verger** was on hand to host **Rasputin's Live** with **Michael Timmins, Ian Tamblyn, Ray Bonneville** and **Luann Kowalek**. Next it was time to do a **Blues Boogie Dance** with Kingston's excellent **Georgette Fry Band**. The most popular session of the day was **Burgundy, Bailey's and Bourbon**, a session of torch songs hosted by **Laura Smith**, with **Georgette Fry** and **Margo Timmins**. To end the daytime programming, the **My Hometown** session hosted by **Jennifer Noxon** boasted **Luann Kowalek, John Prince** and **The Angstones**.

Classical-style guitarist **Andrew Mah** was first up on the **Ontario. More to Discover Stage**. Concerts by the **Ottawa Harp Choir** and **Eve Goldberg** followed. Avid picker and tenor **Rick Fielding** appeared in concert. Three double bills were presented on this stage: **Alex Houghton** and **Martina Sorbara**; **Chuck Brodsky** and **Doug Cox**, and **Sherwood Lumsden**; and **Vance Gilbert** and **Colin Linden**.

Young stepdancers and fiddlers.

The Saturday evening concerts on the **Nortel Networks** stage opened with the contemporary country stylings of **The Grievous Angels**. **Georgette Fry** delivered a bluesy and emotive set. Quirky American singer-songwriter **Annie Gallup** was up next with a series of riveting story songs. **Cox, Fines** and **Brodsky** provided excellent instrumentation and vocals. American troubadour **Bill Morrissey** delighted and amused the audience with his charming adventures in song. The lively **Matapat** set included **Benoit Bourque** stepdancing while shaving a volunteer from the audience. The **Jane Siberry** performance held a few surprises including an impromptu opening number with **Jorane Peltier** that held the audience spellbound. The ever popular **Cowboy Junkies** closed the most well-attended day in CKCU Ottawa Folk Festival history with their own special blend of inspired ballads.

Sunday, August 29

The weekend of first-rate folk music continued on Sunday morning, which dawned bright and sunny.

The **Nortel Networks Stage** was first graced with

the presence of **Fireweed** in concert. The group's harmonies are reminiscent of Crosby, Stills, Nash and Young. **Poetry in Motion**, hosted by **Alrick Huebener** of **SugarBeat**, featured **Jane Siberry**, **Annie Gallup**, **SugarBeat** and **Alex Mortimer**. The mood turned to blue when **Sue Foley** appeared in concert with **Tony D**.

Then it was time for **Heartland Live, Part II.** The CBC Radio show was hosted by **Bill Stunt** and showcased the talents of **Big Gravel**, **Eve Goldberg**, **Andrea Karam and Fred Guignion**, and **James Gordon**. The afternoon on the big stage ended with **Vince Halfhide and Larry "The Bird" Mootham** in concert.

The **Ottawa Folklore Centre Stage** had a diverse lineup of talent. A **Singalong Folk Jam** hosted by **Arthur McGregor** kicked off the day. The **Ottawa Folklore Centre Weekend Choir** was onstage for two practices, coached by **Andy Rush**. Workshops teaching participants how to play the harmonica, the didgeridoo, or to learn shape note singing followed. The rocking sounds of **Lucie Idlout** rounded out the entertainment for the day.

Sunday morning was an opportune time for singing **Hallelujah** on the **Phase 2 Stage**. Host **Doug Cox** introduced a spiritually oriented session with **The Unceded Band, Rick Fielding, Andrea Karam, Fred Guignion** and **Peter Kiesewalter**. **Shelley Posen** hosted **Christmas in August**, featuring **Chuck Brodsky, Finest Kind** and storyteller **Ruth Bowen**. **Lynn Miles** was the host of the **I Can Relate to That** session showcasing **Laura Smith, Beth Ferguson** and **Tom Lips**. A concert with **Dar Williams** followed. The mood then shifted to **Celtic** in a session hosted by **Michaela Foster Marsh** with **Rawlins Cross** and award-winning Ottawa Valley fiddler **April Verch**. Verch also joined the next session, **Old-Time Fiddling**, hosted by **James Stephens** and featuring **Shane Cook, Stacey Lynn Read** and **Fast Forward.**

The entertainment on the **US Airways Stage** began with a session called **Wood and Steel**, hosted by **Lynn Miles**. **Andrew Collins, Joey Wright, Andrew Mah** and **Paul Fenton** also appeared. **Dario Domingues** hosted **North Meets South** with **Lucie Idlout, No Reservations** and **Aqsarniit**. **Jane Siberry** next appeared in concert. The final two sessions were acoustically inclined. The **Acoustic Blues** session hosted by **Larry "The Bird" Mootham** featured **Tony D, Sue Foley, Ray Bonneville, Vince Halfhide, Paul Fenton** and **Southside Steve**. **Angela Page** hosted **American Acoustic II** with **Dar Williams, Lucy Kaplansky, Chuck Brodsky** and **Richard Shindell**.

Michael Ball performing.

We've Got Rhythm was the theme for the **Rogers Stage**. Host **Karen Savoca** introduced an eclectic rhythm section including **Ken Harper, Ian Tamblyn, Kebba Jobateh** and **Fast Forward**. **We've Got You Covered** featured **Cry Cry Cry**, **Chuck Angus** and host **Sarah Harmer**. It was time for dancing with two lively sessions: **Modern Square Dancing** with **John Charman** and **Contradance for Everyone** with **Shindigo**. **Jane Siberry** hosted the **Laugh It Up** session with **Tom Lips, Trout Fishing in America** and **Vance Gilbert**. The day's activities ended with **James Gordon** in concert.

The **Ontario. More to Discover Stage** kicked off the day with **Trace Elements** in concert. **Jane Radmore** was onstage next. Four double bills followed: **Karen Savoca** and **Bill Morrissey**, **Michaela Foster Marsh** and **SugarBeat**, **Annie Gallup** and **Luann Kowalek**, and **Matapat** and **Monette et Poisson.**

Sunday evening on the **Nortel Networks Stage** began with the joyous sounds of the **Ottawa Folk Festival Weekend Choir**. Although storm clouds were gathering, the choir proclaimed in song that the storm was going to pass over. And it did! **Big Gravel**, a Toronto-based ensemble exploring fiddle music, swing and new acoustic styles performed next. **Terry Tufts**, a favourite of Ottawa audiences, delighted the crowd with his inspired vocals and intricate guitar playing. The original and amusing story songs of **Vance Gilbert** provided a highly entertaining set. The dynamic Sudbury-based group **No Reservations** was accompanied by a mesmerizing dancer wearing a traditional raven costume.

Young festival volunteer keeps the rain off.

There was barely a dry eye in the park when **Chopper McKinnon** accepted the **Helen Verger Award** for his role in promoting and supporting Canadian folk music. The host of the CKCU-FM Radio show *Canadian Spaces* for 19 years thanked his fans. The Space Cadets were out in full force to cheer on Chopper. Locally based and globally admired singer-songwriter **Ian Tamblyn** entertained the crowd with a sampling of his eclectic material. **Cry Cry Cry**, an American folk dream team, featured **Dar Williams**, **Lucy Kaplansky** and **Richard Shindell**. The singing poetry of the provocative **Laura Smith** stays in your mind long after you hear it and this performance was no exception. The lively sounds of the Newfoundland-based group **Rawlins Cross**, spanning Celtic, rock and traditional Maritime music, ended yet another incredible weekend of folk music at Britannia Park!

Year 7 – 2000

Folk from Coast to Coast to Coast

Beth Ferguson and Dario Domingues were remembered this year.

The CKCU Ottawa Folk Festival marked the millennium by celebrating some special anniversaries, including the 20th anniversary of the CKCU-FM folk music show *Canadian Spaces* (hosted by Chopper McKinnon), the 20th anniversary of **Rasputin's Folk Café** (operated by Dean Verger), and the 10th anniversary of the CKCU-FM traditional country, western and bluegrass music show, *The Back 40* (hosted by Ron Moores). It was also a time to remember two cherished Ottawa performers who died in the past year: **Beth Ferguson** and **Dario Domingues**. The festival was held from **August 25 to 27** at Britannia Park. **Chopper McKinnon** and **Karen Flanagan McCarthy** returned to host the main stage throughout the festival.

The 2000 festival had an outstanding lineup, wonderful weather and record attendance. Approximately 15,000 people visited the festival. "We were thrilled with the good weather, the great music, and the extremely positive audience response to our seventh festival," said Festival Director Gene Swimmer. "The way the community has embraced this event over the years is inspiring for all of us."

"This was our most elaborate festival so far, and also the smoothest," commented Festival Artistic Director Chris White. "The volunteers, performers and festival goers all did their part to create an environment where magic could and did occur."

With the theme of **Folk from Coast to Coast to Coast**, the seventh annual CKCU Ottawa Folk Festival presented at least one artist from each province and territory. Our American neighbours were also well represented by the outstanding talents of singer-songwriter **Greg Brown**, and **Odetta**, who is known as the Queen of American Folk Music. **Odetta** showed remarkable poise when she continued to sing after a power failure plunged the main stage into darkness during her performance. Without the benefit of a microphone, her magnificent voice reached the back of the park. Another highlight was **Garnet Rogers**, who accepted the **Helen Verger Award** for his outstanding contributions to Canadian folk music before delivering a show-stopping performance.

Chopper McKinnon and Karen Flanagan McCarthy with the cake celebrating the 20th anniversary of *Canadian Spaces*.

After Hours at the Avalon

After Hours at the Avalon featured artists in late-evening sessions held on August 24 to 27 at the **Days Inn Ottawa West**. These popular sessions

showcased the following performers:
- **Thursday, August 24**: James Keelaghan, The Herb Girls, and Karen Savoca.
- **Friday, August 25**: Moxy Früvous, Kim Barlow, Oh Susanna, Jacob Two-Two, Emily Celeste, David Keeble, Martina Sorbara, and Christina Smith & Jean Hewson.
- **Saturday, August 26**: The Arrogant Worms, Théodore Fontaine, Melwood Cutlery, Chris Chandler and Magda Hiller, David Francey, Chris MacLean, Eugene Ruffolo, Les Crapaudes, John Charlton and Tannis Slimmon.
- **Sunday, August 27**: The Sunday brunch featured Cowboy X, John Charlton and Tannis Slimmon.

Friday, August 25

Friday evening opened with **Ottawa Folklore Centre** owner **Arthur McGregor** performing his customary acoustic version of "O Canada." Next up was **Great Balancing Act**, a groovy band from New Brunswick that performed a spirited blend of folk and pop with great harmonies. They were followed by another fivesome: **Colores Andinos**, a group of South American origin that charmed the audience with the ethereal sounds of pan pipes, mandolin and Latin-style percussion. Accompanying them was **Nubia**, a passionate vocalist with Venezuelan roots.

The audience was next treated to the refreshing performance poetry of **Chris Chandler & Magda Hiller**. The American duo was a treat to the eyes and ears each time they performed. Chris and Magda were followed by the pulsating rock rhythms of **The Mike Plume Band** making their second festival appearance. The mood shifted to a performance of historical ballads from Prairie performer **James Keelaghan**.

Following intermission, the wacky, adorable and ever-popular **Moxy Früvous** took the stage with a high-energy performance. After a second appearance by **Chris Chandler & Magda Hiller**, **Oh Susanna** delivered a set of Appalachian-tinged ballads. **The Jim Cuddy Band** closed the evening with a mixed set of Blue Rodeo songs and material from Jim Cuddy's first solo album, *All in Time*.

Saturday, August 26

The day began on the **Nortel Networks Stage** with the heavenly sounds of the **Ottawa Harp Choir** in concert. At noon, **Folk from Coast to Coast to Coast** showcased easterners **Christina Smith** and **Jean Hewson**, northerner **Kim Barlow**, and westerners **UHF** (Ulrich, Henderson and Forbes). During the afternoon, CBC producer **Bill Stunt** recorded his session **Heartland Live 1**, which featured **Garnet Rogers**, **Darlene Sovran**, **Jacob Two-Two** and **Melwood Cutlery**. The next session, **Loonie Tunes**, was hosted by **Mike McCormick** and featured the comical antics of the other members of **The Arrogant Worms**, **Moxy Früvous** and **Chris Chandler & Magda Hiller**. The afternoon ended with the session **Acoustic Blues** with blues harpist **Gary Farmer**, **Tri-Continental** and **Ken Hamm**.

The **Rogers Stage** opened with the comical musings of **Laroque & Larolla** (**Richard Patterson** and **Sandy Crawley**). The **Ottawa Citizen Family Concert** with **Heather Bishop** and **The Arrogant Worms** entertained kids of all ages. Next up was **Théodore Fontaine** and **Les Crapaudes** in concert. The audience participated enthusiastically in the next session, **Learn to Samba**, hosted by **Mike Atyeo** and featuring dancers and **Samba Ottawa! The Women of Folk** showcased three generations of women pushing the boundaries of folk: **Odetta**, **Shari Ulrich** and **Martina Sorbara**. The last performance of the day

Two members of Aqsarniit performing Inuit throat singing.

was **Moxy Früvous** in concert.

The **Phase 2 Stage** presented **My Guitar**, an incredible concert featuring the guitar talents of **Ken Hamm**, **Pete Heitzman** and **Bill Bourne**. The **American Acoustic 1** session, named for the CKCU-FM show, boasted the talents of **Lucy Kaplansky**, **Greg Brown** and **Karen Savoca**. **Northern Exposure** showcased traditional Inuit song and dance with **Aqsarniit,** and the northern voices of **Kim Barlow** and **Tracy Riley**. For a change of pace, the **It's Only (Acoustic) Rock & Roll** session presented **Bill Henderson**, **Laroque & Larolla**, **Sarah Harmer**, and **Madagascar Slim**. **Le Mouton Noir** celebrated the popular Wakefield, Quebec club, the **Black Sheep Inn**. Owner **Paul Symes** hosted this session, which presented **Garnet Rogers**, **Sarah Harmer**, **Kathleen Edwards** and **Mike Plume**.

A barefoot Bill Bournes performing on a workshop stage.

The **US Airways Stage** opened with a double bill: **David Francey** and **Martina Sorbara** in concert. **The Next Wave** gave the younger generation of folkies a chance to show their stuff. **Jim Bryson** hosted **Emily Celeste** and **Mad Violet**. A second double bill featured **The Mike Plume Band** and **Great Balancing Act**. The **Prairie Power** session, hosted by **James Keelaghan**, showcased **Greg Brown** and **Heather Bishop**. The stage's last offering of the day was **East Meets East**, a down-home style kitchen party with P.E.I. native **Lennie Gallant** hosting Maritimers **Christina Smith & Jean Hewson**, and **Mad Violet**.

A double bill of **Gary Farmer** and **David Keeble** was the first entertainment of the day on the **Capital Double Decker & Trolley Tours Stage**. Another double bill followed with **Jorane** and **John Charlton & Tannis Slimmon**. The third double bill featured **Karen Savoca** and **Lynn Miles**. **Kathleen Edwards** hosted **Generation F**, a showcase of rising talents **Oh Susanna** and **Jim Bryson**. The final double bill of the day was a session with **Darlene Sovran** and the **Kim Barlow Band**.

The **CS CO-OP Family Area** opened with **Aytahn Ross** (formerly known as Tawny Ross) who juggled crystal balls and performed other amazing feats. The Inuit traditional group **Aqsarniit**, humorists **Laroque & Larolla**, and **Michael Cass-Beggs** also performed material geared towards the young and young at heart.

The **Ottawa Folklore Centre Stage** opened with an hour-long singalong with **Arthur McGregor**, followed by **HeartSong** in concert, a **Folklore Centre Festival Choir Practice**, and a session on **Learn to Play the Pennywhistle** with **Andy Daub**. Next up was a double bill of **Jacob Two-Two** and **Mad Violet**, followed by a double bill with **Oh Susanna** and **Melwood Cutlery**.

The **Nortel Networks Evening Concert** began with **Sarah Harmer**, a fine singer-songwriter who once fronted the Ontario band, Weeping Tile. The group **Aqsarniit** is dedicated to the preservation of Inuit culture. Their performance demonstrated traditional Inuit drumming, dancing and throat singing. Festival favourites, **The Arrogant Worms**, entertained with their usual zany and side-splitting humorous material. **Lucy Kaplansky**, who wowed last year's audience as part of the supergroup **Cry Cry Cry**, performed an engaging solo set that showcased her considerable talents as a singer-

Sarah Harmer was the opening act for the Nortel Networks Evening Concert on Saturday night.

songwriter. The avant-garde ensemble **F'loom** combined social satire, improvisation and poetry with a sophisticated range of acapella vocals. Crowd pleaser, P.E.I. native **Lennie Gallant**, entranced the crowd with his original roots-rock material.

Following the intermission, **Lynn Miles** gave a wonderful performance to a crowd familiar with her music and exceptional singing style. It was a homecoming performance as Lynn had recently moved back to Ottawa. One of the delights of the evening was **Jorane**, who mesmerized the audience with her unique cello and vocal performance. Acoustic guitar wizard **Jesse Cook** demonstrated why he is considered a virtuoso and rising star on the international stage. The crowd warmly welcomed the last act of the evening, the exceptional singer-songwriter **Greg Brown**. It was the American musician's first Ottawa appearance. His magical but all-too-short set, featuring accompaniment from **Karen Savoca**, **Pete Heitzman** and **Garnet Rogers**, closed the evening in fine style.

Sunday, August 27

Sunday morning has become a popular time for lovers of gospel music at the festival. **Voices of Praise**, a local ensemble that offers a refreshing mix of gospel and soul, opened the day on the **Nortel Networks Stage**. They were followed by **Shindigo** in concert, and **Heartland Live 2**, hosted by **Bill Stunt** and featuring **Jesse Cook**, **Chris MacLean**, **John Charlton & Tannis Slimmon**. **When Old Friends Meet** featured good friends **Greg Brown**, **Garnet Rogers** and **Karen Savoca**. **Jesse Cook** followed, dazzling the audience with his acoustic guitar stylings. The wildly original session **Celtic & Klezmer** followed, with host **Nicholas Froment** presenting **Beyond the Pale** and **La Volée d'Castors**.

On the **Rogers Stage**, the day began with **Back 40 Live, 10 Years After**. This session celebrated the 10th anniversary of the CKCU-FM program, *The Back 40*, which features traditional country, western and bluegrass music. Host **Ron Moores** was joined by **Melwood Cutlery**, **Roy Forbes**, **Ball and Chain**, and **Washboard Hank**. This session was followed by the **Ottawa Citizen Family Concert**, a fun-filled session that featured the whimsical bells, washboard and whistles of **Washboard Hank**, and the stepdancing youngsters of **Fast 4-Ward**. The young Ottawa Valley stepdancers stayed onstage for the participatory session **Stepdancing 4 Everyone**. After that, the wild and wonderful local ensemble, **The Herb Girls**, were joined by veteran western performer **Heather Bishop** in concert. Dance was the theme of the next participatory session, **Contradance for Everyone**, led by **Shindigo**. The afternoon ended on a resounding note with a **Drumming Circle** featuring **Rob Graves** of Shindigo.

Fine Old Traditions was the session that opened the **Phase 2 Stage** on Sunday. **Christina Smith**

Festival goers loved to sit beneath the beautiful willow tree for daytime performances over the years.

& Jean Hewson hosted a session showcasing Canadian traditions with **Russell Levia & Mary Gick** and **Les Crapaudes**. One of the most well-attended afternoon sessions of the festival was **20 Years of Uninterrupted Folk**, celebrating the 20th anniversary of *Canadian Spaces*, the popular CKCU-FM show hosted by **Chopper McKinnon**. Joining Chopper were some of his favourite "Space Cadets": **Lynn Miles, Garnet Rogers** and **Roy Forbes**. Plenty of well-wishers stayed on hand to congratulate Chopper and share some 20th anniversary cake. The **Songs of the Land** session hosted by **Luis Abanto**, explored the relationship between geography, climate and cultural expression, and featured **Tracy Riley, Hart Rouge** and **Colores Andinos**. The fast-paced session, **Battle of the Bards** pitted poets **F'loom** with **Chris Chandler & Magda Hiller**. That was followed by **The Leading Edge**, hosted by **Tom Stewart** and presenting **Jorane** and **Darlene Sovran**. The last session of the afternoon was **Slo' Tom (Tom Stewart)** in concert.

The cheery first aid team.

In the Beginning kicked off the afternoon sessions on the **US Airways Stage**. Host **Bill Bourne** explored the diverse roots of Canadian music, dance, story and song with **Tri-Continental** and **La Volée d'Castors**. **American Acoustic 2** was hosted by **Angela Page**, who introduced **Odetta, Magda Hiller** and **Eugene Ruffolo**. **Lynn Miles** hosted **The People You Love** session featuring **Lennie Gallant, Lucy Kaplansky** and **Jorane**. The **Vox** session hosted by **Mike Regenstreif** celebrated the wonders of the human voice as demonstrated by **UHF, Hart Rouge** and **Ball and Chain**. A special session celebrating the 20th anniversary of **Rasputin's Folk Café** was hosted by owner **Dean Verger** and featured **Lynn Miles, Eugene Ruffolo, David Keeble** and **Melwood Cutlery**. Plenty of fans were on hand to enjoy a spirited session celebrating the legendary Ottawa café that is an essential component of the local folk scene.

The Ragged Flowers kicked off the music on the **Capital Double Decker & Trolley Tours Stage** with a short concert. Host **James Keelaghan** guided us on an historical journey with the help of **Ken Hamm, Gail Anglin** and **Gary Farmer**. **Christina Smith & Jean Hewson** appeared next in concert. **Ken Hamm** stayed to host the **West Meets West** session, which featured an outstanding crew of westerners: **Bill Bourne** and **Lester Quitzau** of **Tri-Continental**, and **Oh Susanna**. Then it was time for a change of pace with the **New York, New York** session with Festival Director **Gene Swimmer** hosting fellow New Yorkers **Lucy Kaplansky** and **Eugene Ruffolo**. The day wound down with a splendid combination of **Words and/or Music** as **David Francey** presented **F'loom** and singing duo **Russell Levia & Mary Gick**.

The **Ottawa Folklore Centre Stage** began and ended the day with practices for the **Folklore Centre Festival Choir**. The second session was one close to the heart of the Folklore Centre: **The Folk Process in Canada**. **Michael Cass-Beggs** hosted an hour of entertainment illustrating the evolution of music, dance, story and song in different parts of the country, as demonstrated by **Les Crapaudes** and **Great Balancing Act**. In keeping with the Canadian theme, **Shari Ulrich** hosted the **Strong & Free** session, showcasing some of our most evocative singer-songwriters: **James Keelaghan, David Francey** and **Michael Cass-Beggs**. **Remembering Dario** was a moving tribute to Ottawa's much-loved musician, **Dario Domingues**, who died during the past year. **Dan Artuso, Ian Tamblyn, Nubia** and **Colores Andinos** joined with host **Jennifer Cayley** to share stories and songs of remembrance. Dario provided many magical moments during the first six festivals, whether playing his pan pipes on the main stage, performing in daytime sessions, or helping children explore the wonders of a wide array of instruments in the family area. A concert featuring **Lennie Gallant** followed.

The **CS CO-OP Family Area** began Sunday morning on a high note, with **Dean Verger**'s fun-filled session, **Storytime with Uncle Dean**. **Russell Levia, Les Crapaudes** and **Gail Anglin** followed with music and stories for the whole family.

The evening of concerts on the **Nortel Networks Stage** opened with the energetic stepdancing of **Fast 4-Ward**. The **Folklore Centre Festival Choir**, directed by **Jann Maloney-Brooks**, delivered a beautiful set of heartfelt songs. **La Volée d'Castors**, a twenty-something ensemble of six Quebec musicians, demonstrated why they are one of the province's most popular young groups. **UHF**, otherwise known as **Shari Ulrich**, **Bill Henderson** and **Roy Forbes**, share common musical roots stretching back three decades in British Columbia. As always, they delivered a tuneful and harmonious set, as one might expect from musical friends who all happen to be excellent musicians.

Garnet Rogers was awarded with the Helen Verger Award.

After a brief intermission, the group **Tri-Continental**, consisting of **Bill Bourne**, **Lester Quitzau** and **Madagascar Slim,** delivered an excellent and eclectic set. **Garnet Rogers** gave a gracious speech when he accepted the **Helen Verger Award** for his valuable contributions to Canadian folk music. He completely won over the crowd with an energized, rocking set that exemplified his musical genius as a master storyteller and a singer of songs from the heart.

Odetta amazed everyone when she continued performing during a power failure on Sunday evening.

Some of the brightest moments of the millennium CKCU Ottawa Folk Festival, however, took place in almost total darkness during a performance by folk music veteran, **Odetta**. She opened her set by leading the audience in a rousing singalong rendition of "This Little Light of Mine" and was just beginning the song "Careless Blues" when a power failure plunged the main stage and surrounding area into darkness. The audience spontaneously broke into "This Little Light" once again as people shone their flashlights to illuminate her, while backstage, workers scrambled to find portable lanterns to provide some light onstage. The effect was exhilarating, as the diminutive woman led the audience in song for half an hour, without the benefits of elaborate lighting or a sound system. Her unamplified voice rang strong and true, carrying to the edge of the crowd.

Odetta seemed undaunted by the disruption and graciously continued her performance, asking the audience to call out a request for a song they could all sing together. She settled on "Swing Low, Sweet Chariot" and led the willing audience in several verses as they swayed back and forth in time with the music.

The audience was entranced by **Odetta**, who was resplendent in a maroon and yellow turban and a bejeweled scarf. She also sang two "field hollers", getting the audience to help out on the choruses. Drummer **Kebba Jobateh** accompanied her from the audience on one song before partial power was restored and Odetta's piano accompanist rejoined her onstage. Odetta picked up where she had left off, with the song "Careless Love" and followed with blues standards including "St. Louis Woman" and "Weeping Know How". She finished the set with "This Little Light of Mine" and was greeted for her encore of "Willow Blues" followed by "Poor Man Blues" and "You Got To" with a well-deserved standing ovation.

Odetta's performance was followed by a short set from Canadian supergroup **Hart Rouge**, who opened the performance with an evocative acapella version of the Neil Young classic, "Helpless". And so ended the seventh annual CKCU Ottawa Folk Festival.

Financial Support

The festival received financial support from the proceeds of a series of benefit concerts held at a variety of venues in Ottawa. The 1999-2000 CKCU Ottawa Folk Festival concerts included the following shows:

- November 27, 1999: **Fred Eaglesmith** and **Fireweed** at Barrymore's
- December 11, 1999: **The Arrogant Worms** and **Chris White** at First Unitarian Congregation
- January 28, 2000: **Cindy Church** and **J.P. Cormier**, National Library Auditorium
- February 18, 2000: **Karen Savoca** and **Vance Gilbert**, National Library Auditorium
- March 24, 2000: **Connie Kaldor** and **David Francey**, National Library Auditorium
- April 14, 2000: **Bill Morrissey** and **Kathryn Briggs**, National Library Auditorium
- May 27, 2000: **Laura Smith** and **Terry Tufts**, National Library Auditorium

The CKCU Ottawa Folk Festival thanks the following sponsors, partners and suppliers: Nortel Networks, the *Ottawa Citizen*, CS CO-OP, Days Inn Ottawa West, Phase 2, The Ottawa Folklore Centre, Canadian Heritage, National Library of Canada, City of Ottawa, Regional Municipality of Ottawa-Carleton, Human Resources Development Canada, Ontario Arts Council, CKCU-FM, Rogers Television, *XPress*, CBC Radio One, Canada, NewsWire, Steve's Music Store, Indigo, Nutshell Music, The SOCAN Foundation, Integral Acoustics, Bell Mobility, Chapters, LoonySaver, The Ottawa Food Bank, VIA Rail Canada, US Airways, Capital Double Decker & Trolley Tours, Michael Davies Plymouth Chrysler Limited, D'Arcy Moving and Storage, The Loeb Glebe, Ginn: The Photography Store, Alexander Keith's, Coca-Cola and Key West Loaded Soda.

Year 8 – 2001

2001: A Folk Odyssey

The 2001 Headliners

The McGarrigles: Anna (left) and Kate (right).

Stuart McLean, Jesse Winchester,
John Prine and Ashley MacIsaac.

The 2001 CKCU Ottawa Folk Festival, held **August 24 to 26** at **Britannia Park**, had a stellar lineup of performers. American folk hero **John Prine** thrilled the capacity audience with a two-hour concert. Canadian folk icons **Kate and Anna McGarrigle** were awarded the **Helen Verger Award**, while up-and-comer **Evalyn Parry** was presented with the first annual **Beth Ferguson Award**. CBC broadcaster and storyteller **Stuart McLean** was on hand throughout the weekend, including a session where he read letters from overseas CUSO volunteers.

Festival organizers were over the moon. "It was our most successful festival ever," commented Festival Director **Gene Swimmer**. "Seeing the crowd waiting for John Prine was awesome. I couldn't help thinking about a rainy Sunday morning eight years ago when I was pretty sure nobody would show up, and there would never be a second Ottawa Folk Festival."

Co-founder and Artistic Director **Chris White** said the 2001 Ottawa Folk Festival was the most elaborate one ever presented in terms of the number of performers, the number of stages, the diversity of the program, and the number of attendees. "In spite of this unprecedented scope, the festival was also the smoothest one ever," said White. "I love the way all aspects of the festival have evolved over the years, and the way the audience embraces the variety of programming we present."

With the theme of **One Canada, Many Cultures**, the eighth annual festival presented five special theme sessions and showcased First Nations, Québécois, African, Asian, Latin American and Caribbean musicians. The featured musicians included **Celso Machado**, **Juan José Carranza**, **The Mighty Popo**, **Galitcha**, **George Sapounidis**, **Jeremy Moyer**, **Qiu Xia He**, **Women Ah Run Tings**, **Ball and Chain**, **El Hadi** and **Pierre Schryer**. **Chopper McKinnon** and **Karen Flanagan McCarthy** returned to host the main stage throughout the festival.

During the 2001 festival, we also paid tribute to **Ottawa Folklore Centre** co-founder **Terry Penner** and blues musician **Larry "The Bird" Mootham**, who both passed away since the last festival. The festival's choir was renamed **The Terry Penner Weekend Choir**, and a one-hour tribute session to Larry called **The Bird Still Flies**, was held on Sunday.

Friday, August 24

Friday evening opened with the thundering rhythms of Japanese traditional drumming group, **Oto-Wa Taiko**, followed by **Ottawa Folklore Centre** owner **Arthur McGregor** performing an acoustic guitar version of our national anthem. **Raggamuffin**, a lively reggae fusion band, next took the stage. The audience was then treated to a reunion of the folk band **Pied Pumkin**, whose members include **Rick Scott**, **Shari Ulrich** and **Joe Mock**. The group's last Ottawa festival performance was at the **Festival for the Folks** in 1976.

Shari Ulrich onstage as part of the reunion of Pied Pumpkin.

Following the intermission, festival goers warmly applauded a captivating performance by **Jesse Winchester**, a popular American-born musician and songwriter who has lived in Canada since the sixties. **The Wyrd Sisters** performed with their usual aplomb, their set running the gamut of styles from jazz to folk. Controversial Cape Breton fiddler **Ashley MacIsaac** caused a sensation when he launched into a whirlwind-paced set accompanied by **John Allan Cameron** on guitar. Hard pressed to keep up with MacIsaac's frenetic fiddling, Cameron displayed characteristic Maritime humour when he opened a song with the comment "Now I'm going to do a song Ashley has never heard." The evening ended with a set of hard-driving story songs by **Fred Eaglesmith**, to the delight of the many Fredheads in the crowd. His six-piece band included both **Willie P. Bennett** and **Washboard Hank**.

Saturday, August 25

This year, the festival added a new daytime stage located in the food court area. In all, there were eight daytime stages, which started at 11:00 a.m. and ran all afternoon. Festival goers had to make sometimes difficult choices of which session to attend in a given time period. Fortunately, because of the informal nature of the festival, it was possible to move between the stages during daytime sessions.

Artistic Director **Chris White** was happy to see so many people arrive at the festival early in the day to enjoy the myriad opportunities for participation, as well as the performances. "There is a definite element of magic in the spirit of community that exists in that beautiful park by the river, and in the activities that take place there during the day," White commented.

The **CS CO-OP Family Area** offered a variety of entertainment, workshops and activities, including face painting, instrument making, hat and jewellery making, bubble blowing, tie-dyeing and papier-mâché making.

On the **Nortel Networks Stage**, Saturday morning opened with a special live broadcast of the longest-running folk show on community radio in Canada: CKCU-FM's *Canadian Spaces*. The session was hosted by **Chopper McKinnon**, with guests **Joe Bishop & Kendall Sullivan**, **Roy Forbes**, **Selina Martin** and **Terry Tufts**. **Ron Moores** hosted the second half of the broadcast, billed as **CKCU-FM Back 40**, with guests **David Francey**, **Jenny and Dan Whiteley**, **Michele & John Law** and **Willie P. Bennett**. The next session, CBC Radio's **Bandwidth Live**, was hosted by **Bill Stunt** and showcased the talents of **Don Ross**, **Ember Swift** and **The Cash Brothers**. **Shari Ulrich** hosted the session **Shari and Her Boyfriends**, with **Rick Scott**, **Joe Mock**, **Roy Forbes** and **Jesse Winchester**.

The **Ontario. More to Discover Stage** located inside **Lakeside Gardens**, offered a diverse range of performers. The session **alt.folk@saturday.com** featured host **Ember Swift** with **First Chance Saloon** winners, **alicide** and **Darlene**. **Dean Verger** hosted **Rasputin's Folk Café** with guests **Kevin Cardamore**, **Nicholas Williams** and **Shari Ulrich**. The **Rick Scott for Kids** family concert was well attended. **My Favourite Things** was hosted by **Dan Whiteley** and **Joey Wright**, with guests **Joe Bishop** and **Selina Martin**. The participatory session **Dansez** was led by **Joséphine**. **Derek Debeer**, a former member of the South African band Jonny Clegg and Savuka, led a drumming circle with enthusiastic audience participation.

The **Phase 2 Stage** on the hill opened with the lively session **Six Strings, Many Cultures,** hosted by **The Mighty Popo** and featuring **Celso Machado** and **Juan José Carranza**. **Stephen Fearing** hosted the session **Sharing Our Stories** with **Kris Northey**, **Marcel Bénéteau** and **Willie Dunn**. The **Jay Willis Band** and the **Jenny Whiteley Band** performed in a double bill. The **Have Song, Will Travel** session featured host

Ron Moores, host of the CKCU-FM show Back 40 talking with Oliver Schroer.

Jim Bryson, Fred Eaglesmith, Kendall Sullivan and Stephen Fearing. The fast-paced **Fiddle Fever** session showcased the music of host **Oliver Schroer, Anne Lindsay, Ashley MacIsaac, Pierre Lessard, Pierre Schryer** and **Valerie Vigoda**. **Mary Gick** appeared in the last session of the day.

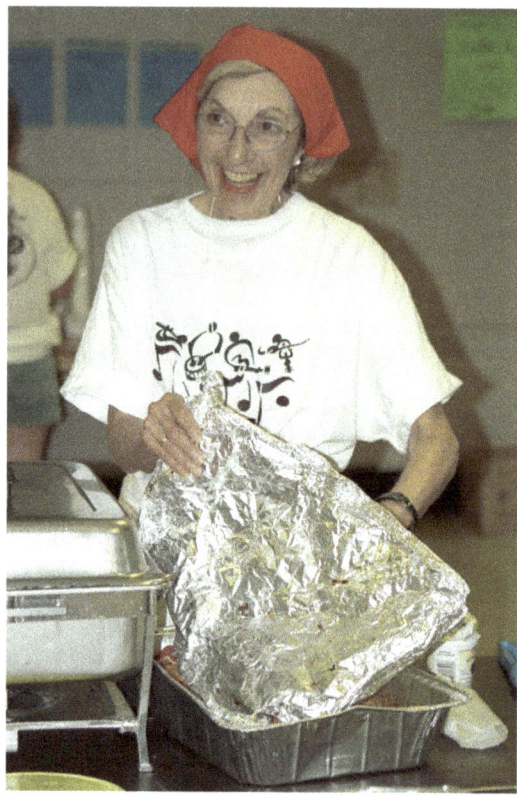

A volunteer preparing food for the volunteers.

The **Rogers Stage**, located around the corner from the **Phase 2 Stage**, opened with a double bill featuring the Ottawa bands **Siobhan** and **Satellite**. A tribute to the popular Quebec club, **The Black Sheep Inn,** was hosted by **Paul Symes** and featured **Darlene, Fred Eaglesmith, Susan Werner** and **Jim Bryson**. The **East Coast Kitchen Party** was a spirited musical celebration. It featured host **Greg T. Brown, Ashley MacIsaac, Siobhan,** and surprise guest **Pierre Schryer**, who was rushed in from the airport just in time to join in the fun. **Spirit Wind** hosted the **Harmony** session with **The Cash Brothers** and **The Wyrd Sisters**. **Jesse Winchester** earned a standing ovation at the finale of the **Beyond Borders** session with **Michele & John Law** and host **David Francey**. The daytime entertainment ended with the eclectic **Anne Lindsay Band**.

The **Capital Double Decker & Trolley Tours Stage** wins the award for longest stage name! The stage, located in the west field, opened with a double bill featuring **Jason Fowler** and **Kris Northey**. **Spirit Wind** hosted the session **When the Spirit Moves You** featuring **El Hadi** and **Kiva**. The entertainment also included two more double bills: **Anne Lindsay Band** and **Michele & John Law**, as well as **Terry Tufts** and **Willie Dunn**. Guitarist extraordinaire **Don Ross** hosted the session **A Sense of Place** with **Oliver Schroer** and **Marcel Bénéteau**. **Michael Jerome Browne**'s half-hour concert was the final performance of the day.

The **OFC Music Stage**, sponsored by the **Ottawa Folklore Centre**, offered a splendid afternoon of participatory sessions. The first session, **Sacred Harp Singing** with **Shelley Posen**, introduced the audience to this American style of singing. **Wendy Moore** hosted an **Introduction to Stepdancing**, **Willie P. Bennett** led the **Harmonica Workshop**, and **Arthur McGregor** presented the **Rise Up Singing** singalong. There was also a rehearsal of the **Terry Penner Weekend Choir** and a **Musical Mentor Showcase** featuring **Terry Tufts** and teachers and students of the **Ottawa Folklore Centre Canadian Musical Mentor** program.

The **CKCU-FM 93.1 Stage** located in the food court, held captivating concerts with **Ian Bell**; Chinese pipa player **Qiu Xia He; Joséphine**; First and Last Chance Saloon winners: **alicide, Kevin Cardamore,** and **The Jay Willis Band**; and **Spirit Wind**. The **Hot, Hot, Hot** session featured a spicy menu of performers, including **Juan José Carranza** (host), **Celso Machado** and **Women Ah Run Tings**.

The **CS CO-OP Family Stage** in the family area opened the day with a **Drumming and Music** session with **Spirit Wind**. **Nicky Brodie** of **Salamander Theatre** hosted **A World of Stories,** followed by **Just Kidding** with **George Sapounidis**. **Michael Jerome Browne** appeared in the wonderfully named **Tap, Clap, Snap** session.

Fit as a Fiddle featured **Pierre Lessard**. **Ian Bell** hosted **The Good Old Days** session. The afternoon entertainment ended with Dean Verger's **Storytime with Uncle Dean**.

The **CS CO-OP Family Crafts** area featured demonstrations on how to make sun-catchers (**Thomas and Naomi Burke of Glass Works**), jewellery (**Heather Boyd of Filament**), wood plaques (**Ron Tremback of Solar Woodcuts**), and sock puppets (**Phil Boyko of Valen Enterprises**).

The featured concerts on the **Nortel Networks Stage** began on Saturday afternoon with concerts featuring the jazzy alternative music of **Ember Swift** and the country-tinged rock from **The Cash Brothers**. The vibrant group **Women Ah Run Tings** exploded onstage in bursts of colour and sound, with their heady mixture of reggae, hip-hop, R&B and funk/rock. Gypsy-flamenco guitarist **Juan José Carranza** performed with his six-piece band. Bluegrass was the predominant theme of an evocative set by the **Jenny Whiteley Band**.

Jane Keeler presents Evalyn Parry with the Beth Ferguson Award.

The first **Beth Ferguson Award**, honouring the late singer-songwriter, was presented to **Evalyn Parry** for her ability to convey human experiences with relevance, intensity and wit through her music. Singer-songwriter **Beth Ferguson**, who died in 1999, was widely admired for the beauty and clarity of her songs, and for her commitment to communicating honestly about women's experiences.

Passionate singer-songwriter **Stephen Fearing** was in fine form during his set, wowing the audience with his inimitable guitar playing and intense lyrics. The zany francophone duo **Polly-Esther** captivated the audience with their folk-rock music.

After sunset, **John Prine** came onstage to a wildly cheering sold-out crowd, many of whom were thrilled to see the American folk music legend for the first time. With his excellent band, Prine maintained the excitement for two hours, playing hit after hit, recent tunes, a four-song encore, and a duet with **Jesse Winchester**. The evening didn't end there for some of John Prine's fans. About a dozen of them stayed on long after the concert ended, singing his songs under the stars.

Sunday, August 26

On Sunday morning, the entertainment on the **Nortel Networks Stage** began with **Galitcha in Concert**. This eminently listenable group performed East Indian folkloric music fused with jazz, classical Indian and Latin styles. The **Family Ties** session included, appropriately enough, **Kate & Anna McGarrigle**, **Northern Sons**, and **The Wyrd Sisters**. The **One Canada, Many Cultures** session echoed the theme of this year's festival and featured a variety of styles presented by host **Pierre Schryer**, **El Hadi**, **George Sapounidis Trio** and **Ball and Chain**. **Kathy Grant Mahon & Chosen** hosted the gospel-influenced **Sing Out** session. **The Northern Sons** session featured a set with this Ottawa Valley bluegrass band. Ottawa singer-songwriter **Jim Bryson** presented his well-crafted songs blending rock and folk. The Ottawa band **Cheza** performed some of their danceable, African-inspired music.

The **Ontario. More to Discover Stage** started the day with a session titled **3 x 2**, which featured three sets of duos: **Clear (Christian Patterson & Sue Johnson)**, **Joe Bishop & Kendall Sullivan**, and **Michele & John Law**.

The **Phase 2 Stage** started the day with the fascinating session **Speaking Out**, with host **Elana Harte**, **Evalyn Parry**, **Kris Northey** and **Susan Werner**. **Musical Journeys**, hosted by **Marcel Bénéteau**, included **Pangur Ban** and **Zainab**

Amadahy of **Spirit Wind**. The joyful **Acoustic Waves Turns 20** session was hosted by **Joe Reilly** and featured performers who had appeared in this renowned Ottawa folk music series: **Celso Machado**, **Oliver Schroer** and **The Wyrd Sisters**.

The Bird Still Flies was a moving musical tribute to the life of the late blues musician **Larry "The Bird" Mootham**. Hosted by **Vince Halfhide**, this session featured Larry's former student **Southside Steve**, **The Mighty Popo** and **Johnny Russell**.

East Meets West showcased the talents of host **George Sapounidis**, **Galitcha**, **Jeremy Moyer** and **Qiu Xia He**. The daytime entertainment on the **Phase 2 Stage** closed following a half-hour concert with **Ball and Chain** (**Michael Ball** and **Jody Benjamin**).

Enjoying the shade of an umbrella.

Darlene performs in a daytime workshop.

Just around the corner, the **Rogers Stage** drew a capacity crowd at **The Vinyl Café Live** with host **Stuart McLean**, **Arnie Naiman & Kathy Reid**, **Ian Bell** and **Michael Jerome Browne**. The youthful session **alt.folk@sunday.com** featured host **Selina Martin**, **Jim Bryson** and **Polly-Esther**. **The Celtic Rathskallions** hosted **Electicism(e)**, which also showcased **Joséphine**. **Ian Bell** led the **Musical Traditions** session with **Arnie Naiman & Kathy Reid** and **Kate & Anna McGarrigle**. Host **Michael Jerome Browne**, **Darlene**, **Southside Steve**, **Suzie Vinnick** and **Vince Halfhide** were featured in the **Blues Everywhere I Go** session. The day wound down with **Nicholas Williams** in concert.

The **Capital Double Decker & Trolley Tours Stage** opened with a double bill featuring **Marcel Bénéteau** and **Pierre Lessard**. Next, famed fiddler **Pierre Schryer** took to the stage. Host **Vince Halfhide**, **Southside Steve**, **Lady Luscious** (**Women Ah Run Tings**) and **Michael Jerome Browne** performed in the session **Music Moves Me**. Three double bills followed, showcasing the following performers: **Selina Martin** and **VSH**; **Joe Bishop & Kendall Sullivan** and **Susan Werner**; and **Evalyn Parry** and **Polly-Esther**.

The **OFC Music Stage** down by the water opened with a **Terry Penner Weekend Choir Rehearsal** led by **Andy Rush**. **Andy Daub** presented the session **Tin Whistle for Beginners**. The **Gospel Sing** session was hosted by **Anna Williams**. **Duncan Gillis** demonstrated during the **Bodhran for Beginners** session. **The Celtic Rathskallions Kid's Show** was up next, followed by a second **Terry Penner Weekend Choir Rehearsal**. **Tracy Vilbert's** session, **Learn to Belly Dance**, wound down the day's entertainment.

The **CKCU-FM 93.1 Stage** in the food court featured a series of concerts with the following excellent performers: **Pangur Ban**, **VSH**, **Darlene**, **Arnie Naiman & Kathy Reid**, **George Sapounidis Trio**, **El Hadi**, **David Francey** and **Clear**.

The **CS CO-OP Family Stage** began the day with the **Music Plus** session featuring **The Celtic Rathskallions**. **Celso Machado** followed with a **Children's Concert**. **The Rag & Bone Puppet Theatre** staged a kid's show titled *Secrets of Puppeteers*. **Monica Wolfe** presented two **Kindermusik** sessions. A **Sunshine Parade** ended the day's entertainment. Kids young and old walked across the grounds playing instruments and displaying articles made in the craft workshops.

The **CS CO-OP Family Crafts** featured demonstrations on how to make the following crafts: sun-catchers (**Thomas and Naomi Burke of Glass Works**), clay whistles (**Brian Harper of Harper Pottery**), and candles (**Greg Brayford of Doozy Candle**).

As the song goes, some days the rain must fall. And Saturday evening, the rain came down in torrents, which shut down the main stage for two hours. Undaunted, many of the festival goers crowded into **Lakeside Gardens**, returning when the entertainment resumed on the **Nortel Networks Stage**. While indoors, the audience was treated to a magical performance from the **Terry Penner Weekend Choir**, whose enthusiasm had not been dampened by the rainstorm.

The entertainment on the **Nortel Networks Stage** opened with **Joséphine**. CBC Radio's **Stuart McLean** was up next, followed by singer-songwriter **Susan Werner**. **Celso Machado** and **Qiu Xia He** performed an exotic set combining music played on the guitar and the pipa, a traditional Chinese instrument. **Kate & Anna McGarrigle** performed and were also presented with the **Helen Verger Award** for their valuable contributions to Canadian folk music. Since releasing their first album in 1976, the sisters have won two Juno Awards and attained international renown for their delicate harmonies, sensitive lyrics and rootsy North American sound. The festival wrapped up with a set from fiddling sensation **Pierre Schryer**.

Benefit Concert Series
The festival held a series of benefit concerts at a variety of venues in Ottawa.

Financial Support
The CKCU Ottawa Folk Festival thanks the following sponsors, partners and suppliers: Nortel Networks, Ottawa Citizen, Rogers Television, OFC Music (The Ottawa Folklore Centre), Days Inn Ottawa West, Canadian Heritage, City of Ottawa, National Library of Canada, Ontario. More to Discover, Human Resources Development Canada, Ontario Arts Council, CKCU-FM, CBC Radio One, Xpress, Canada NewsWire, Steve's Music Store, allgorithms Inc., Nutshell Music, Roger's AT&T Wireless, Phase 2, The Ottawa Food Bank, Dr. John L. Kershman, Hampton Inn, Integral Acoustics, CS CO-OP, The SOCAN Foundation, Bowie Electrical Services, Capital Double Decker Trolley Tours, Michael Davies Plymouth Chrysler Ltd., D'Arcy Moving and Storage, Loeb Glebe, Herb & Spice Shop, Alexander Keith's, Coca-Cola and Key West Loaded Soda.

Year 9 – 2002

East Meets West at Britannia Park

The year 2002 brought both Eastern and Western musical traditions and performers to the ninth annual CKCU Ottawa Folk Festival. "Our theme this year is 'East Meets West', both geographically and culturally," said Artistic Director **Chris White** in an interview in the *Ottawa Citizen*, "and I think that stimulated us to be even more adventurous in our programming."

In beautiful **Britannia Park**, festival goers were treated to musical acts from Eastern and Western Canada as well as to performers whose music combined Eastern and Western musical influences. The East Coast was represented by **Blacks Mountain** and **Les Muses**, two female groups from New Brunswick; as well as Nova Scotia acts **The Cottars** and **Slàinte Mhath**, and Newfoundland's **Ron Hynes**. Ottawa's own finger-picking guitarist **Terry Tufts** was an example of the fine talent featured from Ontario. Performers from Western Canada included **The Bill Hilly Band** and **Mae Moore** from British Columbia, and **The Wailin' Jennys** from Manitoba. **Chopper McKinnon** and **Karen Flanagan McCarthy** returned to host the main stage throughout the festival.

Diverse musical styles combining Eastern and Western influences included three groups with East Indian and North American influences: **Toronto Tabla Ensemble**, **Harry Manx** and **Galitcha**. Ottawa performer **George Sapounidis** sings in eight languages and he and his group perform music from Greek, Chinese, African and Western traditions. The **Khac Chi Ensemble** from Vancouver mesmerized the audience with traditional Vietnamese music.

Legendary performer **Buffy Sainte-Marie** was presented with the **Helen Verger Award** and was very well received by the crowd during her Sunday evening performance.

Festival goers seem pleased with both the location and atmosphere of the CKCU Ottawa Folk Festival. In an informal audience poll, emcee **Karen Flanagan McCarthy** asked the crowd if they wanted the festival to stay at Britannia Park or move downtown. The crowd indicated it wanted the festival to stay put. "I think we have the best quality of life of any festival," said Festival Director Gene Swimmer in the *Ottawa Citizen*. "We don't want to be the biggest festival, we want to be a good middle-sized festival."

Friday, August 23

The 2002 festival kicked off with the Afro-Brazilian rhythms of the percussion group **Samba Ottawa**, which drummed and danced its way in a lively procession from the festival gates to the main stage. Ottawa Mayor **Bob Chiarelli** welcomed the crowd and gave a short speech and was followed by **Arthur McGregor**, who performed his customary charming acoustic version of "O Canada". The evening's entertainment began with **Khac Chi**

A member of the Khac Chi Ensemble performing Vietnamese music.

Ensemble, a Vancouver husband-and-wife duo who perform traditional Vietnamese music. Engaging American singer-songwriter **Bill Morrissey** was followed by **Les Batinses**, a Quebec world music group and **Blacks Mountain**, a female bluegrass quartet from New Brunswick.

After the intermission, **Harry Manx** brought the crowd to its feet with his unique blues guitar playing seasoned with East Indian influences. The music swung to traditional Celtic with **The Cottars**, a group of four youngsters from Cape Breton. The evening ended with a bluesy set from the two "Colins" – guitar wizards **Colin James** and **Colin Linden**.

The after hours entertainment included **Chris MacLean, Rachael Sage** and **Harry Manx** at the **Days Inn Ottawa West**. **The Wailin' Jennys**, **Les Batinses** and **Slàinte Mhath** performed after hours at **D'arcy McGee's Bells Corners**.

Saturday, August 24

Daytime entertainment was provided on seven stages. The **CKCU-FM Family Area** hosted a variety of crafts, music and activities for children and their families. Another popular festival feature was the **Craft Village**, showcasing 20 artisans.

The **CUPE Main Stage** featured a "live-ly" instalment of the CKCU-FM folk show, *Canadian Spaces*, hosted live by **Chopper McKinnon**. The stellar talent on hand to perform for an appreciative audience included **Mae Moore, Garnet Rogers** and **The Anne Lindsay Band**. This was followed by **Back 40 Live** hosted by **Ron Moores**. **Blacks Mountain, Ron Hynes** and **The Bill Hilly Band** joined Ron and performed for an enthusiastic crowd. The afternoon also included an infusion of energy with **Espresso Music** featuring **Norouet**, a Quebec trio that plays a blend of French, Irish, Swedish and Eastern European music. Manitoba trio **The Wailin' Jennys** sang original tunes with breathtaking harmonies, followed by New Brunswick female quartet **Les Muses**, **Norouet** and **The Anne Lindsay Band**.

Over on the **Phase 2 Stage**, the fun kicked off with **Heather McLeod**, an eclectic singer-songwriter from Montreal who combines jazz, flamenco, Aboriginal rhythms and sixties folk influences in her charming compositions. British guitar icon **Richard Thompson**, a founding member of the influential folk-rock band **Fairport Convention**, amazed the audience with his intriguing lyrics and stunning guitar playing. Violin music featured prominently in the double bill with **GrooveLily** and **The Anne Lindsay Band**. The session **Madly Off…** featured madcap performers including host **Nancy White, Lorne Elliott** and **Jack Grunsky**. The **Hook, Line and Sinker** session was hosted by **Bill Morrissey** and included two talented fishermen: **Garnet Rogers** and **Greg Brown**.

Richard Thompson appealed to fans of British folk-rock band Fairport Convention.

The first session on the **Rogers Stage** was the **Vocal Beauty** session, hosted by **Catherine Crowe**, a traditional singer who combines modern expression and Old World restraint. The bevy of vocal beauties featured included **Les Muses** and **The Wailin' Jennys**. Next up was a set with **Mad Violet**, a guitar/fiddle duo, consisting of singer-songwriter **Brenley MacEachern** and fiddler **Lisa MacIsaac** (Ashley's sister). This was followed by **Keith's Kitchen Party 1**: a lively session sponsored by Alexander Keith's featuring hosts **Mad Violet**, three members of the contemporary Celtic group **Slàinte Mhath**, and **The Cottars**, four Cape Breton youngsters who specialize in traditional material. The next session, **The Story Behind the Song**, featured three masters of songwriting representing different countries: host

Garnet Rogers (Canada), Richard Thompson (England) and Bill Morrissey (United States). The humorously named Flamingo Double Bill showcased the talents of flamenco guitarist James Cohen and guests. Another double bill ended the day with sets from American singer-songwriter Karen Savoca, whose music combines soul, R&B and world rhythms, and sisters Nerissa & Katryna Nields, a duo known for its sublime harmonies.

The Kershman-Wasserlauf Stage kicked off the day with the flamboyant Rachael Sage, an American singer-songwriter who was a recent winner in the John Lennon Songwriting Contest. Quebec world music ensemble Les Batinses followed. A Family Concert featured children's performer Jack Grunsky and juggler and "nouveau vaudevillian" Aytahn Ross. Crowd participation was encouraged at A Contra Dance for Everyone with musical accompaniment by Flapjack and caller Catherine Burns. The Power of Love was the theme of the next session, which was hosted by Harry Manx and presented satirical songwriter Nancy White, Rachael Sage and Newfoundland singer-songwriter Ron Hynes. The day ended on an upbeat note with a dance with the irrepressible Maritime traditional band Slàinte Mhath.

The Bowie Electrical Stage opened with a set by Patricia Murray and was followed by a session with Les Muses. Tara MacKenzie performed next, in a duo featuring voices, harp and cello. The David Woodhead Trio played a set fronted by the trio's leader, who is a master of the fretless electric bass. That performance was followed by sets with Serena Ryder and Mad Violet.

The CKCU-FM Family Stage was the ideal place for people of all ages. Sessions included World of Wonders 1 with Aytahn Ross; Uncle Dean's Storytime featuring storyteller and Rasputin's Folk Café owner Dean Verger; Kindermusik, an early childhood movement and music program; Songs for All Ages with Heather McLeod; World of Wonders 2 with Aytahn Ross; The Cottars for Kids; and Hocus Pocus with Doctor Magic (George Sapounidis).

The algörithms inc. Stage opened with a session titled Inn the Black Sheep, hosted by Paul Symes, owner of the popular Wakefield, Quebec venue The Black Sheep Inn. Peterborough vocalist Serena Ryder, singer-songwriter and acoustic guitar player Cliff Eberhardt and guitarist extraordinaire Harry Manx performed in this eclectic session. The Sister Song 1 session, hosted by Mae Moore, also showcased the talents of singer-songwriters Heather McLeod and Serena Ryder. This session was followed by a set with world music ensemble, the George Sapounidis Trio. The American Acoustic session, named for the CKCU-FM radio show, was hosted by Karen Savoca and featured Nerissa & Katryna Nields and singer-songwriter Greg Brown. The day ended with a double bill with Flapjack, a group whose four members play a blend of fiddle tunes, original songs and early swing, and Patricia Murray, a native of Prince Edward Island who is a singer-songwriter in the folk and Celtic traditions.

Harry Manx was a great example of this year's theme, East Meets West.

The Ottawa Folklore Centre Teaching Stage provided participatory sessions in several musical forms including Learn to Play Middle Eastern

Rhythms with **Devin Johnstone**, **Learn to Play the Didgeridoo** with **Rob Pelletier**, **Learn "Shape Note Singing"** with **John Henderson**, **Learn to Play the Bodhran** with **Duncan Gillis**, **Rise Up Singing for Everyone** with Ottawa Folkore Centre owner **Arthur McGregor** and **Learn to Play the Tin Whistle** with **Andy Daub**. A choir rehearsal was also held for the **Terry Penner Memorial Festival Choir**, named in memory of the late **Terry Penner**, co-founder of **The Ottawa Folklore Centre**.

The **CKCU-FM Family Craft Area** hosted sessions teaching you to make a Native American ash basket (with **Marilyn Kromberg-Todd** and **Robert Todd of Tribal Spirit**), and how to make stained glass mosaics (with **Thomas and Naomi Burke of Glass Works by Burkes)**.

The Saturday evening entertainment on the **CUPE Main Stage** opened with a sensational set with melodic Canadian singer-songwriter **Mae Moore**, followed by the innovative and energetic New York City trio **GrooveLily**, featuring the violin stylings of **Valerie Vigoda**. CBC Radio favourite, comedian **Lorne Elliott**, entertained the crowd with his hilarious comedy routine. The **Beth Ferguson Award** was presented to **Darlene**. **Nerissa and Katryna Nields**, two sisters whose music has been described as sublime harmonies and Generation X angst, also performed.

Lorne Elliot was his usual madcap self.

The Toronto Tabla Ensemble performed an entrancing set following the intermission, combining the traditional music of the tabla, a North Indian drum, with world music influences including jazz. American singer-songwriter **Greg Brown** demonstrated why his music has inspired an intensely loyal fan base across North America. The crowd enthusiastically greeted the legendary British guitar virtuoso **Richard Thompson**, whose intriguing lyrics and stunning guitar skills have won him a huge following worldwide. *Ottawa Sun* reporter Denis Armstrong described Thompon's performance as follows: "In a dazzling, funny and touching solo performance, Thompson proved to still be the quintessential folkie, the aging artist at the height of his powers, who still burns with a telling story and a sense of social justice that hasn't aged in 40 years." Armstrong added that "Thompson had all 5,500 fans, including many of the weekend's featured performers, hanging off his every word." The evening ended with a lively set from **Slàinte Mhath**, the Canadian Maritime group who perform traditional Celtic music with a twist on tradition.

The Wailin' Jennys.

The after-hours entertainment at the **Days Inn Ottawa West** included **Les Muses**, **Cliff Eberhardt** and **Ron Hynes**. **The Wailin' Jennys**, **Les Batinses** and **Slàinte Mhath** performed after hours at **D'arcy McGee's Bells Corners**.

Sunday, August 25
The entertainment on the **CUPE Main Stage** began with **Bandwidth Live**, a recording for the CBC Radio show, *Bandwidth,* hosted by **Bill Stunt**. The participants included guitar virtuoso **Terry**

Tufts, duo **Mad Violet** and flamenco guitarist **James Cohen**. **Mike Regenstreif** hosted the **Short Stories that Rhyme** session with songwriters **Ron Hynes**, **Cliff Eberhardt** and **Bill Morrissey**. **Calasaig**, an energetic five-piece band from Scotland, which performs traditional music from the British Isles as well as original compositions, performed next. They were followed by a session showcasing vocalist and percussionist **Karen Savoca**, accompanied by her partner, guitarist **Pete Heitzman**. Ottawa blues musician **Tony D** and duo **Mad Violet** also performed individual sets. The daytime entertainment ended with a performance by the **Terry Penner Memorial Festival Choir** directed by **Michael MacDonald**.

Anne Lindsay, Valerie Vigoda and Ivonne Hernandez were featured in the Femmes Fiddles workshop Sunday morning.

Michael MacDonald directed the Terry Penner Memorial Festival Choir.

In the Tradition was the opening session on the **Phase 2 Stage**. It was hosted by **Tara MacKenzie** and featured **Châkidor**, a Québécois band showcasing the talents of acoustic guitar player and singer **André Varin** and violinist **Valérie Pichon**. **Sister Song 2**, hosted by **Rachael Sage**, featured American "rock-folk" performer **Melissa Ferrick** and Australian singer-songwriter **Emma Wall**. Ottawa Valley folk music aficionado **Brian Crook** was the host of a session called **Traditions Coast to Coast** featuring **The Bill Hilly Band** and **The Cottars**. A double bill with **Châkidor** and **Patricia Murray** followed. The day ended on a Celtic note with **Keith's Kitchen Party 2** with host **Calasaig**, **Tara MacKenzie**, **Patricia Murray** and Grand North American Fiddle Champion **Ivonne Hernandez**.

The **Rogers Stage** began the day with **The Flower Hour**, hosted by CBC *Radio Noon* host **Dave Stephens** and featuring garden guru **Ed Lawrence**, festival co-emcee **Karen Flanagan McCarthy** and **GrooveLily**. **Femmes Fiddles** featured female fiddlers **Anne Lindsay**, **Valerie Vigoda** and **Ivonne Hernandez**. The **Global Guitars** session showcased the instrumental brilliance of host **Terry Tufts** and **Harry Manx**. Finally, the thought-provoking **Songs with a Message** session hosted by **Melissa Ferrick** featured two stellar songwriters: **Greg Brown** and **Garnet Rogers**.

The **Kershman-Wasserlauf Stage** opened with a lively set from the **Toronto Tabla Ensemble**, which also hosted the next session, **East Meets West 2**, featuring the **George Sapounidis Trio**. A **Family Concert** followed, showcasing **Jack Grunsky**, the **Inuit Cultural Performers** and Ottawa music therapist **Kim Kilpatrick**. The cleverly named session, **You Say Savoca, I Say Savuca**, featured percussionist **Derek Debeer** (formerly of the African band Johnny Clegg and Savuca), and American singer and percussionist **Karen Savoca**. The passionate rhythms continued with the session **Drum-Along with Derek** hosted by **Derek Debeer**.

Diverse cultural elements were in evidence on the **Bowie Electrical Stage**. Champion teenage fiddler **Ivonne Hernandez** started the day off and was followed by **Inuit Cultural Performers**, **Galitcha**, **GrooveLily**, **Calasaig**, **The Cottars**, and the upbeat ensemble **Offbeat**, a 25-member percussion group that uses unconventional instruments.

The **CKCU-FM Family Stage** started with the session **Silly Songs**, featuring humorous tunes composed and performed by Festival Artistic Director **Chris White**. **Kim Kilpatrick** followed with **Dog Tales**, while **Nancy White** performed hilarious songs during the **Momnipotent** session, which showcased songs from the album of the same name. A session with **Kindermusik** was followed by **Move to the Music** featuring **Toronto Tabla Ensemble**. **Inuit Cultural Performers** hosted the **Dance to the Beat** session. The day concluded with a **Sunshine Parade**, where the young and young at heart could participate in a happy and noisy procession leading to the main stage.

The **algörithms inc. Stage** hosted five double bills featuring **Emma Wall** and **Rachael Sage**; **Chris McLean** and **Mae Moore**; **Jim Bryson** and **Nerissa & Katryna Nields**; **Ron Hynes** and **Melissa Ferrick**; and **Cliff Eberhardt** and **Harry Manx**. The **East Meets West 3** session was hosted by **Galitcha**, an Ottawa ensemble that combines traditional East Indian music with contemporary and world influences, and featured **Harry Manx**.

The **Ottawa Folklore Centre Teaching Stage** opened with a rehearsal of the **Terry Penner Memorial Festival Choir.** This was followed by various teaching sessions including **Learn to Play Acoustic Blues Guitar** with **Vince Halfhide**, **Learn to Play Harmonica** with **Southside Steve**, and **Learn to Belly Dance** with **Tracey Vibert**. The day's fun also included a **Musical Mentor Showcase** with **Terry Tufts**, and **Gospel Singing for Everyone** featuring local blues vocalist **Maria Hawkins**.

At the **CKCU-FM Family Craft Area**, participants had the opportunity to make several different crafts, including jewellery (with **Heather Boyd** of **Filament)**, a piece of wooden fretwork (with **Ron Tremback** of **Solar Woodcuts**), and stained glass mosaics (with **Thomas and Naomi Burke** of **Glass Works by Burkes**).

Châkidor, a Québécois guitar/violin duo featuring **André Varin** and **Valérie Pichon** kicked things off on Sunday evening on the **CUPE Main Stage**. Virtuoso guitar player **Terry Tufts** was followed by acoustic blues player **Guy Davis**. The mood changed to hilarity with the satirical singer-songwriter **Nancy White**. Ever-popular singer-singwriter **Garnet Rogers** performed the next set to the great pleasure of the assembled audience.

Following the intermission, rocky folk artist Melissa Ferrick performed. After the presentation of the Helen Verger Award to the legendary Buffy Sainte-Marie, the veteran singer-songwriter performed an amazing set in a rare Ottawa performance. Backed by an accomplished full band, she performed protest and love songs that she had written and released throughout her long and prestigious career as well as more recent material. The audience responded very warmly to her evocative performance that included insightful commentary and renditions of favourites including "Universal Soldier", "Up Where We Belong", "Until It's Time for You to Go", and "Bury My Heart at Wounded Knee". The Bill Hilly Band's

Learn to Bellydance was one of the daytime workshops on the Ottawa Folklore Centre Teaching Stage on Sunday.

lively bluegrass-inspired set was followed by a set from guitarist James Cohen, concluding what was perhaps the most eclectic CKCU Ottawa Folk Festival to date!

Legendary singer-songwriter Buffy Sainte-Marie was the recipient of the Helen Verger Award.

Year 10 – 2003
Ten Years of Uninterrupted Folk Festivals

The little festival that could! From its humble beginnings as a one-day event in 1994, the CKCU Ottawa Folk Festival has developed into one of the best folk festivals in Canada. In 2003, we celebrated the sheer joy of showcasing Canadian culture through music, dance, storytelling and crafts for the 10th consecutive year.

Max Wallace, then station manager of community radio station CKCU-FM, discussed the idea of a folk festival on the CBC Radio show *All in a Day*. Wallace was soon contacted by **Chris White**, an Ottawa performer who headed the local songwriting collective, **Writer's Bloc**. They met to discuss the idea and on a September evening in 1993 at Carleton University bar Mike's Place, the CKCU Ottawa Folk Festival was born.

Finest Kind were well-known to the festival audience for their traditional material.

The organizing committee met regularly for a year to organize the first festival. The committee included **Gene Swimmer, Chris White, Max Wallace, Pam Marjerrison, Sheila Ross, Barry Pilon, Roberta Huebener, Chris Brown, Suzanne Lauzon** and **Joyce MacPhee**. Local businesses such as the **Ottawa Folklore Centre** offered financial sponsorship, while individuals such as **Chopper McKinnon**, host of the CKCU-FM folk radio show *Canadian Spaces*, and **Dean Verger**, owner of **Rasputin's Folk Café**, offered valuable advice and support. **Karen Flanagan McCarthy**, the arts reporter on the CBC Radio show *All in a Day* agreed to co-host with Chopper and they have become regular hosts on the evening main stage.

The festival was launched on August 28, 1994, with a full day of entertainment on **Victoria Island**. The five afternoon stages featured Ottawa Valley fiddling and stepdancing, world music, a tribute to **Stan Rogers** and a ceilidh. The main stage performers included **Valdy, David Wiffen, Ian Tamblyn, Lynn Miles** and **Dario Domingues**. In comparison, the 2003 festival featured eight daytime stages and, for the first time, a fourth evening of entertainment.

A cake celebrating the tenth anniversary.

Gene Swimmer, who took over as Festival Director in 1996, remembers his dismay when the first day of the festival began with pouring rain. "It rained all morning," he recalled. "But by noon, the sun came out and we had a very good turnout."

In its second year, the

festival moved to **Britannia Park**, known for its scenic location on the Ottawa River, as well as for gorgeous sunsets. Then in 1996, the festival ran into its first major challenge. In the fall, CKCU was forced to withdraw its organizational support, putting the 1997 festival in serious jeopardy. The crisis was averted when **Arlo Guthrie** performed two sold-out benefit concerts at the National Library Auditorium in December. A group of volunteers led by **Carol Silcoff** raised additional funds by organizing a silent auction in conjunction with the concerts.

The parking volunteers became the "festival greeters" in later years to recognize their role in welcoming the public.

Volunteers continue to play a vital role in the festival's continued success. Each year as the festival approaches, the core team of approximately 20 grows to more than 400 volunteers who work hard to make the event run smoothly. Some of the volunteers plan their vacation time around the festival, and there are a number of families who have been volunteering since the first year.

Part of the success of the festival lies in the positive media coverage it has received over the years. Allan Wigney, an entertainment writer with *XPress*, wrote that the festival had grown to be "one of the premier North American events of its kind." **Lynn Saxberg**, an entertainment writer with the *Ottawa Citizen*, has covered the folk festival for most of the 10 years. In her opinion, "…the folk festival has developed its own unique vibe. It's not the biggest festival in town, but it's the nicest."

Chris White echoes this sentiment. "It's the whole environment of what happens down there, not just because of the (musical) lineup but because of the atmosphere," says White. "It's an experience that has value beyond simply going to a concert."

Ottawa Folklore Centre owner **Arthur McGregor** opens each festival by performing his trademark acoustic version of "O Canada". He was not the only first-year performer who returned in year 10. **Lynn Miles**, **Ian Tamblyn**, **Terry Tufts**, **Finest Kind** and **Tony Turner** were among the many 1994 performers who returned in 2003. Our wonderful emcees, **Chopper McKinnon** and **Karen Flanagan McCarthy**, who have contributed enormously to the success of the festival since day one, made their usual spirited contributions to the festival. They were joined in their emcee duties by **Michel Dozois**, producer of the National Arts Centre's Fourth Stage, and **Rachel Hauraney**, a professional writer and radio host who has been a festival volunteer since 1994. Rachel's parents, **Phil and Cari Hauraney**, are among the scores of volunteers who returned for a tenth year to help the festival run smoothly.

A photo exhibit celebrated Café Le Hibou, which ran from 1960 to 1975.

Thursday, August 21

The first-ever Thursday evening concert at the CKCU Ottawa Folk Festival opened with **Arthur McGregor's** acoustic guitar rendition of "O Canada". Ottawa Mayor **Bob Chiarelli** welcomed the crowd. **Shauntay Grant**, a young performance poet from Halifax, delivered her spoken-word compositions to an appreciative crowd. **Jesse Zubot** and **Steve Dawson**, two brilliant Vancouver performers, demonstrated why they are rising stars of the folk and roots music scene. Their high-energy acoustic music is infused with elements of jazz, bluegrass, world music and folk.

Following the intermission, Prince Edward Island fiddler and stepdancer **Richard Wood** entertained with his instrumental virtuosity and stunning showmanship. **Dar Williams** received a warm welcome. Her evocative voice and beautifully crafted songs captivated the audience. The evening ended on a high note with the young Calgarian twins **Tegan and Sara**, whose performance showed a punkier, poppier edge to their acoustic sound. The twins were given a loud and enthusiastic reception, especially from the young fans who turned out for their show.

Friday, August 22
The evening entertainment on the **CUPE Main Stage** began with **Leela Gilday**, a singer from Yellowknife whose classically trained voice touches audiences on spiritual and emotional levels. Leela was followed by the traditional Québécois band **Le Vent du Nord** whose members sing and play instruments such as the hurdy gurdy, piano, violin, guitar and accordion. Many festival goers were familiar with stepdancer/accordionist **Benoit Bourque**, who had previously performed at the festival with the band **Matapat**. Juno Award-winner **David Francey** charmed one and all with his poignant and moving story songs. The singer-songwriter accompanied himself on guitar and was joined by guitarist **Dave Clarke** and multi-instrumentalist **Geoff Somers**. The mood next shifted to the infectious world-beat rhythms of **The Mighty Popo** who appeared with his seven-piece band. Influenced by the music of his native Burundi, the guitarist and singer combined blues, reggae and African styles in his set.

Two celebrated female performers, one Canadian and one American, followed the intermission. **Lynn Miles** entertained her loyal following with melancholy songs of love and longing. The singer-songwriter demonstrated her enormous talents, which won her a well-deserved Juno Award earlier in the year.

Many festival goers were thrilled to see the legendary Emmy Lou Harris perform on the main stage.

Emmylou Harris is an icon of contemporary American roots music. She was greeted with great warmth by the crowd, many of whom were hearing the veteran songstress in concert for the first time. Emmylou's elegant set blended elements of country, folk, bluegrass and pop, and was punctuated by her commentary delivered in a charming Southern accent. The audience witnessed an outstanding performance by the queen of alternative country music.

After Hours Music at the Travelodge included performances from **Alise Marlane**, **Angie Nussey**, **Harmony Trowbridge**, **Steel Rail**, **The Toasted Westerns**, **Kim Barlow** and **The Laws**.

Saturday, August 23
The daytime sessions took place on eight stages starting at 11:00 a.m. Another popular festival feature was the **Craft Village** featuring 23 artisans.

The **CUPE Main Stage** kicked off with **Here's to Rasputin's**, a session hosted by Rasputin's owner **Dean Verger**. Performers **Ian Tamblyn**, **Lynn Miles** and **Terry Tufts** have appeared frequently at the legendary folk café. **Emmylou and Friends**, hosted by **Rich Warren**, featured **Emmylou Harris**, **Jane Siberry** and **The Laws**. **Michel Dozois** hosted **Québexplosion**, showcasing the talents of **Le Vent du Nord**, **Éric Beaudry**, **André Brunet**, **Sandy Silva** and **Pierre Belisle**. The tribute to *Canadian Spaces* session was led by **Chopper McKinnon**, host of the longest-running folk show on community radio in Canada. Artists who have appeared on the show, including **Aengus Finnan**, **David Francey**, **Jane Siberry** and **Steel Rail**, were on hand to help Chopper and the Space Cadets in the audience celebrate.

The **Ottawa Folklore Centre Stage** debuted with **Fiddle Plus**, hosted by **Nathan Curry**, a veteran Celtic musician who was joined by **André Brunet**, **Gordon Stobbe**, **Olivier Demers** and **Soozi Schlanger**. **Arthur McGregor** hosted a folky singalong titled **Rise Up Singing**, named after the songbook of the same name. Exotic rhythms and expressive dance next took centre stage with a **Learn to Bellydance** workshop. The **Terry Penner Memorial Festival Choir** had a rehearsal before piano wizard **Peter Kiesewalter** hosted **Keyboard Basics**. The day's activities ended on a gentle note with **Kindermusik** led by **Barb Smith**.

The **CKCU-FM Family Area**, located in the main field, was a busy, fun place for kids of all ages. The crafts, games and storytelling began at 11:00 a.m. and went on until late afternoon. Mini-workshops that allowed family members to create their own masterpieces were hosted by **Glass Works**, **Filament** and **Solar Woodcuts**.

On the **Bowie Electrical Stage**, the **Taking Turns** sessions allowed performers to strut their stuff. **Mike Plume**; **Alise Marlane** and **Leela Gilday**; and **Alicide** and **Christine Fellows** entertained throughout the afternoon. **Raven Kanatakta**, an eclectic young singer-songwriter from Northern Quebec whose influences include his native Algonquin heritage as well as jazz, blues and folk traditions, and **ShoShona Kish**, a singer-songwriter, spoken word artist and dancer originally from Toronto, performed solo sets. **Kim Barlow**, a Whitehorse-based artist who plays guitar, banjo and cello, appeared with her trio. The New Brunswick duo **Isaac and Blewett** closed the day's entertainment with music that featured **Tim Isaac** on cello and **Jim Blewett** on guitar.

A talented hooper.

The **Kershman-Wasserlauf Stage** in the **Ron Kolbus Lakeside Centre** kicked off with **Galitcha and Friends** featuring **Benoit Bourque**, **Kathy Armstrong** and the **Kim Barlow Band**. **Planet Drum** was a rhythmic event hosted by **Kathy Armstrong** showcasing the percussive talents of **Kebba Jobateh**, **Pepe Danza** and **Wayne Hamilton**. The **Ottawa Citizen Family Concert 1**, hosted by **The Celtic Rathskallions** presented the hilarious **Trout Fishing in America**. **JouTou** hosted **Around the World in 60 Minutes**, a workshop with an eclectic lineup of **Dean Verger**, **Galitcha** and **Tracey "Halyma" Vibert**. **Dance with Popo** challenged anyone within hearing distance to stay still during a set from the irrepressible bluesman **The Mighty Popo**.

Entertainment on the **Nutshell Music Stage** opened with **Out of Left Field** with **Ann Downey** (host), **Angie Nussey** and **Bob Snider**. **Guitar Delights** featured an impressive trio of guitar heroes including host **David Woodhead**, **Dave Clarke** and **Roddy Ellias**. **Leela Gilday** hosted **Northern Exposure**, a session with a roundup of northern artists that included **Kim Barlow**. **All the**

News That's Fit to Sing (Phil Ochs' Legacy) was the intriguing title of a session that explored the music of the late great American folksinger. Phil's sister **Sonny Ochs** hosted the session with **Arthur McGregor** and **Maria Dunn** paying homage to **Phil Ochs**. **Ron Moores**, host of the CKCU-FM traditional country, western and bluegrass music show *The Back 40*, led a session of the same name featuring **Keith Glass**, **Steel Rail** and **The Laws**.

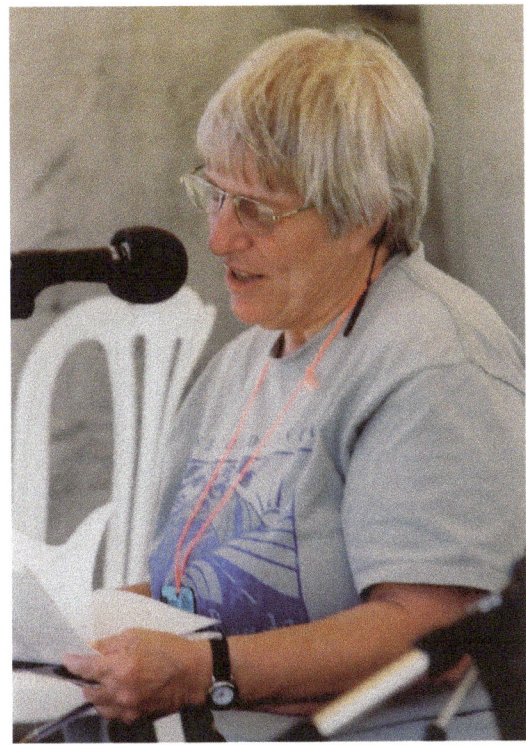

Sonny Ochs hosted a workshop exploring the music of her late brother, Phil Ochs.

On the **Rogers Stage**, **Karen Flanagan McCarthy** hosted the **Gardening Show** with gardening expert **Ed Lawrence** and the poetry and music of **Susan McMaster & Geode**. **Gord Peeling**, host of the CKCU-FM Celtic music show *Music from the Glen*, led a session of the same name with **Bobby Watt**, **Finest Kind**, **Linda Miller & Nathan Curry**, and **Nicolas Boulerice & Bernard Simard**. **Carolyn Sutherland** hosted **Heart Strings**, an evocative session with string-y professionals **Buddy Miller**, **Lynn Miles**, **Mike Plume** and **Wendell Ferguson**. **Atlantic Scene Revisited**, hosted by **Heather Moore**, featured **Gordon Stobbe**, **Harry Martin**, **Isaac and Blewett** and **Shauntay Grant**. **Shelley Posen** hosted the **Funny, Eh?** session with punsters **Bob Snider** and **Trout Fishing in America**.

The **algörithms inc. Stage** rolled out with **The Edge of Folk** featuring **Shauntay Grant** (host), **Alicide** and **Harmony Trowbridge**. The latter performer hosted **Generation F**, showcasing young performers **Amanda Rheaume** and **Stephanie Clement**. **Morna Ballantyne** hosted **Working Folk**, a session with songs about work performed by **David Francey**, **Ian Robb** and **Maria Dunn**. **Words Plus Music** presented spoken word and musical accompaniment from host **Sheila M Ross & Scot P Dunlop** as well as **David Woodhead**, **Sandra Nicholls & Roddy Ellias**. The day wound down with a **Gordon Lightfoot Tribute**. The tribute, hosted by **Aengus Finnan**, featured **Ian Tamblyn**, **Alise Marlane** and **Terry Tufts**, who shared their favourite memories and tunes of one of Canada's most beloved folksingers.

Betty and the Bobs delivered an hilarious set.

The Saturday evening entertainment on the **CUPE Main Stage** began with the rollicking supergroup **Betty and the Bobs**. The band had the audience grooving and swaying with their smorgasbord of country, jazz, blues and R&B. The energy level remained high with talents from far away: the Australian band **Fruit**, and the British-born singer-songwriter **Zoë Lewis**, who was accompanied by **Roxanne Layton**. Audience favourite **Ian Tamblyn** next entertained with some of the classic Canadian folk songs he has written, including "Woodsmoke and Oranges". Between numbers, Ian reminisced about his performance at the first festival.

Following the intermission, festival favourites **The Arrogant Worms** delivered their own wacky take on Canadian life and culture. Audience participation was encouraged! The **Helen Verger Award** was presented to **Jane Siberry** before she performed a mesmerizing, moving set. The main stage performances ended with **La Bottine Souriante**, an exuberant nine-member group that performed numbers ranging from traditional Québécois tunes to jazzy originals.

Jane Sibery, who was a great fan of CKCU-FM for its support of her music, received the Helen Verger Award.

The festival goers who weren't ready to sleep yet on this particular Saturday night went to the **After Hours Music at the Travelodge** to groove with **Bob Snider**, **Betty and the Bobs**, **The Arrogant Worms**, **Aengus Finnan** and **Isaac and Blewett**.

Sunday, August 24

On the **CUPE Main Stage**, the day opened with **Tony Turner** hosting **This Land of Ours**, a session celebrating songs about Canada and featuring singer-songwriters **Keith Glass** and **The Laws**. **Bill Stunt**, host of the CBC Radio show *Bandwidth*, hosted **Bandwidth Live 1**, a session showcasing the talents of **Ron Sexsmith**, **Sarah Harmer** and **Ray Montford**. **Simply the Song** featured veteran songwriters **Buddy Mondlock**, **Ian Tamblyn** and **Jane Siberry**, and was presented by **Mike Regenstreif**, host of the Montreal radio show *Folk Roots/Folk Branches*. Two supergroups, **Betty and the Bobs** and **VSH**, as well as **Bob Snider** appeared in the session **CBC Bandwidth Live 2**, hosted by CKCU-FM station manager and CBC arts journalist **Matthew Crosier**.

Jane Sibery looks on as Ian Tamblyn performs.

The **Ottawa Folklore Centre Stage** entertainment began and ended with the **Terry Penner Memorial Festival Choir** rehearsing with choir director **Mike MacDonald**. The **All in the Family** session was hosted by **Searson**, a talented Ottawa Valley family quintet specializing in traditional music, and featured **Ivonne & Kalissa Hernandez**. **Roxanne Layton** led the **Learn to Play the Recorder** session. Livewire **Zoë Lewis** presented **There's Music in Everything (for kids)**. Banjo player **Mary Gick**, a lover of traditional American styles, hosted the **Old-Time Music** session with other trad fans including **Ann Downey**, **Gordon Stobbe** and **James Stephens**.

The **CKCU-FM Family Area** provided ongoing crafts, games and storytelling. Three nifty **Crafts for Kids** sessions were hosted by **Kinsella Crafts**, **Glass Works by Burkes**, and **White Trash Ink**. Costumes and musical instruments were optional, but fun was mandatory in the **Sunshine Parade**, which wound its way from the Family Area to the **CUPE Main Stage** and back. **Kathy Armstrong** led kids of all ages in a joyful and noisy parade.

Kids large and small gather outside the Saunders Farm inflatable train.

The **Bowie Electrical Stage** opened with the traditional sounds of **Red Wood Central**, otherwise known as **Michelle "Red" April** and **Al Wood**. Three **Taking Turns** workshops featured solo sets by **Bobby Watt** and **Bob Snider**, **Tony Turner** and **Suzie Vinnick**, and **Amanda Rheaume** and **Angie Nussey**. The whimsical **Magoo** was followed by **Searson**.

The **Kershman-Wasserlauf Stage** in the **Ron Kolbus Lakeside Centre** was the setting for sessions featuring an array of traditional music. The entertainment kicked off with **Linda Miller** and **Nathan Curry** (host) and **Magoo**. The **Contra Dance for Everyone** session was led by **The Old Sod Band** with caller **Catherine Burns** and encouraged audience participation in a traditional folk dance. In a different flavour, the **Cajun Dance Party** featured **Poutine Étouffée**. **One Instrument, Many Cultures** was a session featuring guitarists **Juancho Herrera** (host), **André Thibault**, **Nathan Curry** and **Ray Montford**. The **Mother Earth** session featured the band **Fruit** (host), **Shauntay Grant** and **Wolf Moon** (**Sheila M Ross** and **Scot P Dunlop**).

The **Nutshell Music Stage** opened with **Strings Unlimited** featuring **Ray Montford** (host), **Isaac and Blewett** and **Qiu Xia He**. Things turned comical with **A Laugh and a Half**, a session hosted by **The Arrogant Worms** and featuring **Magoo** and **Zoë Lewis**. World music was the focus of **Music of the Diaspora** with **Kleztory** (host), **Juancho Herrera & Michal Cohen**. **Paul Symes**, owner of **The Black Sheep Inn**, hosted a session with performers who had played at the popular Wakefield, Quebec club including **Alise Marlane**, **Mike Plume**, **Ron Sexsmith** and **Stephanie Clement**. The day ended on a tasty note with **Cajun Bagels** showcasing the talents of **Poutine Étouffée** (host) and **Kleztory**.

The entertainment on the **Rogers Stage** began with the session **Voices in Harmony** with **Finest Kind** (host), **Fruit** (trio) and **VSH**. **A Mighty Wind Instrument** was hosted by **The Celtic Rathskallions** and showcased **Mel Watson** and **Peter Kiesewalter**. There was definitely something fishy going on during the **Fishing with Worms** session that brilliantly paired funsters **Trout Fishing in America** (host) with **The Arrogant Worms**. The mood shifted from the ridiculous to the sublime with the session **Sources of Inspiration** with **Alicide** and **Christine Fellows**. CKCU-FM Ottawa Folk Festival Director **Gene Swimmer** hosted the final session of the afternoon with the **Director's Choice** session featuring **Buddy Mondlock** and **Zoë Lewis & Roxanne Layton.**

Christine Fellows and **Maria Dunn** were the first entertainers on the **algörithms inc. Stage** with the **Prairie Sirens** session. The **Adventures**

Sheila Ross and Scott Dunlop perform as Wolf Moon. Sheila recites her poetry and is accompanied by Scott.

in Music session hosted by **Amanda Rheaume** featured **Maria Dunn** and **Raven Kanatakta & ShoShona Kish**. Rocker **Mike Plume** hosted the **Lost and Profound** session with **Christine Fellows**, **Elana Harte** and **Kim Sheppard**. The adventure continued with the **Acoustic Blues** session hosted by **Isaac and Blewett** and featuring **Raven Kanatakta** and **Red Wood Central**. The entertainment for the day ended with **The Travelling Musician** session showcasing **Aengus Finnan** (host), and **Juancho Herrera & Michal Cohen**.

The final evening performances on the **CUPE Main Stage** began with the wonderful three-part harmonies of **VSH** (**Suzie Vinnick**, **Kim Sheppard** and **Elana Harte**), whose group members are also solo performers in their own right. **JouTou** gets its name from the French phrase meaning "play everything". And they do! Their exciting blend of influences includes Chinese, South American, Irish and Québécois cultures. American singer-songwriter **Buddy Mondlock** and the American folk festival favourites **Trout Fishing in America**, delivered sets before the **Terry Penner Memorial Festival Choir** performed, led by **Mike MacDonald**. A highlight of their music was the Stan Rogers classic "Bluenose".

After the intermission, the trio **Finest Kind** gave a rousing performance of their traditional material. **Ron Sexsmith**, the wildly popular singer-songwriter from Toronto who is gaining international acclaim, delivered an evocative set.

Rising star **Sarah Harmer** was received warmly by the audience throughout her spirited performance.

Near the end of the evening, many of the Festival organizers joined the **Terry Penner Memorial Festival Choir** onstage to sing "Happy Birthday". The audience joined in and so ended the 10th annual Ottawa Folk Festival.

Celebrating the tenth anniversary on the main stage.

Incredible singer-songwriter Ron Sexsmith.

Year 11 – 2004
Most Diverse Lineup yet at the 11th Annual CKCU Ottawa Folk Festival

Three of the four headliners of the 2004 Ottawa Folk Festival – Michael Franti, Judy Collins and Arlo Guthrie.

The roster of the 11th annual CKCU Ottawa Folk Festival was studded with superstars of three generations, including **Michael Franti**, **Arlo Guthrie**, **Judy Collins** and **Jackie Washington**. These talented and accomplished performers exemplified the diversity of this year's festival lineup. Festival goers had an opportunity to applaud artists from across Canada and the United States and to celebrate the richness of folk music, which today sits at the crossroads of numerous cultural influences. The recipient of the 2004 **Helen Verger Award** was **Jackie Washington**.

Anticipation for the festival was high. "With reggae activists Spearhead, the indie-rock collective Broken Social Scene and 1960s pioneers Judy Collins and Arlo Guthrie booked as headliners, the CKCU Ottawa Folk Festival unveiled the coolest, most eclectic lineup of its decade-long existence," said Lynn Saxberg in the *Ottawa Citizen*. "We felt we had to go for the best talent we possibly could," said Festival Director Gene Swimmer, "and when these people were available, we just went for it."

Two new festival awards were presented during the weekend. On Friday evening, **Joe Grass** received the **Galaxie Rising Stars Award** from **Roch Parisien**, programmer and producer of the **Folk Roots** channel on the **Galaxie** network of the CBC. **Lis Harvey** and **Dave Carmichael** were awarded the **One Fret Less Award** on Saturday evening. This award was made possible by a **Community Foundation of Ottawa** endowment established by **Harvey and Louise Glatt**, long-time supporters of folk music and singer-songwriters.

Thursday, August 26

Ottawa Folklore Centre owner **Arthur McGregor**, who opens each festival with an acoustic version of "O Canada", delivered a well-executed rendition of our national anthem. **Chopper McKinnon** and **Karen Flanagan McCarthy** returned to host the main stage throughout the festival. **Frida's Brow**, a group named after Mexican artist Frida Kahlo, consists of **Chris MacLean**, **Alise Marlane** and **Jennifer Noxon**. The trio charmed the audience with gorgeous harmonies and songs reflecting a range of musical influences. **Gérald Laroche** entertained one and all with unique storytelling, accompanying himself on a variety of harmonicas and percussive instruments. Senegalese brothers **Karim** and **El Hadji Diouf** fronted the energetic band **Diouf**, an ensemble that combined vocal harmonies, percussion, guitars and drums, and performed a mix of traditional and contemporary tunes. Next up was singer-songwriter **Ember Swift**, who with co-creator **Lyndell Montgomery** on violin, bass and bowed guitar, delivered politically charged folk-jazz-funk music. **Broken Social Scene**, the ultra-hip dynamic collective of Toronto's vibrant experimental music scene, closed the evening with a series of eclectic jams. The music proved infectious for many in the first-night crowd, who jumped to their feet and danced long into the warm summer night.

Friday, August 27
Friday night opened on a dramatic note with **Eagle & Hawk**, a group that combined hard-driving rock with traditional Aboriginal vocals and rhythms. The audience soon warmed up to the Juno Award-winning group, which incorporated Native dance and costumes in its performance.

American singer-songwriter **Rachael Davis** contributed an eclectic set that illustrated influences ranging from jazz to folk to pop. She was followed by Winnipeg native **Joel Kroeker**, whose set featured alternative folk, rock and jazz.

The excitement was palpable when fiddler **Eileen Ivers & Immigrant Soul** opened with a dynamic set of traditional Irish music interlaced with African, Latin and American roots rhythms. **Eileen Ivers** amply demonstrated the talent that stood her in good stead when she starred in *Riverdance*. It was almost impossible not to dance!

The high energy and dancing continued with **Michael Franti & Spearhead**. The phenomenally popular group dazzled the crowd with hip-hop roots fusion music championing peace and social justice. After putting in an intense and highly danceable performance that particularly appealed to the young members of the audience, the charismatic Franti was not ready to go home. He generously signed autographs for nearly an hour after his performance and offered kind words and hugs to his many fans.

Saturday, August 28
Saturday Daytime Workshops
The entertainment on the **CUPE Main Stage** opened at 11:00 a.m. with the well-attended *Canadian Spaces* **Live** session hosted by **Chopper McKinnon**. This popular session featured two singer-songwriters of East Coast extraction: **Joe Grass** and **Gordie Sampson**, humorist **Nancy White**, and newcomer **Liam Titcomb**. Another live CKCU-FM show followed with the **Back 40 Live** session hosted by **Ron Moores**. It featured **Corb Lund**, **Rachael Davis**, **Rae Spoon** and **Michael Jerome Browne**.

The excitement mounted for fans of both veteran singer **Judy Collins** and Canadian icon Leonard Cohen with the **Collins Sings Cohen** session. Collins performed selections from her just-released album *Judy Collins Sings Leonard Cohen: Democracy*. The performance was enriched by her many anecdotes about their long friendship. Collins related how she met Cohen in the mid-sixties when he was a fledgling songwriter. She helped to launch his career by recording his songs, most notably "Suzanne", which was a major hit. The afternoon continued with **NAC Alberta Scene Preview** hosted by **Heather Moore** and featuring **Corb Lund, Lindsay Jane, Rae Spoon** and **The McDades**. The entertainment wound down as it had begun, with a CKCU-FM host. **Laurie-Ann Copple** hosted the **Musical Connections** session featuring **Eve Goldberg**, **Wendell Ferguson** and **Sandy Scofield**.

Taking Turns was the first session on the **Bowie Electrical Stage** and showcased the music of **Dave Carmichael** and **Mark Reeves**. **Changing the World with a Song** featured the Ottawa-based choir **Just Voices** led by **Greg Furlong**. **Lonesome Paul** was featured in the **Welcome Back!** session. Three successive **Taking Turns** sessions allowed the crowd to sample the talents of **Art Turner, Shane Simpson & Paul Bourdeau**; **The Vanity Press** and **Ana Miura**; and **Joe Grass** and **Kate Weekes**.

At the **Kershman-Wasserlauf Stage**, a lively **Dance** session showcased the music of **Eagle & Hawk**. The ever-popular **Connie Kaldor** was featured in the first **Ottawa Citizen Family Concert** and performed songs from her hit children's album, *A Duck in New York City*. CKCU-FM alumnus **Roch Parisien** hosted

Galaxie Rising Stars, sponsored by the CBC digital music network **Galaxie**. Featured artists were **Joe Grass**, **The Vanity Press**, **Ana Miura** and **Ryan Schneider**. **Sonny Ochs**, the sister of the late American folksinger **Phil Ochs**, hosted the **American Women** session with **Zoë Lewis**, **Lis Harvey** and **Natalia Zukerman**. Another **Dance** session featuring **Corb Lund** and his band ended the afternoon performances.

The fun on the **CKCU-FM Family Stage** began with **Music Together** led by **Liz Benjamin**. Ottawa songwriter **Russell Levia** appeared next, followed by the **Stories for Everyone** session hosted by master storyteller **Gérald Laroche**. **Barb Smith** and **Chris Moore** hosted the participative **Kindermusik** session. The Celtic-influenced band **The Gruff** appeared to the delight of the assembled children of all ages. The breezily named session **World Winds** hosted by **Ron Korb** featured **Bruce Fontaine** of **Eagle & Hawk** along with **Duncan Cameron** and **Joe Phillips** of the **Pierre Schryer Band**.

Kids enjoying the performance.

On the **Ottawa Folklore Centre Stage**, **Arthur McGregor** hosted **Rise Up Singing**, a session titled after the songbook of the same name. The **Terry Penner Memorial Choir**, directed by **Michael MacDonald**, had its first rehearsal. Instructional workshops included **All About Flutes** with **Ron Korb**, and **Learn How to Play the Tin Whistle** with **Anj Daub** and **Jeremiah McDade**. Other "how-to" sessions included **How to Write a Song** hosted by **Connie Kaldor** with **Gordie Sampson**, **Shelley Posen** and **Mike McCormick**, and **How to Play Music Together** with **The McDades**. The day ended with a half-hour session of a spiritual nature: **Getting Started with Taoist Tai Chi**.

First on the **Nutshell Music Stage** was **Joel Kroeker**, who hosted the **Self Expression** session including **Ryan Schneider** and **Art Turner**. The lively **Pierre Schryer Band** performed next. **Down East Pudding** was hosted by **Cam Wells** and featured **Dave Carmichael**, **Gordie Sampson** and **Nancy White**. **Morna Ballantyne** hosted **Songs of Struggle and Hope**, which showcased the considerable talents of **Eve Goldberg, Vince Fontaine** of Eagle & Hawk, **Ember Swift** and **Just Voices**. The jovial **Laugh It Up** session featured host **Nancy White**, **Connie Kaldor**, **Washboard Hank**, and **Jay Bodner** and **Spatch Mulhull** of **Eagle & Hawk**.

The wonderful East Indian-influenced music of **Galitcha** was the first offering on the eclectic **Rogers Stage**. **Dean Verger**, owner of **Rasputin's Folk Café**, hosted **Rasputin's Presents** with **Frida's Brow**, **The Vanity Press** and **Ember Swift**. The **Black Sheep Live** session featured musicians who had appeared at the Wakefield, Quebec folk club and included **Rae Spoon**, **Rachael Davis**, **Joel Kroeker** and **Lindsay Jane**. The **Pierre Schryer Band** and **The Old Sod Band** performed in the **Celtic Crossroads** session. Festival Director **Gene Swimmer** hosted the **Director's Choice** session with **Joel Kroeker**, **Mark Reeves** and **Zoë Lewis**.

Canada's folk, roots and world music magazine, *Penguin Eggs,* sponsored the **Penguin Eggs Stage**. The entertainment began with **From Far and Wide**, featuring host **Sandy Scofield**, **The Gruff** and **Kate Weekes**. The **Silly Songs** session featured funsters **Mike McCormick**, **Eve Goldberg** and **Wendell Ferguson**. The mood turned more serious with the session titled **The Art of Justice** with host **Chris MacLean**, **Oni the Haitian Sensation**, **Sandy Scofield** and **Alise Marlane**. Long-time festival emcee **Karen Flanagan McCarthy** hosted the **Across Cultures** session with **Gérald Laroche** and **Ron Korb**. The day ended with the **Guitars R Us** session showcasing the talents of host **Shane Simpson**, **Paul Bourdeau**, **Kristin Sweetland** and **Ray Hickey Jr.** of the **Ron Korb Band**.

Wendell Ferguson kept the crowd in stitches.

The **CUPE EnviroTent**, sponsored by the **Canadian Union of Public Employees**, featured ongoing displays, discussions and hands-on activities related to environmental issues and responsible living. Sessions included **Organic Food and You** with **Laura Telford** of **Canadian Organic Growers**; **Vermicomposting** with **Lori Watt** of **The Worm Factory**; **An Environmental Festival** with **Kathryn Briggs (EcoRail Tour)**; **The Fair Trade Movement** with **Chantal Havard** of **TransFair**; and **Alternative Energy Sources** with author **Bill Kemp**.

Saturday Evening CUPE Main Stage
The Saturday evening entertainment on the **CUPE Main Stage** opened with Vancouver-based singer-songwriter **Sandy Scofield**, whose compelling material reflected her Métis roots. **The McDades** delivered a set of rootsy music that blended Celtic, world and jazz influences. The band includes fiddler, singer and producer **Shannon Johnson** and her brothers **Jeremiah** and **Solon McDade**. Albertan roots-country cowboys, the **Corb Lund Band**, performed a lively set that set toes a tappin' in the audience.

Arlo Guthrie and **Judy Collins** were contemporaries on the American folk scene in the sixties and onward. The capacity crowd at Britannia Park was thrilled to witness back-to-back performances from these legendary silver-haired performers. **Arlo Guthrie** is an old friend of the Ottawa Folk Festival. His performances in two benefit concerts in 1996 made it possible for the festival to survive a difficult period. Arlo charmed the audience with amusing anecdotes and performed hits such as "City of New Orleans" and "Coming Into Los Angeles" as well as some Woody Guthrie songs. The performance **Judy Collins** gave was nothing less than extraordinary. Her pure, beautiful voice proved as lovely as ever as she performed a variety of material from her long career. Collins also touched on her connection with Canadians Joni Mitchell and Leonard Cohen. The evening ended with Dominican Republic artist **Joaquin Diaz**, who performed contemporary and traditional merengue tunes filled with syncopated accordion rhythms.

Ember Swift and Lyndell Montgomery at a daytime stage.

Other Saturday evening venues included the **Alt-Folk Café**, located onsite at the **Kershman-Wasserlauf Stage**, and off-site at the **Travelodge Hotel Ottawa West** located on Carling Avenue. The **Alt-Folk Café** was hosted by **Ember Swift** and included sets with **Spiral Beach**, **Joe Grass**, **Liam Titcomb**, **Lindsay Jane**, **Kate Weekes** and **Rae Spoon**. **After Hours at the Travelodge** featured **Pierre Schryer**; **Scarlett, Washington and Whiteley**; **Natalia Zukerman**; and **Zoë Lewis** and **Mark Reeves and Friends** in the **Beachcomber Room**. **Galitcha** hosted a jam session in the **Acoustic Room**.

Sunday, August 29
Sunday Daytime Workshops

On the **CUPE Main Stage**, the morning opened with the **New Voices** session with host **Sam Baijal**, **Natalia Zukerman**, **Rachael Davis**, **Mark Reeves** and **Darryn Grandbois**. The soulful session **Blues Without Borders** was hosted by eclectic guitarist **Harry Manx**, and featured **Jackie Washington**, **Ken Whiteley**, **Michael Jerome Browne**, **Solon McDade**, **Gérald Laroche** and **Joe Grass**. **CBC Bandwidth Live** was a live version of the CBC Radio show focusing on Ontario performers, and was hosted by **Bill Stunt**. The diverse lineup included **Oni the Haitian Sensation**, **Jane Bunnett**, **Eve Goldberg** and **Kristin Sweetland**. DJ **Mike Regenstreif** hosted the **Folk Roots/Folk Branches** session with **Jane Bunnett**, **Harry Manx**, **Rachael Davis** and **Jay Bodner** of **Eagle & Hawk**. The **Fiddle Focus** session with host **Pierre Schryer** featured **Valérie Pichon** and **André Varin** of **Châkidor**, **Samantha Robichaud**, and **Shannon Johnson** of **The McDades**.

The entertainment on the **Bowie Electrical Stage** opened with three **Taking Turns** sessions. First up were **The Gruff** and **Ball and Chain** followed by **Kristin Sweetland** and **Lis Harvey,** and **Lindsay Jane** and **Ryan Schneider**. Other sessions showcased the talents of **Rae Spoon**, **Michael Jerome Browne** and **The Twin Rivers String Band**, **The Gruff** and **Junkyard Symphony**.

A **Tribute to the Past** was the first session on the **Kershman-Wasserlauf Stage**. Host **Eve Goldberg** performed and introduced **Mose Scarlett**, **Michael Jerome Browne**, and folklorist-musician **Shelley Posen**. The second **Ottawa Citizen Family Concert** called **Music in Everything** highlighted the music of host **Zoë Lewis** and a presentation of **Junkyard Symphony's Garbage and Guitars**. Audience participation was highly encouraged at three **Dance** sessions led by **Sandy Scofield**, **Joaquin Diaz** and **Ball and Chain**.

A member of Eagle & Hawk hoop dancing amidst the crowd.

The **CKCU-FM Family Stage** performances began with the **Music Together** session led by **Liz Benjamin**. **Hoops and Flutes** was a session with **Bruce Fontaine** of **Eagle & Hawk**. **Kate Weekes** performed in the **Songs I Like** session. **Splash'N Boots** performed two interactive sets. The **Kindermusik** session was led by **Barb Smith** and **Chris Moore**. The **Celtic Rathskallions with Wendy Moore-McGregor** performed an enjoyable and lively set. Kids of all ages were

Ontario singer-songwriter extraordinaire Eve Goldberg.

invited to participate in the **Sunshine Parade**, which involved marching and dancing with musical instruments. The happy and noisy celebration made its way to the main stage, gaining participants en route.

The **Ottawa Folklore Centre Stage** opened and closed the day with rehearsals of the **Terry Penner Memorial Choir** directed by **Michael MacDonald**. **How to Sing in Harmony** featured the talented musicians of **Frida's Brow** along with **Ball and Chain**. **Miles Howe** and **Roxanne Layton** hosted sessions teaching participants how to play the harmonica and recorder respectively. **Rev. Ernie Cox** led the session titled **About Gospel Music**. More harmonica tips were provided in the session **Advanced Harmonica Techniques** hosted by **Gérald Laroche**.

Kids getting crafty in the Kidzone.

Sources of Inspiration was the first session of the day on the **Nutshell Music Stage**. It featured host **Kristin Sweetland**, **Wendell Ferguson** and **Lis Harvey**. The **Taking Turns** session included sets by **Darryn Grandbois**, and **Valérie Pichon** and **André Varin** of **Châkidor**. **The Gruff** and **The McDades** teamed up in the session **Western Celtic**. **Galitcha** led the spirited **Learn East Indian Dancing** session. The day ended on a spiritual note with the **Gospel Unlimited** session showcasing host **Ken Whiteley**, **Connie Kaldor**, **Eve Goldberg**, **Rev. Ernie Cox** and **Mark Reeves**.

On the **Rogers Stage**, festival emcee **Karen Flanagan McCarthy** hosted **The Flower Hour** with celebrity gardener **Ed Lawrence** and humorist **Nancy White**. The laughter continued with **Funny Folk** with host **Morna Ballantyne**, **Arlo Guthrie**, **Nancy White** and **Mike McCormick**. **A Tribute to Leonard Cohen** was hosted by **Nancy White** and featured **Gordie Sampson**, **Connie Kaldor**, **Spiral Beach**, **Jay Bodner** of **Eagle & Hawk**, and **Liam Titcomb** singing their favourite Cohen songs. **An Extraordinary Life (A Musical Conversation with Jackie Washington)** featured veteran performer **Jackie Washington** and was hosted by his good friend **Ken Whiteley**. The day's entertainment closed with the **Window of Opportunity** session with host **Laurie-Ann Copple**, **Natalia Zukerman**, **Lindsay Jane** and **Darryn Grandbois**.

Arlo Guthrie's well-travelled guitar case.

Rise and Shine was the appropriately titled first session on the **Penguin Eggs Stage** and showcased the talents of **Galitcha and Friends**. **Now That's a Stretch – Yoga and Music** was a participatory session pairing gentle yoga movements and music featuring yoga teacher **Jo-Ann Osterman** and musician **Ron Korb**. **Shelley Posen**, who leads a shape note singing group in Ottawa, hosted the participatory session **Shape Note Singing for Everyone**. The **Doc's Pick** session was named for the popular segment on the CKCU-FM radio show *Canadian Spaces*. The mysterious Doc (**Peter Conway** of McCrank's Cycles, a local business that is a long time sponsor of *Canadian Spaces*) was on hand, as were musical guests **Jennifer Noxon**, **Gordie Sampson** and **Wendell Ferguson**. To wind down the day, the **Taking Turns** session showcased **Zoë Lewis** and **Shelley Posen**.

The **CUPE EnviroTent** featured more displays, discussions and hands-on activities related to environmental issues and responsible living. Sessions included **Sun Power** with **Sean Twomey** of **Arbour Environmental Shoppe**, **Getting Involved** with **Mike Kaulbars** of the **Peace and Environment Resource Centre**, **An Environmental Festival** with **Arthur Goldsmith** of **EcoRail Tour**, **Fair Trade in Action** with **Nicole McGrath** of **Peri Dar**, and **Pesticide Safety** with **Mari Wellman** of **Coalition for a Healthy Ottawa**.

Sunday Evening CUPE Main Stage

The Sunday evening entertainment on the **CUPE Main Stage** began with the **Terry Penner Memorial Choir** led by director **Michael MacDonald**. The choir consisted of festival goers who attended three rehearsals during the weekend and performed for an appreciative audience. An exceptionally high-calibre evening exemplified the festival's diverse lineup. The five-piece Quebec band **Châkidor** regaled the audience with a high-energy set that included Irish, bluegrass, Celtic and classical influences. **Connie Kaldor** has appeared at several festivals and as usual she wowed the crowd with a cross-section of her vast repertoire.

Musical treasures **Scarlett, Washington and Whiteley** performed a set of their warm-hearted and sometimes amusing tunes that blended their talents in the world of folk, blues and swing. **Jackie Washington** was awarded the **Helen Verger Award** for his valuable contributions to Canadian folk music. Washington, who has an exceptional memory, recalled how he began his musical career as a child growing up in the 1930s in Hamilton, Ontario. His many accomplishments include becoming Canada's first black disc jockey, participating in the 1960s coffee house scene, and composing more than 1,200 songs. He has toured and recorded with Scarlett, Washington and Whiteley since the 1980s. The group's first CD, *Where Old Friends Meet*, received a Juno nomination in 1993.

Harry Manx & the Urban Turban was one of many diverse groups at the festival.

Harry Manx & The Urban Turban delivered an exhilarating performance under the stars. Manx is a master of the slide guitar and mohan veena, an instrument that combines elements of the guitar and sitar. His music meshes blues with India ragas and this unlikely combination of styles is nothing less than magical. Manx was ably accompanied by **The Urban Turban**: **Niel Golden** on tabla, **Wynn Gogol** on keyboards and backup singer **Emily Braden**.

The festival ended with a powerful performance from one of Canada's top jazz musicians, **Jane Bunnett**, who appeared with her band, **The Spirits of Havana**. Bunnett is a virtuoso on the saxophone and flute and is passionate about Cuban music, which features prominently in her repertoire. On this warm summer evening the ethereal music of Bunnett and her band provided unforgettable memories for the audience. And so ended the most culturally diverse CKCU Ottawa Folk Festival.

Year 12 – 2005

*Canadian Talent Shines Brightly
at 12th Annual Ottawa Folk Festival*

Canadian talent shone as brightly as the stars over Britannia Bay at the 12th annual CKCU Ottawa Folk Festival. **Willie P. Bennett**, the **Jim Cuddy Band** and **Natalie MacMaster** reminded us why our folk tradition is so worthy of our support. Celebrations for the 25th anniversary of *Canadian Spaces*, the longest-running folk radio show in Canada echoed this sentiment.

Chopper McKinnon and **Karen Flanagan McCarthy** returned to host the main stage throughout the festival. Some controversy arose over the appearance of Alberta singer-songwriter **Kalan Porter**, who won the Canadian Idol competition in 2004. Porter was seen as a pop performer rather than a folk performer by some people. But Porter, who is classically trained, held his own when he performed on the main stage and in a workshop.

Peter Katz and **Layah Jane** were co-winners of the **Galaxie Rising Stars Award**. They were presented with the award on the **CUPE Main Stage** on Saturday evening by **Roch Parisien**, music programmer for Galaxie's Folk Roots channel. Katz and Jane shared the award and a $1,000 cash prize.

Also on Saturday, the wonderfully named **Terry Joe Banjo** was given the **One Fret Less Award** and a $1,000 cash prize. This award is made possible by a **Community Foundation of Ottawa** endowment established by **Harvey and Louise Glatt**, long-time supporters of folk music and singer-songwriters. The winners were selected at the annual auditions held at **Rasputin's Folk Café** and the **NAC Fourth Stage**.

Other features at the festival were the artisans at the **Craft Village**, who offered a wide array of handmade items, ranging from pottery to furniture to jewellery. The ever-popular **CKCU-FM Family Area** presented musical performances, craft workshops, face painting and a puppet playhouse. The **CKCU-FM Stage** featured music, dancing and magic shows. The **Family Craft Area** had workshops led by festival artisans. Participants could make colourful hats and percussion instruments for the **Sunshine Parade** on Sunday evening. The **CUPE EnviroTent** offered environmental demonstrations and discussions. The festival continued its **green initiatives** with reusable plates in the **Food Court**. A beer cup recycling program was created by the CKCU Ottawa Folk Festival and **Arbour Environmental Shoppe**. Prizes including a rain barrel from Arbour. Tickets to upcoming folk festival concerts were offered to participants of the beer cup recycling program.

A festival documentary film, *River Tales*, created by Gemini Award-winning filmmaker **Scott Troyer** and journalist **Rose Simpson** was shown in the **Ottawa and District Labour Council** tent. The film looks behind the scenes at the 2004 Ottawa CKCU Folk Festival, and includes interviews with

Willie P. Bennett was presented with the Helen Verger Award.

organizers, volunteers and artists such as **Judy Collins**, **Arlo Guthrie**, **Michael Franti** and **Jackie Washington**. The documentary creators were available on Saturday and Sunday afternoon to chat with viewers.

Thursday, August 18

Of course, **Arthur McGregor**, owner of the **Ottawa Folklore Centre**, opened the festival with his customary acoustic stringed instrument rendition of our national anthem. The first evening of the 12th CKCU Ottawa Folk Festival was graced with an inspired set by veteran Canadian performer **Willie P. Bennett**, who was presented with the **Helen Verger Award**. Bennett performed with aplomb. He kept the audience entranced with a crowd-pleasing cross-selection of material from his long musical career that stretched from the mid-70s to the present day. This performance is a special memory for his fans as he tragically passed away in 2008 at the age of 57.

Popular American singer-songwriter Eliza Gilkyson.

The lively Quebec trio **Genticorum** performed with their blend of traditional music and original songs delivered with strong vocals and an impressive range of acoustic instruments. Halifax roots-rocker **Joel Plaskett**, whose album *Truthfully Truthfully* was named best rock recording at the 2005 East Coast Music Awards, gave a heartfelt and well-received performance. The esteemed American folk performer **Eliza Gilkyson** treated the audience to a set showcasing her poetic and sometimes political folk tunes.

Following Willie P. Bennett's performance, the amazing veteran British performer **Joan Armatrading** closed the evening with a high-energy set that had the audience dancing beneath the stars. This Member of the Order of the British Empire is a singer-songwriter who plays a mean guitar. Armatrading performed many of her hit songs such as the evocative "Show Some Emotion" as well as newer material.

The audience was thrilled to see British folk-rock performer Joan Armatrading.

Friday, August 19

On the **Nutshell Music & Event Management Stage**, renowned drummer/percussionist **Derek Debeer** led a **Community Drumming Jam**. Many local drummers participated while the audience got into the groove. Debeer was born in Rhodesia (now Zimbabwe). He is well known for his work with **Johnny Clegg**, and with Clegg's bands **Savuka** and **Juluka**, both of which celebrated African rhythms.

Lucie Idlout

CUPE Main Stage
The Texas based duo **The Dreamsicles** (**Cary Cooper** and **Tom Prasada-Rao**) gave us a set of sassy and sweet love songs. **Lucie Idlout**, a powerful Inuit performer from Nunavut who spent many years living in Ottawa, mesmerized the audience with her hard-hitting and emotional tunes. American singer-songwriter **Chuck Brodsky** performed a set that showcased his diverse repertoire of funny and touching story songs.

The Weakerthans were up next with a set that incorporated rock, folk and alt-country with lyrics with a literary bent. **Feist** wowed the crowd with a dynamic and danceable set. The Calgary singer-songwriter's performance featured intimate lyrics, catchy melodies and her seductive, haunting voice. Alternative rock band **The Jim Cuddy Band** includes the co-founder of Blue Rodeo along with **Bazil Donovan**, **Anne Lindsay**, **Joel Anderson** and **Travis Good**. The band country-rocked the park with original tunes by Jim Cuddy and Blue Rodeo standards. It was wonderful to see Anne Lindsay having such a great time playing her fiddle!

The **Beth Ferguson Award** was presented to 16-year-old **Meredith Luce** who received a bursary and an original painting by Geoff Sangster. The award is presented to an Ontario female songwriter under the age of 30 in memory of **Beth Ferguson** (1953-1999) who was greatly admired for her body of work as a solo singer-songwriter and as a member of the acapella group **Malaika**.

Alternative evening programming also took place on the **Kershman-Wasserlauf Stage**. **Catherine Burns**, the regular caller for Ottawa's monthly Old Sod contra dances, performed those duties at a **Contra Dance** featuring **Genticorum**. Beginners were welcome and instruction was provided.

Offsite, **After Hours Folk** at the **Travelodge Hotel's Beachcomber Room** featured New Brunswick trio **Hot Toddy** and Edmonton's **Painting Daisies**, as well as a midnight set with country rebels **The Swiftys**.

Saturday, August 20
Daytime
Things got off to an inspiring start on the **CUPE Main Stage** with a **Gospel Sing** featuring **Linda Tillery & the Cultural Heritage Choir**, **Penny Lang** and host **Ken Whiteley**. There was more inspiration at the **Sources of Inspiration** session featuring **Lucie Idlout**, **Harmony Trowbridge**, **Jason Fowler** and host **Anne Lindsay**. **Genticorum** hosted **Vocal Focus** with **Linda Tillery & the Cultural Heritage Choir**. **Ron Moores**, host of the CKCU-FM old time country show *The Back 40*, led **Back 40 Live**, **Part 1**. His country dream team included **The Dreamsicles**, **Crescent and Frost**, and **Sarah Lee Guthrie & Johnny Irion**.

On the **Bowie Electrical Stage**, the fun began with a concert showcasing the talents of **Peter Katz**. Three **Taking Turns** sessions featured **Crescent and Frost** and **The Swiftys**, followed by **Tito Medina** and **Casadore**, and ended with **Layah Jane** and **Meredith Luce**. **Cam Wells** hosted the **Musical Friends** session with **Chris Frye**, **Dave Clarke** and **Penny Lang**.

Folka Voca, a community choir led by **Lee**

Hayes opened the day with a concert of popular contemporary tunes at the **Kershman-Wasserlauf Stage**. **Dave Clarke** hosted **Expect the Unexpected** with **Hot Toddy** and storyteller **Ruth Stewart-Verger**. The **National Arts Centre** sponsored **Alberta Scene Revisited** with **Kehewin Native Performance**, **Painting Daisies**, **The Swiftys** and host **Jen Covert**. The NAC had presented several Alberta performers in its Alberta Scene series earlier in the year. **H'Sao** got the crowd up dancing with the **Danse africaine** session. More dance opportunities followed with a **Latin Dance Party** featuring **Joaquin Diaz**.

The **Nutshell Music & Event Management Stage** entertainment began with a concert with **Crescent and Frost**. The **Guitar Tales** session featured **Yann Falquet** of Genticorum, **Stephen Carroll** of The Weakerthans, and host **Rachelle van Zanten**. The **Rural Roots** session featured **Feist**, **Concession 23** and host **Chris Frye**. A collaboration of musical styles was presented when the **Blues Meets Jazz** session showcased **Hot Toddy**, **Grant Stovel** of The Swiftys, and host **Ken Whiteley**. **Chopper McKinnon** hosted *Canadian Spaces* Live with **Ken Whiteley**, **Harmony Trowbridge**, **Meredith Luce** and **Arthur McGregor**. This session had particular significance as it was the 25th anniversary of the CKCU-FM show *Canadian Spaces*.

A concert with **Casadore** was the first performance on the **Crosstown Traffic Stage**. The **Story Songs and Song Stories** session included musical storytellers **Chuck Brodsky**, **Penny Lang** and host **Dean Verger**. The **Galaxie Rising Stars** session hosted by **Roch Parisien** showcased the music of **Layah Jane**, **Peter Katz** and **Joe Grass**. **CBC Fuse** featured **John K. Samson** of The Weakerthans, **Feist** and co-hosts **Amanda Putz** and **Bill Stunt**. Festival Director **Gene Swimmer** hosted **President's Choice**, a session with **Anaïs Mitchell**, **Tom Prasado-Rao** and **Chuck Brodsky**. Great choices, Gene!

At the **Rogers Stage**, the **Canadian Woman** session hosted by longtime festival volunteer and journalist **Rachel Hauraney** started things off with **Harmony Trowbridge**, **Lucie Idlout** and **Daisy Blue Groff**. Following a concert with **Kehewin Native Performance**, it was time for the Americans to get into the act with the **American Woman** session. This session was hosted by **Angela Page** and presented **Anaïs Mitchell**, **Cary Cooper**, and **Sarah Lee Guthrie & Johnny Irion**. **Anne Lindsay** and **Genticorum** alternated in the **Taking Turns** session. The day's entertainment ended with a concert with **Linda Tillery & the Cultural Heritage Choir**.

Bluegrass and blues music were the themes in the **OFC Music Tent**. Performances by bluegrass artists **Leavin' Train**, **Jan Purcell & Pine Road**, **Handsome Molly** and **Concession 23** were followed by blues musician **Miles Howerd** and friends.

A dedicated festival volunteer from year one, Peter Zanette.

The participatory sessions on the **Ottawa Folklore Centre Stage** got off to a lively start with the **Rise Up Singing** session led by **Arthur McGregor**. The session was named for the popular folk music songbook. **David Keeble** hosted the **Songcraft** session with **Pat Moore, Lee Hayes** and **Tom Lips**. **Miles Howe** led a crowd with his

Harmonica Basics workshop, while **Terry Joe Banjo** hosted the **Banjo Basics** session. **Folka Voca**, a community choir led by **Lee Hayes**, gave a concert. The **Terry Penner Festival Choir** held its first rehearsal. The session **Spotlight on the Diddley-Bow** with **Crescent and Frost** focused on the unusually named instrument the diddley bow, which is a single-stringed American instrument that influenced the development of blues music.

For the Love of Music with **Kindermusik** was the first bit of fun on the **CKCU-FM Stage**. Other children-oriented entertainment included **Kid Stuff** with **Rich Hinman** of Crescent and Frost and **Magic for Kids** with **Doctor Magic** (**George Sapounidis**). After a **Traditional Dance** performance with **Kehewin Native Performance** it was time for the **Taking Turns** session with **David Keeble** and **Tom Lips**. The day ended on a relaxed note with a **Balance and Stretch** session led by the **Taoist Tai Chi Society of Canada.**

The **Family Craft Area** featured workshops with **Bead-y-licious**, **Jason Bellchamber Celtic and Medieval Goldsmith, Barefoot Toys**, **The Leathersmiths** and **Emily Wood**.

Participatory environmental demonstrations and discussions took place in the **CUPE EnviroTent**. The topics included the upcoming pesticide decision in Ottawa, building a home from car tires, human-powered vehicles, how to make biodiesel fuel, and trading fairly.

Saturday Evening
The **CUPE Main Stage** concerts kicked off with **Sarah Lee Guthrie & Johnny Irion**. Sarah Lee is the daughter of **Arlo Guthrie** and granddaughter of **Woody Guthrie**. She joined with her musical partner and husband **Johnny Irion** to create exhilarating folk-rock. They were followed by **H'Sao,** a Montreal group that fuses traditional African music with soul, jazz, R&B and gospel. Bluesy American folk performer **Chris Smither** treated the crowd to his dazzling guitar work, and philosophical lyrics delivered in his trademark gravelly voice. Ottawa-based blues star **Sue Foley** demonstrated why she is considered one of the finest blues/roots artists by delivering an evocative set. This Juno Award winner had also received a record-setting 17 Maple Blues Awards.

Linda Tillery & the Cultural Heritage Choir is a six-voice ensemble from San Francisco whose mission is to preserve Black American music. They performed a variety of percussion-driven vocals rooted in the deep South and in their West African and Caribbean traditions. Canadian favourite **Natalie MacMaster** had the crowd buzzing with her high-energy performance of Cape Breton fiddle music. The evening ended on a soulful note with **Hothouse Flowers**, a Dublin-based band that has been described as "Ireland's finest folk-rock export" by BBC Radio.

Natalie MacMaster

Alternative evening programming included the **Alt-Folk Café** on the **Kershman-Wasserlauf Stage** featuring **Painting Daisies** (hosts), **Harmony Trowbridge**, **Anaïs Mitchell**, **Layah Jane**, **Meredith Luce** and **Peter Katz**. **After Hours Folk** at the **Travelodge Hotel Ottawa West** showcased **Crescent & Frost**, **Lucie Idlout** and **The Weakerthans.**

Sunday, August 21
Daytime
On the **CUPE Main Stage**, **The Black Sheep Live** session was hosted by **Paul Symes**, owner of the Black Sheep Inn in Wakefield, Quebec. It featured **Ana Egge**, **Jeremy Fisher**, **Chris Smither** and **The Swiftys**. **Laurie-Ann Copple** hosted the next session, **Words and Music**, featuring **Jason Fowler**, **Doreen Stevens**, **The Dreamsicles** and **Arthur McGregor**. Humour was the theme of the

next session, titled **A Funny Thing Happened**. Fun-loving performers were **The Arrogant Worms**, **Jean-Marc Lalonde**, **Chuck Brodsky** and host **Carolyn Sutherland**. Folk enthusiast **Mike Regenstreif** hosted the **Musical Influences** session with **Natalie MacMaster**, **Anne Lindsay**, **Kalan Porter** and **Derek Sharp**.

A festival volunteer finds out what worked and didn't work for the festival-goers.

The **Bowie Electrical Stage** had four **Taking Turns** sessions: **Terry Joe Banjo** and **Jean-Marc Lalonde**; **Anaïs Mitchell** and **Ana Egge**; **Concession 23** and **Hurry Up and Wait**; and **Jeremy Fisher** and **Harmony Trowbridge**.

Guitar Styles was the theme of the first presentation on the **Kershman-Wasserlauf Stage**. **Michel Dozois** hosted the session, which featured **Tony McManus**, **Jason Fowler**, **Slavek Hanzlik** and **Dave Clarke**. There were two **Cross-Cultural Sound Exchange** sessions. The first featured **Mushfiq Ensemble**, **Anne Lindsay**, and the **George Sapounidis Ensemble**. The second showcased **Mushfiq Ensemble** in a second appearance, **Derek Debeer** and **Tito Medina** (host). There was also an **African Roots** session with **Baobab Tree Drum Dance Community**, hosted by **Linda Tillery & the Cultural Heritage Choir**.

The Wailin' Jennys hosted **People and Places**, the first session on the **Nutshell Music & Event Management Stage**, featuring **Chuck Brodsky** and **Chris Frye**. **The Wailin' Jennys**, whose name is a play on the name of country star Waylon Jennings, returned for the second session, **Rasputin's Live**. It was hosted by **Dean Verger** and also showcased the talents of **Rick Fines** and **Ian Robb**. The **Life Changes** session included performances by **Anaïs Mitchell**, storyteller **Ruth Stewart-Verger** and **Penny Lang**, and was hosted by **Karen Flanagan McCarthy**. The **Country Style** session featured music that was just that and included **Slavek Hanzlik** and **Dave Clarke**, **Pat Moore**, **Hurry Up and Wait** and host **Zita Murphy-Brascoupé.**

At the **Crosstown Traffic Stage,** the **Doc's Pick** session, named after a regular segment on the CKCU-FM folk show *Canadian Spaces*, was hosted by Doc himself (**Peter Conway** of McCrank's Cycles, a local business that is a longtime sponsor of the show). The session included **Rick Fines**, **Joe Grass** and **Sue Foley**. Things took an historical turn with the **Ottawa 150 Anniversary Celebration** featuring **Alex Sinclair**, **Jean-Marc Lalonde**, **7IM-VWA**, **Jim McIntyre** and **Victor Emerson** (host). **Shades of Blue** was the theme of a session hosted by **Rick Fines** and featured **Sue Foley** and **Joe Grass**. The day ended on a philosophical note with **What Was I Thinking?** Lighthearted responses were provided by participants including **The Arrogant Worms**, **Lee Hayes**, **Alex Sinclair** and host **Bruce Steele**.

Songs for the Earth was the first offering on the **Rogers Stage.** Hosted by **Arbour Environmental Shoppe** owner **Sean Twomey**, the session featured the talents of **Doreen Stevens**, **Alex Sinclair**, **Chris Whiteley** and **The Dreamsicles**. **Songs of Hope and Freedom** was an inspiring session with **Linda Tillery & the Cultural Heritage Choir**, **The Original Sloth Band**, **Sarah Lee Guthrie & Johnny Irion**, and host **Morna Ballantyne**. **Music from the Glen** was a session named for the CKCU-FM British traditional music show. It was led by the show's host **Gord Peeling** and included **Tony McManus**, **Ian Robb**, **Genticorum** and **Natalie MacMaster**. **Ron Moores,** host of the CKCU-FM old time country show *The Back 40*, hosted **Back 40 Live, Part 2** with **The Swiftys**, **Southside Steve Marriner** and **Genticorum.**

Bluegrass and blues music were again offered in the **OFC Music Tent**. In four separate sessions, performers **Jan Purcell & Pine Road**, **Concession 23**, **Handsome Molly** and **Leavin' Train** treated us to bluegrass performances. **Miles Howerd** performed with friends in the second blues session.

At the **Ottawa Folklore Centre Stage**, first up was the **Terry Penner Festival Choir Rehearsal**. The **Taking Turns** session saw **Chris Smither** and **Joe Grass** delighting the audience with their original tunes. After another **Festival Choir** rehearsal, the **George Sapounidis Ensemble** performed in the session titled **A World of Music**.

The Arrogant Worms recruiting a young fan before their Sunday evening performance.

The **CKCU-FM Stage** kicked things off in the **Family Area** with **Kindermusik** in the session **For the Love of Music**. The **Taoist Tai Chi Society of Canada** presented a **Balance and Stretch** session. The **Kid Stuff** session featured **Terry Joe Banjo**. **Chris Frye** joined hosts **The Original Sloth Band** in the **Jazzin' It Up** session. The **Moving to the Beat** session showcased **Baobab Tree Drum Dance Community**. This group led the annual **Sunshine Parade**, a happy and noisy celebration that wends it way from the Family Area to the main stage. Children and adults are encouraged to dress up and march along, making as much noise as possible with a variety of percussion instruments.

The **Family Craft Area** gave children the chance to create their own treasures. Participants included **Brighid's Bard** (papier mâché vases), **Emily Wood** (bubble play), **Filament** (flip-flop necklaces with beads and wire), **The Leathersmiths** (custom leather keychains and barrettes) and **Barefoot Toys** (traditional wool felt mats).

More participatory environmental demonstrations and discussions were held in the **CUPE EnviroTent**. The topics included **Keeping Rivers Healthy** (Ottawa Riverkeeper), **Safe Alternatives to Pesticides** (Coalition for a Healthy Ottawa), **Renewable Solar and Wind Power** (Arbour Environmental Shoppe), **The Peace Kitchen Project** (Ottawa Peace Kitchen) and **The Ethical Consumer** (Peri Dar).

Sunday Evening
CUPE Main Stage

The entertainment began with **The Original Sloth Band**, a folk-rock group that formed 40 years ago in North York, Ont. featuring brothers **Chris and Ken Whiteley** and **Tom Evans**. They were joined onstage by **Bucky Berger** and **Victor Bateman** on drums and string bass. Next up was **Tony McManus**, a virtuosic Celtic guitarist who performed songs that incorporated tunes from Cape Breton, Scotland and Brittany. The popular group **Painting Daisies** dazzled the crowd with its incredible harmonies, inspired instrumentation and heartfelt lyrics. The **Terry Penner Festival Choir**, whose members included festival goers who come together at each festival, performed to an enthusiastic audience. Festival favourites **The Arrogant Worms** injected laughter and levity to the evening's entertainment with their humorous songs and onstage antics. Vancouver-based **Jeremy Fisher** spent the last four years touring and performing across the country travelling by bicycle. He performed a spirited set that had toes tapping. The evening ended with **Kalan Porter** who gave us a set that incorporated covers, original tunes and fiddle playing. He was a delight to the hordes of teenage fans who were on hand.

Kalan Porter

Alternative evening programming on the **Kershman-Wasserlauf Stage** featured a blockbuster **Super Session** with **Rick Fines** (host), **Penny Lang**, **Slavek Hanzlik**, **Dave Clarke**, **Chris Frye**, **Rachelle van Zanten** and **Joe Grass**.

Monday, August 22
The **Festival Wrap-Up Concert** was held at the **Black Sheep Inn** in Wakefield, Quebec and showcased the talents of **The Dreamsicles** and **Painting Daisies.**

Year 13 – 2006
CKCU Ottawa Folk Festival Has Something for Everyone!

The 2006 CKCU Ottawa Folk Festival presented an appealing variety of entertainment ranging from American alt-country sensation **Steve Earle** to singer-songwriter **Ferron** to the Burundi-inspired **The Mighty Popo Band**. Blues, Celtic, klezmer and gospel artists and a ukulele virtuoso demonstrated the diversity of folk music. The 25th anniversary of **Rasputin's Folk Café** was celebrated in fine style, while former Bronson Avenue neighbour **Arthur McGregor** of the **Ottawa Folklore Centre**, received the **Helen Verger Award**.

This year also marked the departure of Executive Director **Gene Swimmer** who had made an exceptional contribution to the festival in this role since 1996. Gene, who was involved since 1994, was recognized by many people on the main stage and was presented with mementoes for his many years of dedicated volunteer service.

Festival goers had many different ways to participate, whether singing with the **Terry Penner Festival Choir**, performing at the Ottawa Folklore Centre's open mic session, joining a singalong, or learning to play the harmonica, ukulele or pennywhistle. There were also chances to dance to musical styles from Cuban to Cajun to klezmer, and to perform with a community drumming circle.

The **CKCU-FM Family Area** was bigger and better than ever and featured two of the best children's acts on the circuit: **Fran Avni** and **Sho Mo and The Monkey Bunch**. As usual, kids could make musical instruments, and participate in crafts workshops. **Kathy Armstrong** organized the **Kids Weekend Drumming Ensemble**, giving kids a chance to learn and rehearse African drumming and perform during the **Sunshine Parade** held on Sunday afternoon.

The **CUPE EnviroTent** offered ongoing talks, demonstrations and hands-on activities for adults and children. Topics included renewable energy, raw vegan foods, attracting butterflies to your backyard, water, patchwork quilting, terminator seeds, and rekindling our relationship with Mother Earth.

Thursday, August 17

On Thursday, August 17 two separately ticketed downtown shows launched the 13th festival. An all-star song circle of **Lynn Miles**, **Ian Tamblyn**, **Bill Bourne** and **Erick Manana** celebrated the 25th anniversary of **Rasputin's** at **Library and Archives Canada**. Many wonderful memories and amusing anecdotes were shared at the tribute and owner **Dean Verger** was in great spirits. A lively show at the **Capital City Music Hall** featured a dynamite quadruple bill of **The Sadies**, **Ridley Bent**, **The Agnostic Mountain Gospel Choir** and **Amy Millan**.

Intrepid festival goers

Friday, August 18

Friday afternoon in Britannia Park at the **Metro Ottawa Stage** began rhythmically with a **Community Drumming Circle** with **Kathy Armstrong**, **Leo Brooks** and **Rusty Eckland**. The evening main stage opened with **Ottawa Folklore Centre** owner **Arthur McGregor** performing an acoustic version of "O Canada" in his inimitable ragtime style. Arthur was followed by the **Kelli Trottier Band**, the wonderfully named ensemble

The **Agnostic Mountain Gospel Choir**, **Erick Manana**, ukulele virtuoso **James Hill**, festival staple **Ian Tamblyn**, and bluesy duo **Dawn Tyler Watson & Paul Deslauriers**. **Steve Earle** received a rousing welcome from the enthusiastic crowd who responded to his extraordinary and deeply personal brand of country music.

Local musician Fred Guignion accompanied Ian Tamblyn on the CUPE Main Stage on Friday evening.

Alternative evening programming took place in the **World Harmony Stage** inside the **Ron Kolbus Lakeside Centre**. A song circle was held with **Mark Wilson**, **Old Man Luedecke** (a surprisingly young banjo songster), **Zach Stevenson** (well known for his interpretations of Phil Ochs material), **Rachelle van Zanten** and **Amy Millan**. At an **After Party** held at the **Travelodge Hotel Ottawa West**, the entertainment included **Jan Purcell and Pine Road**, **Erynn Marshall & Chris Coole**, and **Robert Michaels**.

Saturday, August 19
On the **CUPE Main Stage**, the day opened with a **Family Concert** with **Sho Mo and The Monkey Bunch**. **Mike Regenstreif** hosted the **Fiddle Frenzy** session with **Dirk Powell**, the **April Verch Band**, **Sarah Burnell**, **Erynn Marshall & Chris Coole**, and the **Kelli Trottier Band**. **Dawn Tyler Watson & Paul Deslauriers**, **DiggingRoots**, **Rachelle van Zanten** and **Andy Cohen** participated in the **Saturday Blues** session hosted by **Rich Warren**. The *Canadian Spaces* session hosted by **Chopper McKinnon** featured artists often featured on the CKCU-FM folk music show of the same name: **Charlie Sohmer**, **Ferron**, **Paul Mills**, **Holmes Hooke** and **Stella Haybukhai**. The magnificent ensemble, **The Maple Leaf Brass Band**, performed with great gusto beside the main stage.

Over at the **Bowie Electrical Stage**, four separate groups appeared in concert: a double bill with **Mike Evin** and **Zach Stevenson**, the funky Indian-jazz fusion band **Autorickshaw**, **Sarah Burnell**, **Paul Mills & Friends**, and **Tiiu Millistver** and **ElizaBeth Hill**. An excellent spoken word session, **Word Play**, followed with the wordy talents of master storyteller **Holmes Hooke**, beat poet **Lillian Allen** and lowercase poet **bill bissett**.

At the **World Harmony Stage** in the **Ron Kolbus Lakeside Centre**, a **CBC Live Fuse** show hosted by **Alan Neal** was taped featuring **Ridley Bent** along with **Ndidi Onukwulu & Madagascar Slim**. **Nubia Cermeno** hosted a lively **Cuban Dance** session with **Valle Son**. Later in the day, there was more dancing when **Steve Pritchard** hosted **Cajun Dance #1** session with **Grouyan Gombo**. Two separate concerts showcased the talents of **Erick Manana, The Agnostic Mountain Gospel Choir** and **Dan Frechette**. **Kathy Armstrong** also hosted a **Kids Participatory Drumming Ensemble**.

A family enjoying the entertainment at the Metro Ottawa Stage.

A diverse day of entertainment took place on the **Metro Ottawa Stage**. Two groups of musicians appeared in concert: **Balfa Toujours** and the

Kelli Trottier Band, and **The Supers** and **DiggingRoots**. **The Nature of Things** session hosted by **Karen Flanagan McCarthy** featured **Ian Tamblyn, Sheila M Ross** and **ElizaBeth Hill**. **The Nature of Strings** session, on the other hand, showcased **James Hill, Old Man Luedecke** and **Silk Road Duo** and was hosted by **Rachel Hauraney**. The day ended with a session titled **It's Latin to Me** featuring **Valle Son** and the **Robert Michaels Band**.

Qiu Xia Ha, along with her husband Andre Thibault, comprise Silk Road Duo.

At the **Loeb Glebe Stage**, many musical explorations took place, beginning with the **Musical Journeys** session hosted by **Steve Pritchard** featuring **Tiiu Millistver, Andy Cohen** and **Dan Frechette**. **Gene Swimmer** hosted the **Director's Choice** session with **Ridley Bent, James Hill**, and **Dawn Tyler Watson & Paul Deslauriers**. Two separate concerts showcased **Eileen Laverty** and **Silk Road Duo**. **Erin Barnhard** hosted the **Appalachian Echoes** session with the **Dirk Powell Band, Erynn Marshall & Chris Coole**, and **Old Man Luedecke**. The fascinating **East Meets West** session hosted by **Rachel Hauraney** included **Autorickshaw, Silk Road Duo** and renowned sitar player **Vishwa Mohan Bhatt**, who was once the teacher of **Harry Manx**.

There was plenty happening at the **Rogers Stage**. **Colin Henein** hosted the **Music from the Glen** session inspired by the CKCU-FM radio show, which featured **Orealis, Eileen Laverty, Sarah Burnell** and **April Verch**. **Pat Moore** hosted the **Salutin' Rasputin's** session with **Charlie Sohmer, Stella Haybukhai, Rick Hayes** and **Don Fletcher**. **The Big Smoke** session hosted by **Bill Stunt** featured Toronto performers **Ron Sexsmith, Mike Evin** and **Amy Millan**. **Ron Moores** hosted the **Back 40 Live** session inspired by his traditional country, western and bluegrass music show on CKCU-FM, featuring **Amy Millan, Ridley Bent**, and **Dallas & Travis Good** of The Sadies. The **Songwriters' Songwriters** session featured the calibre of songwriters you might expect: **Eliza Gilkyson, Ferron, Ron Sexsmith** and **Rich Warren**. The day ended with a solo concert from **Eliza Gilkyson**.

The **CKCU-FM Stage** hosted music as diverse as the station's programming. **MaryLou Hulan** and **Monica Wolfe** kicked things off with the **Kindermusik** session. Separate concerts were performed in a range of styles by **Fran Avni, Sho Mo and The Monkey Bunch, Folka Voca, Silk Road Duo, ElizaBeth Hill** and **Andy Cohen**.

The **Ottawa Folklore Centre Stage** entertainment opened with a concert with **Folka Voca**. Two educational sessions followed: **Singing Tips for Everyone** hosted by **Lee Hayes**, and **Learn to Play the Harmonica** with **Miles Howe**. **Arthur McGregor** hosted the song circle session **Rise Up Singing**. The day ended with an **Open Mic** session allowing participants the opportunity to perform onstage to a receptive audience.

In the **CUPE EnviroTent**, sessions were held to educate people in environmental topics including **Renewable Energy for Home Owners** with **Sean Twomey** of **Arbour Environmental Shoppe**, **Healthy Lifestyles with Raw Vegan Food** with **Natasha Kyssa** of **SimplyRaw, Bringing Your Garden to Life** with **Sandy Garland** of **Fletcher Wildlife Garden**, and **Environmental Politics** with **David Chernushenko** of the **Green Party**.

The **Family Craft Area** provided lots of fun for

Chopper McKinnon looking good on the CUPE Main Stage.

families including the following sessions: **Drum Making for Kids** with **Gaelen Hart**, **Making Paper Bag Puppets** with **Liz Murphy**, **Making Jewellery** with **Heather Boyd** of **Filament**, and **Making Wire Art** with **Emily Wood**.

On the **CUPE Main Stage** the night kicked off with the lively French-Canadian ensemble **Mauvais Sort** and continued with **Ridley Bent**, the Cajun group **Balfa Toujours**, and the accomplished flamenco guitarist **Robert Michaels**. Two superb singer-songwriters at the top of their game, **Ferron** and **Ron Sexsmith**, followed with excellent solo sets.

Alternative evening programming on the **World Harmony Stage** opened with the mesmerizing **Autorickshaw** whose music is a wonderful melange of South Indian classical music, Bollywood-tinged jazz standards and Indo-jazz originals. **The Supers** and the popular alt-folk group **The Sadies** rounded out the night's entertainment.

The **After Party** at the **Travelodge Hotel Ottawa West** showcased a diverse cross-section of roots music with **Ndidi Onukwulu & Madagascar Slim, April Verch** and **DiggingRoots**.

Ndidi Onukwulu and Madagascar Slim performed throughout the festival weekend.

Crowd favourite Ferron appeared on the CUPE Main Stage Saturday evening.

Sunday, August 20

On Sunday morning, the **First Annual Musical Festival Brunch** featured great food and the talents of **Frida's Brow, Ndidi Onukwulu & Madagascar Slim, Michael Munnik, Ann Downey** and host **Cam Wells**. An **Ottawa Folklore Centre Celebration** featured **Ian Tamblyn, Eliza Gilkyson, Jan Purcell and Pine Road, Eileen Laverty, Chris MacLean** and host **Arthur McGregor**. An **Afternoon Raga** showcased the renowned sitar player **Vishwa Mohan Bhatt**. The **East-West Extravaganza** hosted by **Eric Stein** featured **Beyond the Pale**, **Silk Road Duo** and **Galitcha**.

The festival was fortunate to have internationally recognized sitar player Vishwa Monan Bhatt on the roster.

Four excellent concerts were held on the **Bowie Electrical Stage** featuring **Dan Frechette** and **Old Man Luedecke**; **Kelli Trottier Band** and **Pat Moore**; **Jan Purcell and Pine Road** and **Zach Stevenson**; and **Vishwa Mohan Bhatt** and **Galitcha**. The session **Speaking Words** featured poets **John Akpata, Sheila M Ross, Lillian Allen**, and **bill bissett**.

The **World Harmony Stage** in the cool confines of the **Ron Kolbus Lakeside Centre** was a happening place. The entertainment started with concerts with

John Akpata was one of the poets featured in the Speaking Words session on Sunday.

Mostly Harmless and **Mark Wilson**, as well as a group comprising **Erynn Marshall & Chris Coole** and **Andy Cohen**. Two dance sessions celebrated dance styles: **Klezmer Dance** (**Susan Watts & KlezKanada All-Star Dance Band** with instructor **Michael Alpert**); and **Cajun Dance #2** (**Balfa Toujours** and **Jody Benjamin**).

The Cajun Dance session, shown here with Balfa Toujours onstage, was held on the World Harmony Stage Sunday evening.

Sho Mo and The Monkey Bunch were the first group to appear in concert on the **Metro Ottawa Stage**; **Mauvais Sort** was the second. The **Tout le Monde** session hosted by **Karen Flanagan McCarthy** featured **Balfa Toujours, Mauvais Sort** and **Erick Manana**. **Sharon Fernandez** hosted the session **2 Pianos, 6 Hands** with **Marilyn Lerner** of **KlezKanada, Braydis (Valle Son)** and **Mike Evin**. **Cam Wells** hosted the **Musical Traditions** session with **Ndidi Onukwulu & Madagascar Slim, Kelli Trottier Band**, and **Erynn Marshall & Chris Coole**.

Laurie-Ann Copple hosted the **Lost and Found** session on the **Loeb Glebe Stage** with **Eve Goldberg, Eileen Laverty** and **Holmes Hooke**. The **East-West Blues** session showcased the considerable talents of **Vishwa Mohan Bhatt, Rachelle van Zanten, Rick Fines** and host **Sharon Fernandez**. **Carolyn Sutherland** was the host of the session titled **African Guitar Pinnacle** with **Madagascar Slim, Erick Manana** and **The Mighty Popo**. The amusingly titled **Stringed**

Things session was hosted by CKCU Ottawa Folk Festival volunteer **Zita Murphy-Brascoupé** and featured **Vanya Zhuk**, **Robert Michaels** and **The Mighty Popo**. The day ended with the **Galaxie Rising Stars** session featuring musical luminaries **Mark Wilson**, **Rachelle van Zanten** and **Michael Munnik**.

Folk festival audiences are always happy to see local singer-songwriter Ian Tamblyn.

On the **Rogers Stage**, **Morna Ballantyne** hosted the **Politically Direct** session with **Eliza Gilkyson, Lillian Allen, John Akpata** and **Alise Marlane**. A **Phil Ochs Tribute** was hosted by his sister **Sonny Ochs** and featured **Zach Stevenson** (who had formerly appeared in a Phil Ochs musical play), **Eve Goldberg** and **Alise Marlane**. Host **Mike Regenstreif** led the **Common Ground** session with the **Dirk Powell Band, Dan Frechette** and **Robert Michaels**. **Doc** (Peter Conway) was on hand to host the **Doc's Pick** session showcasing **Eliza Gilkyson, Rick Fines** and **Jennifer Noxon**. The **First Verses Only** session, hosted by **Mitch Podolak**, featured **Sneezy Waters, Arthur McGregor, Andy Cohen, Ann Downey, Dan Frechette, Eve Goldberg** and **Rick Fines**.

The audience at **the CKCU-FM Stage** was treated to concerts with **Silk Road Duo, Fran Avni, Old Man Luedecke, Holmes Hooke** and **Klezmer: The Next Generation**. The last item on the folk agenda was the annual, always fun, noisy and wonderful **Sunshine Parade**, a musical percussion-rich procession of kids of all ages that wound its way to the main stage.

Arthur McGregor was given the Helen Verger Award for his many contributions to the Canadian folk community.

On the **Ottawa Folklore Centre Stage** several instructional sessions were presented: **Blues Guitar for Beginners** with **Andy Cohen, Learn to Play the Ukulele** with virtuoso **James Hill**, and **Learn to Play the Tin Whistle** with **Andy Daub**. The day ended with an **Open Mic** session.

The **CUPE EnviroTent** was the site of several information sessions with environmental themes: **Water: A Basic Human Right?** with **Tony Clark** of the **Polaris Institute, Food Security** with **Juniper Turgeon** of **Just Food, Patchwork Quilting** with **Joanne Hyslop, Terminator Seeds** with **Pat Roy Mooney** of the **ETC Group**, and **Renewing the Sacred Balance** with **Kristina Inrig** of the **Faith and the Common Good** organization.

Little ones in the **Family Craft Area** were treated to the following sessions: **Drum Making for Kids** with **Gaelen Hart**, and **Making Paper Bag Puppets** with **Liz Murphy**.

The **CUPE Main Stage** evening concert opened with a lively **Klezmer** showcase featuring **Beyond the Pale** and continued with the Cuban sounds of **Valle Son** and American singer-songwriter **Dar Williams**. The **Terry Penner Festival Choir** with **Mike MacDonald** graced the stage with a typically uplifting performance. The Burundi-flavoured pop of **The Mighty Popo** was followed by an American husband and wife who performed separate sets: **Greg Brown** and **Iris DeMent**. Contemporary singer-songwriter **Greg Brown** performed in three previous Ottawa Folk Festivals, while this was the first performance here by his spouse, country folk performer **Iris DeMent**.

Greg Brown appeared in his fourth Ottawa Folk Festival performance.

Alternative evening programming was found on the **World Harmony Stage** in the **Ron Kolbus Lakeside Centre**. The featured sessions were **Cajun Dance** with **Balfa Toujours, Frida's Brow**, and **Super Session 2006** featuring **Rick Fines, Rachelle van Zanten, James Hill, Eve Goldberg** and **Miles Howe**.

The music continued after the festival gates closed Sunday night with two **Festival Wrap-Up Concerts** on Monday night. At the **Black Sheep Inn** in Wakefield, Quebec, a double bill featured singer-songwriters **Dar Williams** and **Dan Frechette**. The **Dirk Powell Band** whooped it up at **The Bayou** in Ottawa.

There was music aplenty at the volunteer party: "O.F.F. Volunteers are the BEST!"

Festival smiles

Year 14 – 2007
The Times They Are A-changin'

Changes were everywhere at the 2007 Ottawa Folk Festival. Following the departure of long-time **Festival Director Gene Swimmer**, **Tamara Kater** came on board as Executive Director, bringing a fresh approach and new ideas to the festival. The layout of the festival changed with the main gate and box office repositioned and the artisans and vendors moved closer to each other. Enhanced bus service made it easier to get to the festival without taking the car, while more visible signage helped folks find their way around. Greater community involvement brought in more local organizations to set up tables, and more green initiatives were introduced. Other changes made it easier to dance and to enjoy the volunteer experience.

Woody Guthrie was celebrated at the festival in many ways. An interactive, multi-media presentation was given by Woody's daughter **Nora Guthrie** on Saturday afternoon. An interview about Woody Guthrie's life and influence featuring **Kris Kristofferson, Nora Guthrie** and **Jimmy LaFave** was conducted by journalist **Mike Regenstreif** on Saturday afternoon. It was followed by a 90-minute main stage tribute to Woody Guthrie entitled "Ribbon of Highway" featuring **Kris Kristofferson, Jimmy LaFave, Eliza Gilkyson, Ray Bonneville** and **Joel Rafael**. A spectacular display was set up in the **Ron Kolbus Lakeside Centre** that included photos from the **Woody Guthrie Archives**, along with samples of Woody's handwritten lyrics and visual art. A concert featuring Woody's children's songs was held on Sunday. Finally, an award-winning film entitled **"Man in the Sand"**, about Woody Guthrie's life and influence was held at the **National Library and Archives** on Monday, August 20.

Other festival highlights included performances by **Kris Kristofferson** and **Buffy Sainte-Marie**, as well as **Penny Lang** receiving the **Helen Verger Award**. **Chopper McKinnon** and **Karen Flanagan McCarthy** hosted the main stage throughout the festival.

Old Man Luedecke holds his own as a solo performer.

Ana Miura appeared with Amos the Transparent.

Thursday, August 16

This year the festival returned to Thursday night programming at Britannia Park. **Arthur McGregor** performed his ragtime-style acoustic guitar rendition of the national anthem on the **CUPE Main Stage,** as he has done each year since the first festival. The **Meredith Luce Band**, calypso band **Kobo Town**, the innovative **Amos the Transparent** and banjo songster **Old Man Luedecke** followed. The evening ended with the danceable music of Ottawa's own jazz-fusion group, **Souljazz Orchestra**.

The soaring vocals of Kiran Ahluwalia interpreting Indian and Pakistani music were an enchanting addition to the Friday night lineup.

Friday, August 17

The entertainment on the **CUPE Main Stage** opened with an Ottawa bluesman and his musical pals: **Tony D & Friends**. A spellbinding performance from **Kiran Ahluwalia** followed. The Canadian singer specializes in ghazals and Punjabi folk songs, and her soaring vocals were one of the highlights of the festival. **Oh Susanna**, a Canadian vocalist steeped in roots and Appalachian-style traditional music appeared next and was followed by the wonderfully named bluegrass band **The Foggy Hogtown Boys**. The greatly anticipated performance by the legendary **Kris Kristofferson** ended an exceptional evening of entertainment. The American singer-songwriter extraordinaire wowed the larger than average crowd with a set that included a combination of old and new material. Luckily, Kristofferson also appeared in workshops during the rest of the weekend.

Performances also took place in the **Bowie**

Juliana Pulford impressed the crowd with her flamenco dance moves.

Electrical Hall (in the **Ron Kolbus Lakeside Centre**) including the traditional ensemble the **Carolina Chocolate Drops**, the rootsy

Doug & Jess Band are continuing the tradition of old-time music.

Doug & Jess Band, **Juliana**, and **Mansa Sissoko**, a kora player from Mali.

Peter MacDonald and a second-generation folk fan.

Saturday, August 18

In the **Bowie Electrical Hall**, the excitement began with a **Festival Drumming Workshop** for kids aged 8 to 15 with **Kathy Armstrong** followed by a session with **The Boys and Girls Club Drummers**. The **Results of Cross-Cultural Music Experiment #1** session featured the **Carolina Chocolate Drops, Jah Youssouf** and **Lewis Melville,** and was hosted by **Petr Cancura**. An interview hosted by **Mike Regenstreif** chronicling Woody Guthrie's influences featured a panel of **Kris Kristofferson, Nora Guthrie** and **Jimmy LaFave**. **I Know an Old Lady** was the unusual title of a tribute to **Alan Mills** hosted by CBC arts guru **Alan Neal** that featured **Bram Morrison** and **Lorne Brown**.

The **Penguin Eggs Garden** was named for the Canadian folk magazine *Penguin Eggs*. The entertainment on this stage opened with the **African Morning** session with **Mansa Sissoko**. The session **This Land Is Your Land: The Story of Woody Guthrie** was a multimedia presentation hosted by his daughter **Nora Guthrie**. **The Music of Rev. Gary Davis** was celebrated by **Andy Cohen**. **From the Heart** was a session showcasing the talents of **Mary Murphy** with **Paul Keim, Jimmy LaFave** and **Lewis Melville**.

Over at the **Ten Thousand Villages Beach Stage**, the **Once Upon a Time** session hosted by **Anne-Marie Brugger** included story songsters **Heather**

Dale & Ben Deschamps, **Michelle Desbarats** and **Nathan**. **The Living Traditions** session featured **Andy Cohen, Arthur McGregor** and host **Bram Morrison**. **You Must be Joking** was a jovial session hosted by **Terry Eagan** with **The Arrogant Worms**, and **Karen Savoca & Pete Heitzman**. **Roch Parisien** of **Galaxie**, CBC's Continuous Music Network, hosted the **Rising Stars** session featuring **David Gaudet, Lindsay Jane** and **Rose Cousins**.

Doc, a regular on the CKCU-FM folk music show *Canadian Spaces*, hosted **Doc's Pick** featuring the talents of **Kate Weekes, Oh Susanna** and **Ray Bonneville**. Doc is **Peter Conway** of McCrank's Cycles, a local business that is a longtime sponsor of *Canadian Spaces*.

A member of the production crew hard at work.

The fun in the **CKCU Kidzone** started out with the **Carolina Chocolate Drops** and continued with **Stories for Kids** with **Lorne Brown**, a **Musical Instrument Petting Zoo** and an **Instrument Making for Kids** session. **Curtis Jonnie (Shingoose)** was followed by a wire sculpture workshop for kids with **Heather Boyd** of **Filament** and a craft workshop for kids with **Helen & Ingrid**

Sherling of **Nicbela**. The kids were also treated to a session showcasing **Easy Flamenco Rhythms** with **Juliana**, and a mini-concert with **Penny Lang**.

A volunteer displays a shirt with an impressive number of performer autographs.

At the **Ottawa Folklore Centre Point Stage**, the **All about the Groove** session hosted by **Karen Savoca & Pete Heitzman** included **Pepe Danza** and **Ray Bonneville**. **The Music of South America** session featured **Turpial**. **Juliana** hosted the **Rhythm and Shoes** session with poet **Stuart Ross** and musician **Pepe Danza**. The evocative **Painting Pictures** session was led by master storyteller **Buffy Sainte-Marie** and included **Christian Masotti** and **Kaie Kellough**. A tuneful **Vocal Harmony** session hosted by **Mike McCormick** showcased **The Arrogant Worms**, **Chris Whiteley & Diana Braithwaite**, and **The Good Lovelies**.

The **Loeb Glebe Hill Stage** opened with the **Up North, Down South** session with **Jimmy LaFave** and **Kate Weekes**. The **Back 40 Live** session named for the CKCU-FM radio show featuring traditional country, western and bluegrass music was led by **Ron Moores** and featured **Dirk Powell**, the **Foggy Hogtown Boys**, and the **Doug & Jess Band**. **Steve Pritchard** hosted the **Prestidigitation** session featuring the nimble fingers of the **Foggy Hogtown Boys, Lindsay Jane** and **Miles Howe**. **Cam Wells**, co-host of the CKCU-FM folk music show *Canadian Spaces,* hosted **The Sum of the Parts** session with the **Doug & Jess Band** and **The Gruff**. **The Spoken Word** session showcased spoken word specialists **Kaie Kellough, Michelle Desbarats, Sheila M Ross, Stuart Ross** and host **Sean Wilson**.

The **Rogers Tree Stage** entertainment began appropriately with **New Beginnings**, a session hosted by **Eliza Gilkyson** that highlighted the talents of **Lindsay Jane** and **Martha Scanlan**. **Tales from the Road** was hosted by **Paul Symes**, owner of the Black Sheep Inn and featured **Oh Susanna, Old Man Luedecke** and **Rose Cousins**. **The Songs of Peace** session attracted a huge crowd. It was hosted by **Sonny Ochs**, the sister of **Phil Ochs** and featured the stellar talents of **Kris Kristofferson, Buffy Sainte-Marie** and **Penny Lang**. **Music from the Glen** was a session named for the CKCU-FM Celtic music show and was hosted by **Colin Henein**. It included **Andy Daub, Heather Dale & Ben Deschamps**, and **Mary Murphy** with **Paul Keim**. The day wound down with the **Mountain Music** session hosted by **Dirk Powell** and presenting the **Carolina Chocolate Drops, Martha Scanlan, Michael Jerome Browne** and **Old Man Luedecke**.

The incomparable artist Arthur II in front of one of his many festival murals.

In the **CUPE EnviroTent**, workshops were held on topics including **Switching to Renewable Energy at Home** with **Sean Twomey**, **Speaking Out: Public Speaking Tips** with **Pamma Durin**, **How Technology Affects the Environment** with **John Buschek**, **Green Energy for Everyone** with **Bullfrog Power**, and the **Life, Money and Illusion** session with author **Mike Nickerson**.

The **OFC Music Knoll** featured the **N'Goni Building Demonstration** with **Jah Youssouf** and **Basic Flamenco Rhythms** with **Juliana**, followed by **The Craziest Right Hand Banjo Picking Pattern Ever** session with **Max Cossette**. This was followed by a **Folk Jam with Tony D** session that encouraged audience participation using provided instruments. A second **N'Goni Building Demonstration** was followed by an **Open Mic** session.

Other activities included **Taoist Tai Chi** workshops near the **EnviroTent**.

In the evening on the **CUPE Main Stage**, **Hoots & Hellmouth** opened the evening entertainment. **Ray Bonneville** delivered a wonderful set of his original singer-songwriter material for his third festival appearance. **Penny Lang** received the **Helen Verger Award**. The Canadian singer-songwriter was honoured for her exceptional career that spanned more than 40 years. Her longstanding connection with the festival began with performances at the inaugural festival on Victoria Island in 1994.

Penny Lang was the deserving recipient of the Helen Verger Award.

Karen Savoca & Pete Heitzman performed a rhythmic and tuneful set before **Buffy Sainte-Marie** performed to an appreciative audience. The **Carolina Chocolate Drops** transported us to a bygone era with their rootsy music of the southern U.S. The evening ended with the first Canadian presentation of the magnificent **Ribbon of Highway Tribute to Woody Guthrie.** The 90-minute tribute to the words and music of Woody Guthrie featured **Kris Kristofferson, Eliza Gilkyson, Ray Bonneville, Jimmy LaFave** and **Joel Rafael**, with narrator **Bob Childers**. The tribute celebrated a unique individual whose massive influence continues to be felt.

The festival audience was treated to thrilling performances by Buffy Sainte-Marie on Saturday afternoon and evening.

On the **Bowie Electrical Stage** in the air-conditioned comfort of the **Ron Kolbus Lakeside Centre**, the audience was treated to performances from traditional folk stylists **The Gruff**, singer-songwriters **Nathan**, and **Jason Lang** (son of Penny) along with **Michael Jerome Browne** and **Petr Cancura**. This was followed by a set with **The Good Lovelies.** The evening ended with a rootsy quadruple bill of **David Gaudet, Meredith Luce, Old Man Luedecke** and **Rose Cousins**.

Sunday, August 19
The final day of the festival kicked off in the **Bowie Electrical Hall** with a **Festival Drumming Workshop** for kids aged 8 to 15 led by **Kathy Armstrong**, followed by a performance from **Bram Morrison**. The session **Results of Cross-Cultural Music Experiment #3** showcased **Chris Whiteley & Diana Braithwaite, Mansa Sissoko** and host **Petr Cancura**. The **Blues Sources** session featured **Ray Bonneville, Tony D** and host **Michael Jerome Browne**. The final session of the day was an

energetic **Klezmer Dance** with **Oy Division**.

Over at the **Penguin Eggs Garden**, **Curtis Jonnie (Shingoose)** appeared in concert and was followed by the **Banjorama Unplugged** session hosted by **Ann Downey** featuring the **Doug & Jess Band** and **Old Man Luedecke**. **Making It Up as We Go Along** showcased **Andy Cohen, Christian Masotti, Miles Howe** and **Petr Cancura**.

Longtime volunteer and Photo Crew leader Tim Ladd.

At the **Ten Thousand Villages Beach Stage**, the session **Results of Cross-Cultural Music Experiment #2** showcased the talents of **The Gruff, Mushfiq Ensemble, Pepe Danza** and host **Petr Cancura**. The **African/American** session featured **Dirk Powell, Jah Youssouf, Martha Scanlan** and host **Andy Cohen**. The **Mixed Blessings** session hosted by **Mike Regenstreif** included **David Gaudet, Eliza Gilkyson**, and **Mary Murphy**. The **Good Vibes** session featured **The Gruff** and **Hoots & Hellmouth**. The day ended with **Danse Africaine**, a session with **Elage**.

In the **CKCU Kidzone**, things started with a bang at the **Percussion Petting Zoo** and continued with performances by **Christian Masotti** and **Mushfiq Ensemble**, as well as craft and drumming workshops and performances. **Joel Rafael** led a **Woody Guthrie Songs** session and the day ended with the joyous annual **Sunshine Parade** where everyone was invited to join a musical, percussion-filled procession to the main stage area.

At the **Ottawa Folklore Centre Point Stage**, the day opened with the **Rise and Shine Session** with **Eliza Gilkyson, Jason Lang** and host **Sheila M Ross**. An improvisional dance session by the **Grasshoppa Dance Exchange** was followed by the **A Capella** session showcasing **Mary Murphy, Nathan** and host **Diana Braithwaite**. **Curtis Jonnie** (Shingoose), **Michelle Desbarats** and host **Lindsay Jane** appeared in **This Land Is Our Land** session. **Old Man Luedecke** hosted the session titled **I Quit My Job** with **The Good Lovelies** and **Kate Weekes**. The final session, **Matters of the Heart**, featured **Lindsay Jane, Nathan** and host **Stuart Ross**.

Britannia Park is remote enough that many festival-goers must drive there. The parking crew performs an essential function with a smile!

The **Loeb Glebe Hill Stage** opened for the day with **Looking Back**, showcasing **Michael Jerome Browne, Martha Scanlan, Oh Susanna** and host **Louis Meyers**. **Jennie Stratton** hosted the **Music as a Bridge** session with **Elage, Joel Rafael**, and **Karen Savoca & Pete Heitzman**. The **Human Nature** session featured **Heather Dale & Ben Deschamps, Rose Cousins** and **Kaie Kellough**, and was hosted by **Karen Flanagan McCarthy**. The **Grasshoppa Dance Exchange** showcased improvisional dance. **Chopper McKinnon** hosted the *Canadian Spaces* session with **Chris Whiteley, Karen Savoca & Pete Heitzman**, and **Rose Cousins**. A very special event followed. The Ottawa Folklore Centre distributed 300 free pennywhistles to the audience and **Andy Daub** gave everyone a free introductory lesson on this traditional instrument. How folkie can you get?

The fun on the **Rogers Tree Stage** began with **Celtic Jam** with **Alf Warnock**. **Tom Werbo** hosted the **Spontaneous Combustion** session featuring **The Arrogant Worms** and **Hoots & Hellmouth**. **Grasshoppa Dance Exchange** contributed improvisational dance. The **Music from the Andes** session featured **Turpial**.

Ann Downey was the host of the **Deep Roots** session featuring **Dirk Powell** and **Oh Susanna**. The final session of the day was **Super Blues Jam** hosted by **Tony D** and showcasing the talents of **Andy Cohen, Chris Whiteley & Diana Braithwaite, Jah Youssouf, Penny Lang** and **Ray Bonneville**.

The **CUPE EnviroTent** featured discussions as well as sessions including **Against Uranium Mining** with **John Kittle**, and **Non-Toxic Personal Care Products** with **Patti Murphy & Tamey McIntosh**.

On the **OFC Music Knoll**, **Petr Cancura** was featured in the session titled **Improvising Over Chord Changes**. **Arthur McGregor** led the **Rise Up Singing** session followed by a **Harmonica for Beginners** session hosted by **Catriona Sturton**. **Ellen MacIsaac** introduced Irish music to the crowd at the session **Introduction to Sean Nos**. After improvisational dance with **Grasshoppa Dance Exchange**, an **Open Mic** session ended the day.

Other activities included the **Second Annual Musical Festival Brunch** hosted by **Cam Wells** and featuring the **Doug & Jess Band, Mary Murphy** and surprise guests. The festival goers also had a chance to try out **Taoist Tai Chi** near the **EnviroTent**.

The **CUPE Main Stage** evening entertainment opened with the **Mushfiq Ensemble** performing Afghani and North Indian folk music in many languages. **Andy Rush** and the **Terry Penner Festival Choir** gave a particularly moving performance that included a wonderful version of "This Land Is Your Land" and other Woody Guthrie tunes. Up and coming P.E.I. singer-songwriter **Rose Cousins** was followed by favourite festival funny guys **The Arrogant Worms**, who performed their famous alligator song to the delight of the audience members who got into the act with the usual wild hand motions. Performances by **Dirk Powell & Martha Scanlan** and American songstress **Eliza Gilkyson** were followed with a highly danceable set from **Cheza**, an Ottawa band that blends African styles with rock and folk influences. The final segment brought the evening's performers back to the main stage for a dramatic finale.

The music in the **Bowie Electrical Hall** opened with

A folk festival meet-up: Rose Cousins & Sean Hoots onstage.

A beautiful festival evening with a crescent moon.

Heather Dale & Ben Deschamps. It was followed with **Pepe Danza and Friends, Jah Youssouf**, and **Chris Whiteley & Diana Braithwaite**. The festival wrapped up with the female trio of **Ann Downey, Kate Weekes** and **Lindsay Jane.**

The Arrogant Worms and their fans.

Year 15 – 2008

A Party for the People!

The construction crew at work and play. Two crew members building a fence (left). Chris White accompanying the gang singing a crew song (right), led by Bob Nesbitt, the crew leader.

The 15th **Ottawa Folk Festival** certainly lived up to its billing as a party for the people! And party we did, while listening, singing, dancing, building, painting and celebrating. A 2,000 square foot dance tent, a free ukulele-building workshop, a ParticiPaint mural honouring the late **Willie P. Bennett** and the **Terry Penner Festival Choir** were but a few of the opportunities people had to "party-cipate".

Festival highlights included a moving performance from **Odetta** (who died on Dec. 2, 2008 at the age of 77); and appearances by **The Experimental Farmers, Catherine MacLellan, Don Ross & Andy McKee, Finest Kind** and the **Healing Divas**. A moving tribute to **Rasputin's Folk Café** was particularly well attended after a July 2008 fire at the legendary Ottawa folk club led to its closing.

An exciting feature at this year's festival was the **2008 Cross-Cultural Music and Dance Collaboration** featuring **Anne Davison** (Nova Scotia), **Benoit Bourque** (Quebec), **The Carolina Chocolate Drops** (North Carolina), **Claire Jenkins** (Toronto), **James Hill** (Nova Scotia), **Jaxon Haldane** (Winnipeg), **Mohamed Diarra** (Guinea/Gatineau), **Petr Cancura** (New York/Ottawa), **Radoslav Lorkovic** (Nashville), **Roda de Samba** (Brazil/Ottawa), **Shara Weaver** (Ottawa) and **Timothy Mason** (Boston).

This year's festival was the greenest yet. A festival **Green Team** was established and new initiatives included providing water stations to refill reusable water bottles, making compostable water bottles available on-site, arranging food for a volunteer lunch to be supplied locally from the **Lansdowne Farmers Market**, and composting food scraps. Other innovations included a vehicle-free site, pedal-powered cargo trikes to haul equipment and supplies, and using solar power to wash plates. Green printing materials were used for festival promotional material, banners and T-shirts. A partnership with **Ottawa Riverkeeper** and **Ecology Ottawa** was also established to educate people about local water and watershed management issues.

Continuing initiatives included the reusable dish program, electricity from renewable sources supplied by **Bullfrog Power**, compostable beer cups provided by **Big Rock Brewery** and "cupsucker" receptacles provided by **Blue Heron Solutions**. Folks were encouraged to walk, bike or take public transit to the festival.

Grasshoppa Dance Exchange gave impromptu dance performances all around the site and was joined this year by **Dancing in the Street**, a project of the **Ottawa School of Dance**.

The **Community Corner** was designed to foster discussion and promote awareness. The following organizations had tables this year: Green Party of Canada/Ottawa Greens, ArtsCan Circle, Ecology Ottawa, Ottawa Riverkeeper, Amnesty International, Canada 211, Catholic Immigration Centre of Ottawa, Oxfam Canada, The Ottawa Food Bank, Ottawa Community Immigration Services Organization, and USC Canada.

There were many awards presented at this year's festival. **J. Chalmers Doane** received the **Helen Verger Award**, which is presented to an individual who has made valuable contributions to folk/roots music in Canada. While working as the Director of Music Education in Halifax in the 1970s, Doane developed a method of teaching students to play music using the ukulele. More than 50,000 schoolchildren and adults throughout Canada and in parts of the U.S. learned to play the ukulele as a result of his efforts. He was recognized with the Order of Canada in 2004 and recently collaborated with ukulele virtuoso James Hill to develop the Ukulele in the Classroom program. **Margaret Feuerstack** and **David Johnstone** received the **One Fret Less Award** sponsored by **Harvey and Louise Glatt**. **James Farr** was presented with the **Galaxie Rising Stars Award**. **Ana Miura** was the recipient of the **Beth Ferguson Award**.

Arthur II is a gifted Ottawa artist and musician who designed this year's participatory mural project to honour Canadian folk music legend **Willie P. Bennett**, who died in February. The huge success of the ParticiPaint mural project at the 2007 festival inspired Arthur II to create an 8 foot by 40 foot mural, which he named after one of Willie's best-loved songs, "Music in Your Eyes". The result was a fantastic and heartwarming tribute to one of Canada's finest singer-songwriters and musicians.

Windhorse Yoga offered participatory yoga sessions to help festival goers stretch, relax and breathe while **Santosha Yoga** offered a group singing session.

Thursday, August 14

Ottawa Folklore Centre owner **Arthur McGregor** kicked things off with his acoustic ragtime version of "O Canada". **Colores Andinos**, a Latin-Andean musical ensemble of South American and Canadian extraction, opened the festival with panache on the **CUPE Main Stage**. The wonderfully named group, **The Experimental Farmers,** stole the show that evening. The Farmers included **Lynn Miles** on vocals and mandolin, **Lonesome Paul** on vocals and guitar, and **Keith Snider** on banjo and fiddle. **Finest Kind**, a group who has performed at the festival since the first year on Victoria Island, took the stage next. **Ian Robb, Ann Downey** and **Shelley Posen** performed a mix of traditional songs and original tunes with their usual exquisite three-part harmony. Brilliant fingerstyle guitarist **Don Ross** was joined by percussive guitar sensation **Andy McKee**, renowned for his YouTube rendition of "Drifting" that has garnered over 14 million hits. **Vieux Farka Touré** closed the evening with a lively set that combined traditional Malian blues music with rock and reggae. The group's performance was recorded by CBC Radio for *Canada Live*.

In the **Dance Tent**, the **Carolina Chocolate Drops** set the audience in motion with their old-time string band music of the Carolinas. The delicious Drops were followed by the **D. Rangers**, a band whose music has been described as "mutant bluegrass". The evening closed with **Brisa Latina**, a group known for their enticing fusion of classic and contemporary Latin rhythms, and their ability to get any crowd moving to the beat!

Roberta Huebener (left) presents the One Fret Less Award to David Johnstone and Margaret Feuerstack.

Waiting for the gates to open on Friday.

Friday, August 15

The lovely **Ana Miura** opened the **CUPE Main Stage** with her gentle, acoustic self-penned tunes. **Bryan Bowers**, a native of Virginia now living in California, mesmerized the crowd with his virtuoso autoharp performance. The **Jerry Douglas Band** featured another virtuoso. **Jerry Douglas**, renowned for his resophonic guitar playing, has appeared on a staggering 2,000 albums and has won a dozen Grammies. The audience witnessed a stellar performance from this master picker/slide guitarist and his bandmates. **Dala** features two 20-something vocalists who play guitar and piano. The duo created a set with uplifting sweet harmonies and folk-pop songs. The excitement built as indie favourites **Broken Social Scene** took the stage. The band delivered a free-flowing, guitar-driven and dynamic vocal performance.

Albert Dumont is a traditional Aboriginal leader and elder who grew up in the Algonquin territory.

Ana Miura was awarded with the Beth Ferguson Award.

In the **Dance Tent**, the fun began with a lively, infectious set with **Genticorum**, a Québécois band that has toured in over 15 countries worldwide. They were joined by the ever-popular **Benoit Bourque**. Bourque, who garnered a Juno Award and a Canadian Folk Music Award as a member of Le Vent du Nord, is an exuberant accordion player, a virtuoso percussionist on bones, spoons and feet, and a world-class Québécois stepdancer. **Spiral Beach**, a band that includes the offspring of two well-known folkies, returned to the festival with their rhythmic indie rock and performed a rollicking set that was well received by the dancing throng. **Donna the Buffalo**, a five-member band from upstate New York, were up next with an eclectic offering of folk-rock, country folk, zydeco, reggae and bluegrass tunes. The evening concluded with a wonderful **Big Bad Bluegrass Jam** featuring **Jerry Douglas**, the **D. Rangers**, **Leavin' Train**, **The Experimental Farmers** and **Doug Cox**. We could have danced all night with this gang!

The entertainment on the **Hall Stage** in the **Ron Kolbus Lakeside Centre** kicked off with a round-robin **Good Vibrations** session hosted by **Doug**

Cox. The talented group included **Catherine MacLellan**, the **Healing Divas** and **Radoslav Lorkovic**. They were followed by **Claire Jenkins Avec Band**, featuring the theatrical actress and singer and her accompanists, who performed quirky and catchy tunes in both official languages. The **Doc's Pick** session, named for a regular feature of the CKCU-FM folk music radio show *Canadian Spaces* was hosted by Doc and featured a diverse and talented lineup. Doc is **Peter Conway** of McCrank's Cycles, a local business that is a long time sponsor of *Canadian Spaces*. The **Carolina Chocolate Drops**, whose music is steeped in the string band tradition of the American South, was joined by modern bluesman **Jaxon Haldane**, cellist **Anne Davison**, and Boston-area spoken word artist **Timothy Mason**.

Rhiannon Giddens, vocalist and instrumentalist of the Carolina Chocolate Drops.

Saturday, August 16
Saturday Daytime

Entertainment and activities abounded in the many daytime venues and on the three evening stages.

In the **Dance Tent**, **The Experimental Farmers** got toes tapping and were followed by spirited performances from the **Carolina Chocolate Drops** and **Donna the Buffalo**. **Anne-Marie Brugger**, host of the CHUO radio show *Hop the Fence*, led the **My Chemistry Experiment** session featuring spoken word guy **Timothy Mason**, members of **Broken Social Scene** and **Ana Miura**. The last performance of the afternoon was a Cajun dance featuring **Harlan Johnson & Grouyan Gombo**, **Michael Jerome Browne**, **Jody Benjamin**, **Michael Ball** and **Mary Gick**.

On the **Hall Stage**, a double bill showcased the talents of **Catherine MacLellan** and **Doug Cox**. **Anne-Marie Brugger** hosted the **Hop the Fence** session, named for her CHUO radio show that features Canadian musicians of all genres. Participants included **Chris Velan**, an unplugged **Spiral Beach**, and two members of the **Claire Jenkins** band. **Andy Rush** led the **Terry Penner Festival Choir** in its first rehearsal. **Jowi Taylor** hosted the **Six String Nation Guitar** session featuring pickers and grinners **Shelley Posen**, **Catherine MacLellan** and **Sean Cotton**. The afternoon's entertainment wound down with a supersonic double bill with two fascinating ensembles making their festival debuts. The five Toronto women comprising the **Healing Divas** entranced the audience with their positive energy, primal rhythms and luscious vocal harmonies. They were the best-kept secret of the festival. **Raymundo & Balam** dazzled the audience with their Spanish and Latin guitar styles.

The Healing Divas from Toronto rocked the main stage with their healing vibes.

On the scenic **Beach Stage**, the opening act was **Village Harmony**, a choir made up of 24 teenagers from Ontario and the eastern United States. The group performed music from Bulgaria, Georgia and South Africa. **Roch Parisien**, programmer of Galaxie's Folk Roots channel, hosted the **Full Moon, Rising Stars** session with **James Farr**, winner of the **Galaxie Rising Stars**

Award; emerging artist **Mélisande**; and guitarists **Raymundo & Balam**. **Claire Jenkins** hosted the wonderfully fun **Cheesy Songs We Love** session with guilty pleasure conspirators **Spiral Beach** and **Finest Kind**. The **Unaccompanied Ballad Singing** session with **Riley Baugus** and **Finest Kind** was hosted by CBC Radio 2 host and traditional Newfoundland music enthusiast **Tom Power**. **Genticorum** hosted the **Nos racines musicales** (translation: our musical roots) session and was joined by **Peter Andrée & Natacha Ducharme** and **Mélisande**.

In the **Artisan Village**, audience members were fortunate to have the opportunity to participate in the following hands-on workshops: **Working with Wood – Solar Woodcuts (Ron Tremback); Wear Your Message – Global Aware (Sarah King); Healthy Products for Your Skin – U.fabu (D. Passmore); Reclaiming Old Fabric – Sew Very Vintage (Carol Elchuk); Working with Glass – Miller's Glass Reflections (Randy Miller); and Re-working Jewellery for Metal Allergies – Creations of the Heart (Tunica Haris)**.

On the **Hill Stage**, **Bryan Bowers** hosted the **Story Songs** session. Joining him was **Woody Johnson**, an individual who creates guitar music for a variety of material dating back to the 1800s. **James Hill** hosted the **Words and/or Music** session with **Margaret Feuerstack & David Johnstone** and **Timothy Mason**. The **Hand Me Down** session featured **Tao Rodriguez-Seeger** and **Alexandre de Grosbois-Garand**, and was hosted by **Michael Jerome Browne**. **Don Bird** was the host of the **Hummin' and Strummin'** session with **Dala, Bryan Bowers** and **Doug Cox**. **Maura Volante** led the audience in a **Songcircle** to round out the afternoon entertainment.

The verdant space of the **Tree Stage** set the scene for **A Touch of Jazz**. The session was hosted by **Petr Cancura** and showcased **Radoslav Lorkovic** and **Margaret Feuerstack & David Johnstone**. **Dallas** and **Travis Good** of The Sadies teamed up with members of **Broken Social Scene** for the **Behind the Scenes** session. **Anne Davison** hosted **Sources of Inspiration** with **Woody Johnson** and **Petr Cancura**. **Tao Rodriguez-Seeger** hosted the **Global Villages** session with **Village Harmony**. The day concluded with the first concert in the **2008 Cross-Cultural Music and Dance Collaboration**.

On the **Point Stage**, the afternoon kicked off with the **Banjo Banjo Banjo** session hosted by **Ann Downey** and featuring **Dirk Powell, Riley Baugus**, and **Donna the Buffalo** bandmates **Jeb Puryear & Tara Nevins**. **Ottawa Folklore Centre** owner **Arthur McGregor** led the audience in the **Rise Up Singing** session. **Chopper McKinnon**, host of the CKCU-FM radio show *Canadian Spaces*, led the session honouring his late, great friend **Willie P. Bennett**. Chopper told many anecdotes about his pal. **Remembering Willie P.** also included heartfelt performances by **Jaxon Haldane**, the **D. Rangers, Dallas Good, Travis Good** and **Lonesome Paul**. The **Healing Divas** hosted the **Musical Connections** session with **Peter Andrée & Natacha Ducharme** and **Chalmers Doane**. The **Ukulele 101** session was hosted by virtuoso performer **James Hill** and also included **Chalmers Doane**.

A young banjo picker.

In the **Kidzone**, a wide variety of crafts and activities were available all day. For example, kids could make a kimono or a drum. There were also performances by musicians and jugglers as well as storytelling. **Yoga for Families** gave everyone a chance to stretch and relax.

At the **EnviroTent**, green activities were happening

all day. **Jason Sonier** of **The Otesha Project** presented the session **Cradle to Grave: The Life Cycle of a Banana**. The **Greening the Home** session was presented by **Sean Twomey** of **Arbour Environmental Shoppe**. **Leaf Bellaar-Spruyt** of **Berg en Dal Honey Farms** spoke about **Honey, Health and the Environment**. USC Canada members **Kate Green** and **Sarah Mohan** addressed the topic **Food, Farmer and Climate Chaos**. The session **Muscle Testing Techniques** was presented by **Katherine Willow** of the **Carp Ridge EcoWellness Centre**. **Charles Jonah** of **Jademark** gave the presentation **The E-Bike: A Power-Assisted Electric Bicycle**.

Windhorse Yoga sponsored a number of activities. In the morning the Catholic Immigration Centre's **CIC Community Cup Celebrity Soccer Match** took place in the field behind the Dance Tent. The 30-minute **Yoga Tasters** presentations held in the morning and afternoon included the following flavours of yoga: Hatha, Vinyasa Flow, Yin and Final Relaxation. **Uke Building for Kids** allowed children to make their very own ukuleles. In the Dance Tent there were the **1,000 Cranes: Origami for Everyone** activity and a display of the **Six String Nation Guitar**.

Our main stage hosts deserve special mention. **Chopper McKinnon** and **Karen Flanagan McCarthy** have hosted the festival main stage every year, starting in 1994 when the first festival was held on Victoria Island. **Chopper McKinnon**, an important figure in the Canadian folk roots music scene, was perhaps best known for his CKCU-FM radio show *Canadian Spaces*. The show first aired in 1980 and is the longest-running folk music show on community radio in Canada. **Karen Flanagan McCarthy**, affectionately known as KFM, is a communications expert who has played a significant role in the festival's evolution, having served as a member of the festival's steering committee and board of directors. She is also a former board member of the Ontario Council of Folk Festivals. **Tom Power** is a Newfoundland musician, broadcaster and writer and the host of CBC Radio 2's *Deep Roots*. **Alan Neal** is a journalist and radio personality who hosts two CBC Radio 2 shows: *Canada Live* and *Bandwidth*.

Thanks also to the many hosts who helped things run smoothly at the daytime sessions.

Saturday Evening

The Québécois band **Genticorum** opened the **CUPE Main Stage** and were warmly welcomed by the crowd. **Country Joe McDonald**, the iconic figure who played at Woodstock, sang his famous anti-war anthem, "I-Feel-Like-I'm-Fixin'-to-Die Rag", and showed he still has a radical bent and an unfailing sense of humour. Two blues artists followed. First up was **Roxanne Potvin**, a 26-year-old Gatineau-raised singer who has earned Maple Blues and Juno nominations for her soulful, sultry singing. Her high-energy set was followed by **Colin Linden**, a master of the country-blues guitar, who gave a powerful performance that reverberated throughout the audience. The evening closed with the charming **Sarah Harmer**. It doesn't get any better than listening to Sarah singing under the stars on a Saturday night!

Ron Farmer and Johanna Geuer of the popular Green Door Restaurant, provided a vegetarian food concession.

The **Dance Tent** performances began with **Wil**, a West Coast roots rocker known for his intense live performances. Next up were the **D. Rangers**, a Winnipeg band who served a heaping helping of their "mutant bluegrass" sound. Ottawa favourites **Ball and Chain** are always fun and their set was no exception. Country vocalist **Jody Benjamin** and fiddler **Michael Ball** are **Ball and Chain**. They were backed up by **The Wreckers**, and together they delivered classic country hurtin' heartache with a Cajun twist. Just the thing to dance to on a warm summer night. **The Sadies**, led by **Dallas and Travis Good,** combined hillbilly and punk influences in their set.

In the **Hall Stage**, **Tao Rodriguez-Seeger** drew an audience eager to hear his songs of struggle and hope and stories about his granddad, Pete Seeger. The crowd enjoyed his "subversive acoustic traditionalist" approach to making music. A rousing set by **Village Harmony** rounded out the evening's entertainment.

Sunday, August 17
There was plenty happening in the many daytime venues and on the three evening stages.

Sunday Daytime
In the **Dance Tent**, **Roda de Samba** presented **The Story of Samba**. **Donna the Buffalo** performed next.

Some of the cranes were displayed in the Dance Tent following the 1000 Cranes: Origami for Everyone activity.

The session **Latin Breeze** was led by dance instructor **Nubia Cermeño** who taught festival goers how to samba. The dance floor was jam-packed! **The Experimental Farmers** hosted the **On the Edge** session with the **D. Rangers**, **Wil** and **Lonesome Paul**.

Andy Rush gathered members of the **Terry Penner Festival Choir** on the **Hall Stage** for a second rehearsal. **Claire Jenkins Avec Band** did a showcase set followed by a performance by **Wil**. A session posing the musical question **How Can I Keep from Singing?** featured **Odetta**, **Tao Rodriguez-Seeger** and **Finest Kind** and was hosted by **Mike Regenstreif**, host of the Montreal CKUT radio program *Folk Roots/Folk Branches*. The last choir rehearsal wrapped up the afternoon stage.

On the scenic **Beach Stage** a **Ukulele Jam** featured virtuoso **James Hill** and uke educator extraordinaire **Chalmers Doane**. They were joined musically by audience members. An American patron of the festival for many years, **Terry Eagan** of **Patio Records**, hosted the **Uncommon Ground** session with **Dirk Powell & Riley Baugus, Benoit Bourque** and blues vocalist **Roxanne Potvin**. The **Old Blues** session hosted by **Colin Linden** showcased the talents of **Michael Jerome Browne, Woody Johnson** and **James Farr**. A very inspirational session, **Spirit Connections**, showcased the **Healing Divas** and **Village Harmony**.

A large crowd gathered for the **Here's to Rasputin's** session honouring **Rasputin's Folk Café**. The revered Ottawa folk club was forced to close its doors in 2008 following a fire. **Lynn Miles**, whose musical journey included a close involvement with Rasputin's in the early years, hosted this session and shared the stage with **Colin Linden** and **Catherine MacLellan**. This session provided some of the most poignant moments in the history of the Ottawa Folk Festival. Stories, songs, tears and laughter were shared. Owner **Dean Verger** spoke briefly and was given a standing ovation and many hugs during and following this moving tribute.

In the **Artisan Village**, there were presentations all day. **Heather Boyd** of **Filament** presented a workshop on **Wire Jewellery Techniques**. **The Lo-Down on Chair-Making** was given by **Jonny**

Lo of **Lo-Chair**. **From Cutlery to Jewellery** was the theme of the workshop hosted by **Bloom/Ash/Postart Gallery**. **Ania Geerts** hosted a **Silver Smithing** workshop, while **Robert Webster** of **Maple Leaf Studio** demonstrated **Working with Stone**. **Artisans Around the World** was presented by **Ian Brown** of **Ten Thousand Villages**. The day concluded with **Randy MacNeil** of **Canadian Bluesbook** who discussed **Photo Techniques for Music Events**.

At the **Hill Stage**, the entertainment began with the second concert of the **2008 Cross-Cultural Music and Dance Collaboration**. The **Carolina Chocolate Drops** hosted the **Heaven and Earth** double bill with the **Healing Divas**.

Black Sheep Live was hosted by **Paul Symes**, owner of the famed Black Sheep Inn in Wakefield, Quebec. This session featured **James Hill, Anne Davison, Roxanne Potvin** and **Catherine MacLellan**. **Themes and Variations** was a session with **Laura Cortese** (Tao Rodriguez-Seeger), **Jeb Puryear** of Donna the Buffalo, and hosted by **Pascal Gemme** of Genticorum.

Over at the **Tree Stage**, **Maura Volante** led a song circle. The **20 Something** session showcased two young groups: **Spiral Beach** and **Dala**. **Anne Davison** hosted the eclectic session **Exploratorium** with **Timothy Mason** and **Genticorum**. **Instrumentalism** was a session featuring **Doug Cox, James Farr** and **Aaron Goss** of D. Rangers. The third concert of the **2008 Cross-Cultural Music and Dance Collaboration** was very well received.

The **Point Stage** opened with **Colin Henein** of the CKCU-FM radio show *Music from the Glen* hosting **The Art of Accompaniment** with **Tom Power, Yann Falquet** and **Ann Downey**. **Arthur McGregor**, owner of the **Ottawa Folklore Centre**, hosted the **Songs with a Message** session featuring **Country Joe McDonald** (of Woodstock fame) and **Finest Kind**. **Karen Flanagan McCarthy** led the **Tuned In to Nature** session with **Sarah Harmer, Jaxon Haldane** and **Ana Miura**. The lively **Accordion Overload** session showcased **Benoit Bourque, Radoslav Lorkovic, Harlan Johnson, Tara Nevins** and **Treasa Levasseur** (Claire Jenkins Avec Band), and was hosted by **Dirk Powell**. **Chalmers Doane** and **James Hill** introduced the uke in **Ukulele 101**.

In the **Kidzone**, there were musical performances and many activities including kimono-making, drum making and craft workshops. There was also a session called **Yoga for Kids**.

Radoslav Lorkovic had toes tapping when he performed on a workshop stage.

The **EnviroTent** provided talks and demonstrations throughout the day. **Albert Dumont** (Algonquin, Kitigan Zibi, Anishinabeg) spoke about **The Healing Power of Nature**. **Why Rivers Matter** was the topic addressed by **Christopher Kelly** of the **Ottawa Riverkeeper** organization. **Sean Twomey** of Arbour Environmental Shoppe spoke about **Renewable Resources**. **Practical Mud Pies: Cob for Building and Art Projects** was the theme of a discussion by **Leigh Thorpe** and **Brent Hyde** of **City Repair Ottawa**. **Katherine Willow** of the **Carp Ridge EcoWellness Centre** spoke on **The Soul of Sustainability**. The newly formed **Folk Festival Green Team** presented the **How Are We Doing?** session to discuss the progress of the festival's green initiatives.

Windhorse Yoga sponsored afternoon events including **Uke Building for Kids**, **1,000 Cranes – Origami for Everyone** and the all-day **Six String Nation Guitar** display. The 30-minute **Yoga Tasters** presentations held in the afternoon included the following flavours of yoga: Hatha, Vinyasa Flow, Yin and Final Relaxation. At the **OFC Music Knoll**, educational programs ran all afternoon. In the **Catholic Immigration Centre (CIC) Language Village**, you could get a language passport and learn a few words in up to 10 languages.

James Hill posed with his mentor J. Chalmers Doane, the recipient of the Helen Verger Award.

Sunday Evening

The evening opened on the **CUPE Main Stage** with an exuberant set by **The Duhks** followed by the final performance of the **2008 Cross-Cultural Music and Dance Collaboration**, which was recorded by CBC Radio for later broadcast. The collaboration showcased the talents of more than a dozen performers from across Canada and the United States.

The entertainment continued with **James Hill** and **Anne Davison**. Hill, a virtuoso musician and world-class composer, was accompanied by classically trained cellist Anne Davison. The duo are known for creating magical performances and this one was no exception. **Andy Rush** and the **Terry Penner Festival Choir** performed a wonderful set of songs, including Willie P. Bennett's "Music in Your Eyes".

Festival goers were privileged to see **Odetta** in one of her final performances (she died three months after the festival). Performing in a wheelchair, Odetta was in fine voice and demonstrated why she has inspired so many in the civil rights movement

The audience was charmed by Odetta, in what turned out to be one of her final performances.

Rufus Wainwright, who closed the show Sunday night, was joined on stage by his mother, Kate McGarrigle.

and legions of folkies including Bob Dylan and Joan Baez. Her rendition of "This Little Light of Mine" was particularly poignant because she had memorably sung this song unamplified and unaccompanied during a power blackout at the festival five years before. Odetta's performance was recorded by CBC Radio.

The wild and wonderful **Rufus Wainwright** closed the evening with a thrilling performance. His mother **Kate McGarrigle** accompanied him on the grand piano for a few songs.

The performers in the **Dance Tent** included **Spiral Beach** and Prairie sensations **The Duhks**, whose performance set toes tapping and feet flying. They were followed by Québécois band **Genticorum**.

The evening ended with a **Big Bad Blues Jam** with **Roxanne Potvin, Michael Jerome Browne, Radoslav Lorkovic** and surprise guests.

Country Joe McDonald was the popular first performer on the **Hall Stage** inside the **Ron Kolbus Lakeside Centre**. A set by the luminous singer-songwriter **Catherine MacLellan** followed. The First Annual Ottawa Folk Festival **"Kirtan"**, a participatory session of singing, was hosted by **Santosha Yoga**. There was still time for spirited sets by **Dirk Powell, Riley Baugus and Friends**, and **The Duhks** before the sun set on the 2008 Ottawa Folk Festival.

Members of the organizing committee received a commemorative print of Willie P. Bennett, who passed away in 2008. Arthur II created the print and animated the ParticiPaint mural honouring the beloved Ontario singer-songwriter.

Festival goers could stroll through the Artisan Village looking for creative finds well into the evening.

Year 16 – 2009
Dig Your Roots!

The 16th annual Ottawa Folk Festival gave everyone a chance to "dig their roots" in a glorious community celebration of music, dance, culture and healing.

The festival warmly welcomed **Tatiana Nemchin**, Director of Planning and Operations, who joined Artistic Director **Chris White** and Volunteer and Outreach Manager **Julia Adam**, office staff and more than 700 volunteers to present the "sweet sixteen" edition of the festival.

And sweet it was. In addition to music from a wide array of performers, the festival offered a **Kidzone**, gardening village, sound healing conference and many participatory activities. The latter included learning swing and Cajun dance steps in the beautiful dance tent, singing in the **Terry Penner Festival Choir**, and painting a giant mural.

Some popular traditions continued. The **Third Annual Cross-Cultural Artist Collaboration** featured 25 artists from a range of musical traditions who appeared in groups throughout the festival. The **Artisan and Craft Village** and the **Food Fair** continued to be popular elements of the festival experience.

This year's main stage hosts were CBC broadcasters **Amanda Putz** and **Tom Power**. They were ably joined by **Ana Miura**, a local singer-songwriter who also took on the task of coordinating the gardening theme introduced at this festival.

Each year the festival presents the **Helen Verger Award** to an individual who has made valuable contributions to Canadian folk music. This year's deserving recipient, **Paul Mills**, has been an integral part of the Canadian folk scene for more than 30 years. Paul has worn many hats in his roles as a multi-instrumental musician, performing songwriter, arranger, producer, recording engineer, and founding partner of Borealis Records. He has produced more than 140 albums for artists such as Stan Rogers, Ron Hynes, and Sharon, Lois & Bram. Some of the albums he produced or engineered have reached gold or platinum status, and won both Juno and East Coast Music Awards.

Paul Mills (right) was the recipient of the Helen Verger Award.

Three cheers for the festival's **Green Team**! The greening of the Ottawa Folk Festival continued with the introduction of reusable cutlery and ending the sale of bottled water on-site. Festival goers were encouraged to bring their own water bottles and fill them at hydration stations and thus avoid having plastic bottles filling up the trash. This plastic water bottle-free initiative was achieved with the help of **Ottawa Riverkeeper, CUPE, The Water Store** and **The Council of Canadians**.

In the months leading up to the festival, staff, volunteers participating on the Ottawa Folk Festival Green Team and partner organizations put in many hours of work. They ensured that the festival became the first regional festival to become 100% plastic water-bottle free and to actively promote city water as a healthy, sustainable alternative to bottled water. Hydration stations were provided at key points on the site where people could refill their water bottles. The main hydration station consisted of a mobile water dispenser, a large stainless steel tank with five hoses and nozzles for refilling water bottles. The tank was filled continuously from a hose connected to one of the Ron Kolbus Lakeside Centre's exterior taps.

Thanks to a donation by CUPE local 503 – which represents the city's own water department employees – we were able to sell stainless-steel bottles to those who didn't bring their own. And, in collaboration with Ottawa Riverkeeper, we developed and distributed a fact sheet outlining "10 Reasons to Say No to Bottled Water".

Two partners actively participated on-site at the festival talking with festival goers about the water-bottle-free initiative, distributing educational information at satellite hydration stations, and assisting the Green Team in refilling and dispensing city drinking water to festival goers. The most impressive part of the operation was the low-tech white board where the usage statistics were recorded all weekend. Festival attendees were very interested to see concrete results: by Sunday evening, 3,819 litres (or more than 1,000 gallons) of water had been dispensed.

Gardening demonstrations and workshops blossomed in the **Gardening Village**. Here you could get expert advice and information from master gardeners and gardening guru **Ed Lawrence**, explore a themed patchwork garden or relax in the calming **Zen Garden** created by **Rebecca Cragg**. **The Worm Factory** was also on hand to entertain and educate one and all about worms and the joys of recycling.

Dean Verger, co-founder of Rasputin's Folk Café, enjoying the festival.

The **Matsuri Room** inside the **Ron Kolbus Lakeside Centre** featured aspects of traditional Japanese culture ranging from origami (paper folding) and ikebana (flower arranging) to calligraphy, poetry and music. The **Ottawa Japanese Cultural Centre, Camellia Teas of Ottawa** and **KaDo Ottawa** graciously provided displays and demonstrations at this and other venues.

The **CUPE EnviroTent** was in full swing with talks and demonstrations given by USC Canada and Ottawa's **Arbour Environmental Shoppe**, to name a few. The Sound Cycle performances by the energetic band **Mr. Something Something**, featured Canada's first bicycle-powered sound system.

Bay Ward Councillor Alex Cullen helped open the festival on Friday night.

One of the most exciting festival initiatives this year was Ottawa's first annual **Sound Healing Conference**, which incorporated interactive and experiential workshops, dancing, drumming, singing, chanting, sound healing sessions and a panorama of live indigenous music. Sound healing is a therapeutic practice that makes use of chanting, a variety of bowls, gongs, drums, tuning forks and sound tables. Two stellar examples were **David Hickey** and **Debbie Danbrook**. A popular sound healing practitioner, David gave an exceptional evening performance of meditative healing music presented with crystal bowls, gongs and chimes. Debbie expertly played the shakuhachi, a traditional Japanese bamboo flute. She is one of the first women to have mastered this ancient sacred instrument.

Perennial festival favourites included the **Kidzone** where kids of all ages enjoyed music, storytelling and a variety of crafts and games. A 40-foot mural offered another fun way to get involved at the festival. Young and old took up brushes to paint their favourite festival images to accompany those created by veteran artist **Arthur II**. This was Arthur II's third festival mural in as many years and he was assisted by **Patricia Rodi**.

Friday, August 21
Evening

On the **CUPE Main Stage**, **Arthur McGregor**'s delightful acoustic version of our national anthem opened the 2009 Ottawa Folk Festival. Thanks to Arthur, owner of the **Ottawa Folklore Centre**, for continuing to open the festival with this charming festival tradition!

Sheesham and Lotus using fiddle and banjo to perform old-style music.

A set with great gusto followed with the **Third Annual Cross-Cultural Artist Collaboration.** Old-style performers **Sheesham and Lotus** were up next on fiddle and banjo. The Prince Edward Island group **Vishtèn** got a great response from the crowd with their fiery fiddling and stunning stepdancing. B.C. resident **Kinnie Starr** has performed at the festival both as a poet and as a musician. This time around she introduced the receptive audience to her hip-hop groove.

Following intermission, **Amy Millan**, a member of Stars and Broken Social Scene, took the stage. The evening closed with **Steven Page** (formerly of The Barenaked Ladies) whose spirited set and amusing banter received a rousing response.

In the big, beautiful **Dance Tent**, Toronto alt-country rockers **The Sadies** got the audience up dancing. The crowd was entranced by **Mihirangi**'s soulful hip vocals in English and Maori. **Mr. Something Something**, an ecology-minded band with a bike-powered sound system, closed the evening.

At the **Hall Stage** inside the **Ron Kolbus Lakeside Centre**, the entertainment began with **Asani**, a trio of Aboriginal women from Edmonton. **Victoria Vox**, a ukulele-wielding woman from south of the border followed. Festival favourite **Ray Bonneville** performed an emotive set. **Bryan Bowers** lived up to his reputation as a virtuoso of the autoharp, a stringed folk instrument. Lively piano and accordion wunderkind **Radoslav Lorkovic** and friends had as much fun performing their blues zydeco music as the audience had listening!

Victoria Vox jams with Linsey Wellman.

Saturday, August 22

Festival goers enjoyed music, dance, talks and demonstrations at eight daytime and three evening venues.

The School of Dance's Dancing in the Street troupe performed throughout the festival.

Saturday Daytime

The fun in the **Dance Tent** began with the joyful cacophony of **Junkyard Symphony**. **Debbie Danbrook**, a master of the shakuhachi (a Japanese bamboo flute), was accompanied by **Wendy Morrell** for a session of **Sacred Dance**. The dancing continued with the **Ottawa Ondo Dance** session, presented by the **Ottawa Japanese Cultural Association**. A surprise hit of the festival, the band **Mr. Something Something** entertained with a bike-powered sound system and infectious world beat songs. The **Favourite Colours** session featured **Amy Millan, The Sadies** and newcomer **Charlotte Cornfield**. The next performer was **That 1 Guy**, famous for his homemade instrument The Magic Pipe, which is a seven-foot-high conglomeration of pipes and strings. The day concluded with a performance by **Group 1** of the **Cross-Cultural Artist Collaboration**.

The weatherproof indoor venue known as the **Hall Stage** offered a wide variety of musical experiences. Things kicked off with a double bill featuring guitar-playing duo **Tall Trees** and American ukulele virtuoso **Victoria Vox**. The **Dig Your Roots** session presented **Lyndell Montgomery, That 1 Guy** and brothers **Travis and Dallas Good** of **The Sadies**. The **Uke-Cello Duos** session gave us a chance to see two of the best musical pairs around: ukulele virtuosos **James Hill** and **Victoria Vox**, and cellists **Anne Davison** and **melaniejane**. The mood shifted with the **Life in Japan** session that showcased **Ellen McIlwaine**, who grew up in Japan, and **Debbie Danbrook**, who studied flute there. They were joined onstage by **Linsey Wellman, Catriona Sturton, Ana Miura** and **Kyoko Tsunetomi**. The session **Your Brain on Music** was presented by **Daniel Mauro** and **Gary Baker**. **The Balloon Orchestra** was one of the most amusing sessions ever presented at the festival. University music students "played" balloons using various techniques and achieved surprisingly entertaining results.

New Zealander Mihirangi charmed the audience with her one-woman show.

The wonderfully named **Moon Stage** opened with a lively ukulele jam led by virtuoso **James Hill**. A double bill followed with **Charlotte Cornfield** and **Jason Lang**, son of Penny Lang. **Jeremy Sills** and **Theda Phoenix** followed with a spiritually-centred performance using acoustic instruments, crystal bowls and voice to create healing vibrations. The **Gourd Grooves** session featured **Sheesham and Lotus, Dirk Powell, Christine Balfa** and **Michael Jerome Browne**. **Bryan Bowers, Stewed Roots** and Ottawa Folklore Centre owner **Arthur McGregor** participated in the **Something Old, Something New** session.

Up on the **Hill Stage**, **Amelia Curran, Mihirangi** and **Charlotte Cornfield** took part in the **Sources** of Inspiration session. The **Music to Garden By** session featured master gardener **Ed Lawrence** who was joined by musicians **Penny Lang, Anne Davison, Robbie Anderman** and **Petr Cancura**. **Vishtèn in Concert** showcased this Acadian ensemble from Prince Edward Island. **Tom Power, James Keelaghan** and the **Good Lovelies** graced the stage for the powerful **Deep Roots** session. **Dirk Powell, Vishtèn** and **Troy MacGillivray** joined together for the **Waterbound** session. The day closed with a mother and son collaboration: **Penny Lang and Jason Lang in Concert**.

Preparing food for the volunteer masses.

The **Point Stage** opened with the **Three** session, which featured talented Australian **David Ross MacDonald** and Canadian **Catriona Sturton**. **Joel Plaskett** had been scheduled to perform in this session but was delayed due to transportation problems. A diverse group of musicians was showcased in the **Musical Arrangements** session: newly solo singer-songwriter **Steven Page**, Newfoundlander **Amelia Curran** and piano/accordion player **Radoslav Lorkovic**. There were musical harmonies in abundance at the **Harmony Singing** session with **The Arrogant Worms, The Breakmen** and **Michael Ball and Jody Benjamin**. **Rich Warren** hosted the **Blues and Beyond** session featuring a premier bluesy lineup of **Ray Bonneville, Terra Hazelton** and **Idy Oulu**.

The **VIP Tent** was the site of **Musical Yoga** with **Tanya Nash** and **Jeremy Sills**. Vocal Warm-Up with **Meredith Matthews** preceded a **Terry Penner Festival Choir** rehearsal with **Andy Rush**. **Spins and Needles** led a **Kite-Making Workshop**, where festival goers could make a kite in an hour.

In the **OFC Music Tent**, Ottawa Folklore Centre co-founder **Arthur McGregor** led a vocal session called **Rise Up Singing**, whose name comes from the songbook of the same name. The **Tin Whistle Workshop**, led by **Ross Davison**, offered a free tin whistle to the first 20 participants. Other participatory sessions included **Intro to Irish Stepdance** with **Michael Farrell** and a **Didgeridoo Workshop** led by **Chris Lavigne**. The first 30 participants in the didgeridoo session received free mini-didges. The day concluded with an **OFC Music Open Stage**.

In the **Garden Tent**, a variety of activities came to fruition. **Advice Clinics** were presented by the **Master Gardeners of Ottawa-Carleton**. **Earthworm Choreography** was a session with **The Worm Factory**. The **Just Food** session explored aspects of community gardening. The **Zen Gardening** session was presented by **Rebecca Cragg**. A talk on gardening without pesticides by master gardener **Ed Lawrence** was followed by a question-and-answer session and book signing. The USC session was titled **Seeding for the Future from the Past**. The day's activities concluded

Hometown folk hero Bruce Cockburn was happy to accept the Helen Verger Award.

with a **Kimono Demonstration**, showcasing some beautiful traditional Japanese garments.

Saturday Evening
On the **CUPE Main Stage**, Aboriginal artists **DiggingRoots** wowed the crowd with their musical presentation melding roots, rock, hip-hop and blues. Perennial festival performers **The Arrogant Worms** made us laugh with their silly stories and songs. From the ridiculous we moved to the sublime with renowned ukulele virtuoso **James Hill**, and his life partner, cellist **Anne Davison**. After intermission, the **Good Lovelies** delivered a set of heavenly vocal harmonies. Headliner and Ottawa hometown hero **Bruce Cockburn** offered up a superb set of songs featuring many fan favourites.

Between sets, awards were presented to the winners of the local auditions that precede the festival each year. **Tall Trees** (**Kelly Peltier** and **Trevor Pool**) received the **Galaxie Rising Stars** award given annually to the under-25 winners. In the open

Roch Parisien presented the Galaxie Rising Stars Award to Tall Trees (Trevor Pool and Kelly Peltier).

category, **Stewed Roots** (**Neva Tesolin** and **Jeff [Jennifer] Hale**) received the 2009 **One Fret Less Award** sponsored annually by **Harvey and Louise Glatt**.

In the **Dance Tent**, the entertainment was perfectly suited to dancing the night away. However before the boogeying began, **Crystal Journey with David Hickey** gave a profoundly relaxing presentation of meditative healing music using gongs, bowls and tuning forks. A feeling of peacefulness and spiritual harmony filled the tent. The music then turned to the mellow musings of **Michael Jerome Browne**, a brilliant interpreter of vintage blues and Cajun and Appalachian music. Things really kicked into high gear with a **Saturday Night Cajun Dance Party** with **Ball and Chain & the Wreckers**, featuring **Jody Benjamin** and **Michael Ball**. They were joined by **Christine Balfa** and **Dirk Powell** of **Balfa Toujours**, a traditional Cajun band from southwest Louisiana.

At the **Hall Stage**, **Jody Benjamin** got audience members kicking up their heels with a participatory Cajun dance lesson. **James Keelaghan,** who has delighted festival audiences over the years with his wonderful stories in song, performed next with

The Dance Tent was illuminated with the festival logo.

renowned bass player **David Woodhead**. They were followed by the lovely Newfoundland singer-songwriter **Amelia Curran**. **That 1 Guy** hosted the **Power of One,** which included a mesmerizing vocal performance by **Mihirangi**, a native woman from New Zealand.

Sunday, August 23
Festival goers enjoyed music, dance, talks and demonstrations at eight daytime and three evening venues.

Sunday Daytime
Sunday morning opened in the **Dance Tent** with a performance by **Group 2** of the **Cross-Cultural Artist Collaboration**. The members of **Junkyard Symphony** followed and filled the tent with infectious rhythms created with a variety of funky instruments. No experience was needed

for the **Hip Hop with Frank!** session. Festival goers also got into the swing of things with an **Intermediate Charleston Lesson** presented by the **Swing Dynamite Dance School**. **Geoff & Andrea** presented the **Beginner 1920s Charleston Lesson**. **The Woodchoppers Association with Jah Youssouf** and special guest **Abdoulaye Koné** provided the next dance tracks. The day ended in style with a **Sunday Swingtacular**, presented by **Dance with Alana** and featuring the jazzy **Terra Hazelton & Her Easy Answers**. Terra is a jazz vocalist who was mentored by the late Jeff Healey.

At the **Hall Stage**, the day's entertainment began

Ana Miura playing in the natural setting of the Hill Stage.

Secure bike parking for those who cycled to the festival.

with a double bill featuring **Captain Dirt and the Skirt**, and **The Breakmen**. **Flowing with the Go** was the enigmatic title of the next session featuring sax/flute player **Linsey Wellman**, cellist **Anne Davison** and flute player **Robbie Anderman**. Instructors **Alana & Fred** led two dance sessions: **Beginner Swing Dance Lesson** and **Intermediate Lindy Hop Lesson**. **Focus on the Guitar** was the theme of a session with **Kristin Sweetland** and **Jason Lang** (son of Penny Lang). The afternoon ended with an amazing performance by **Group 3** of the **Cross-Cultural Artist Collaboration**.

On the **Moon Stage,** the **Uke Addiction** session presented an impressive performance by **James Hill, Jason Lang** and **Victoria Vox**. **Theda Phoenix** was up next with her healing and meditative music. She was followed by an eclectic set with **Stewed Roots**. There were sweet harmonies aplenty in the soulful **Sing It Sister** session with **Terra Hazelton, Penny Lang** and the **Good Lovelies**, accompanied by multi-instrumentalist **Radoslav Lorkovic**. **Uke 101** was a participatory session with ukulele master **James Hill**. The final session was a double bill with **Jeremy Sills** and the female Aboriginal group **Asani**.

The **Hill Stage** rang with **Spirit Voices**, which

Joel Plaskett played with Bruce Cockburn, Steven Page and Ana Miura in the Songs From the Road session hosted by Mike Regenstreif.

showcased a diverse group made up of **Raven Kanatakta, ShoShona Kish, Mihirangi, Albert Dumont** and **Asani**. **The Human Condition** was the emotive theme explored in a session with a talented lineup including **Ray Bonneville, Ellen McIlwaine, Michael Jerome Browne** and hosted by Montreal folk DJ **Mike Regenstreif**. **Bruce Cockburn, Joel Plaskett, Steven Page** and **Ana Miura** were featured in the popular session **Songs from the Road**. The **Outstanding in Their Field** session brought together gardener **Ed Lawrence** and "earthy" musicians **The Arrogant Worms, DiggingRoots, Stewed Roots, Tall Trees** and **Charlotte Cornfield**. The afternoon closed with **Albert Dumont**, **Mr. Something Something**, and **Vishtèn** lifting their voices in the **Natural Harmony** session.

The **Point Stage** opened with the **African**

Animating the Kidzone with bubbles.

A volunteer for the folk festival mural facilitated by Arthur II.

Roots session featuring the rhythmic offerings of **Jah Youssouf, Abdoulaye Koné** and **Lewis Melville**. The *Canadian Spaces* session, a salute to the CKCU-FM folk radio show, was hosted by **Chopper McKinnon** and featured **David Ross MacDonald, Captain Dirt and the Skirt**, and **James Keelaghan**. Toes were tapping at the next session showcasing **Troy MacGillivray & Canadian Grand Master Fiddlers**. The **Be the Change** session was hosted by **Peter Conway** and featured **Asani, Catriona Sturton** and members of **The Woodchoppers Association**. The **Participate** session highlighted the talents of **Todd Crowley**,

The Breakmen and **Petr Cancura**.

In the **VIP Tent, Tanya Nash** began the day with a **Musical Yoga** session. **Meredith Matthews** followed with **Vocal Warm-Up**, which led into a **Terry Penner Festival Choir** rehearsal with **Andy Rush**. **Debbie Danbrook**, a virtuoso of the shakuhachi, led the session **Breath Work**. The **Balladry** session brought together two Maritime singer-songwriters, **Tom Power** and **Amelia Curran**, along with **Brian Bowers**, a master autoharp player from the U.S. A second **Vocal Warm-Up** session with **Meredith Matthews** led to the third and final **Terry Penner Festival Choir** rehearsal.

A joyous group during the annual Sunshine Parade.

In the **OFC Music Tent**, **Arthur McGregor** started off the afternoon workshops with a **Jaw Harp** workshop. The first 25 people who attended **Marc Seguin's Harmonica Workshop** were given a free blues harp courtesy of the **Ottawa Folklore Centre**. **Jesse Greene** gave a **Blues Guitar Workshop**, while **Dean Adema** led a **Banjo Workshop.**

Terry Penner Festival Choir members belting it out.

Linsey Wellman accompanying Ellen McIlwaine on the saxophone.

On the **OFC Music Open Stage**, **Jack MacGregor** closed the afternoon with a **Drum Workshop and Free Dance**.

The **Garden Tent** was a popular site that offered a wide variety of information and activities. **Advice Clinics** were given by the **Master Gardeners of Ottawa-Carleton.** This group also presented a session on **Gardening in Hypertufa Troughs**. Tea enthusiasts flocked to the **Zen Garden** for a traditional Japanese tea ceremony.

Ed Lawrence gave a talk about gardening without pesticides, followed by questions and answers and a book signing. **Rebecca Cragg** demonstrated ikebana, the Japanese art of flower arranging. The **Dig Your Roots** session offered advice about gardening in your backyard. The **USC** gave a talk on **Seeding for the Future from the Past**. The day ended with the lively session **Come and Dance the ONDO!**

Sunday Evening

The early evening performances started with one that many people look forward to each year: the **Terry Penner Festival Choir** directed by **Andy Rush**. Thank you to Andy and this dedicated group of singers who volunteered their time and energy to practices throughout the festival. They spread

Idi Oulo performs his mix of African world music and reggae.

a little light and love in song in memory of Terry Penner, the late co-founder of the Ottawa Folklore Centre. The audience was in for a treat with a set by the charming **Ellen McIlwaine**, a master of the slide guitar and a consummate storyteller. The **Circle of Song** was hosted by silver-haired folksinger **Penny Lang**, who shared the stage with **Ray Bonneville** and **James Keelaghan**. **Joel Plaskett** showed us why he is one of the young stars on the Canadian music scene. He performed a folky set accompanied by his father **Bill**. African world music and reggae was the flavour of the last musical guest of the evening. **Idy Oulu** and his band performed with instruments both traditional and modern.

The music in the **Dance Tent** began with **Sunday Swingtacular,** a swing dance extravaganza with **Terra Hazelton & Her Easy Answers**. **That 1 Guy** (a.k.a. **Mike Silverman**) gave us a unique set that only a classically trained one-man band that plays wild and wonderful homemade instruments can. The Vancouver foursome **The Breakmen** dispensed a little bluegrass joy to help the audience get that dancin' feeling.

At the **Hall Stage,** the effervescent **Good Lovelies** showed why they have been described as "the perfect antidote to world gloom and doom". Australian songwriter and fingerstyle guitarist **David Ross MacDonald** amazed the crowd with his nimble-fingered performance. Classically-influenced instrumentalist **Lyndell Montgomery** and singer-guitarist **Kristin Sweetland**, known collectively as **Captain Dirt and the Skirt**, delivered an enjoyable set. The evening closed with a **Kirtan** session featuring **The Bhakti Connection**. This Ottawa ensemble gave participants a chance to experience blissful devotional music.

A member of The Bhakti Connection performing during a Kirtan, a yogic chanting session.

On the Monday night after the festival, a mix of volunteers, staff and general public who hadn't yet had their fill of the wonderful musical array that was the 2009 festival, met at the **Elmdale House Tavern** for the **Festival Wrap-up Concert.** It featured the ever-popular **Ray Bonneville** and one of this year's festival "finds", **Victoria Vox**.

A special thank you to **Chris White** who co-founded the Ottawa Folk Festival with CKCU-FM station manager **Max Wallace** in 1993 and served as artistic director for all 16 festivals before stepping down in the fall of 2009. Chris has passionately and with boundless energy helped the festival grow from a small one-day event to a multi-day event that has earned widespread acclaim. We wish him well in his future endeavours!

We must also express gratitude to the festival's founding hosts, **Chopper McKinnon** and **Karen Flanagan McCarthy,** who co-hosted the main stage from year 1 to year 15. Chopper was an important part of the Canadian folk scene and was the creator and host of Canadian Spaces. Now in its 30th year, it's the longest-running folk show on Canadian community radio and can be heard Saturday mornings on CKCU-FM 93.1. Karen is a lively presenter, experienced broadcaster and communications expert who contributed to the festival in myriad ways, encouraging partnerships and participating as a member of its board and steering committee.

A fond farewell was extended to **Tatiana Nemchin**, Director of Planning and Operations. Thanks also go out to Volunteer and Outreach Manager **Julia Adam**, whose work at the festival over the past two years was greatly appreciated.

Year 17 – 2010
The Final Sunset at Britannia Park

The 17th annual Ottawa Folk Festival was held at Britannia Park for the final year at that location in 2010 with a new Festival Director at its helm. **Dylan Griffith,** from the Dawson City Music Festival, led the event, which ran from **August 13-15**. The streamlined program had no Thursday night concerts or off-site concerts as was the case in many previous years, and operated Friday night and during the day and evening on Saturday and Sunday.

The festival's sustainable practices were further enhanced in 2010. Reusable dishes, solar heating to heat the dishwashing water, and not selling bottled water on the site were just a few of the ways the Ottawa Folk Festival worked toward holding a future zero-waste event. The **EnviroTent** ran sessions on Saturday and Sunday, which included discussions about urban gardening, veggie cars and solar energy. The popular cob-building demonstration returned.

The volunteer dish crew!

Some of the site layout changes, however, were controversial. For the second year, the food vendors and artisans were located in the parking lot where many found the traffic to their booths was reduced. This site change also didn't allow city buses to drive directly to the main gate. OC Transpo buses were rerouted to a nearby back street.

Neema Mugala accompanying the Mighty Popo.

Programming in 2010 focused on community involvement, sustainability and an eclectic mix of acts that included several festival favourites, such as the **Jim Cuddy Band**, and emerging artists or cross-over acts, like **The Weakerthans** and **The Hidden Cameras**. There were many non-traditional choices, including **Arrested Development**, as well as world music offerings **The Mighty Popo, Delhi 2 Dublin** and **Namgar**. The Canadian Aboriginal community was well represented by Inuit singer-songwriter **Tanya Tagaq**, who has a unique style of solo throat singing. With several local choirs performing on the main stage, the festival continued to foster inclusivity and active public participation. American musical legend **Ramblin' Jack Elliott**, a contemporary of Woody Guthrie who influenced Bob Dylan, gave evocative performances throughout the festival with fascinating stories and anecdotes to match.

The sessions and demonstrations were some of the ways our children were involved at the festival. **Todd Crowley** returned to the **Kidzone** with his musical petting zoo, and the **Catholic Immigration Centre** hosted pick-up soccer games outside the **Dance Tent**. The annual children's parade (the **Sunshine Parade**) did not take place because of a rainstorm, but the **Kidzone** had storytelling sessions, a drum circle, and yoga to keep kids occupied.

Kids getting hands on at Todd Crowley's Musical Petting Zoo.

Festival volunteer Carol Noel playing a zither.

Ottawa artist **Arthur II** coordinated and led **Participaint**, which was a great way for both children and adults to create a beautiful large-scale mural during the festival. There were many opportunities to get involved in the music making, dancing and artistic projects, including an instrument lock-up available to festival goers, the **Terry Penner Festival Choir**, the ukulele-building session, and **Librivox**, which is an opportunity for performers, volunteers and audience members to read and record classic Canadian poems. In the food tent and at the trolley station, organized jam sessions continued throughout the day on Saturday and Sunday, and continued long after the scheduled sessions had ended.

Ana Miura giving the Helen Verger Award to Harvey Glatt.

The **Helen Verger Award**, named in honour of the co-founder of **Rasputin's Folk Café**, was presented to **Harvey Glatt**, a major contributor to the Ottawa music scene. Harvey opened the first of 15 Treble Clef music stores in 1957. He went on to finance the legendary folk music venue **Le Hibou** and helped numerous folk musicians with their careers. In 1977, Harvey founded CHEZ-FM, a station notable for its commitment to Canadian artists. Harvey and his wife, **Louise Glatt**, continue to contribute to the Ottawa musical community with major donations to the National Arts Centre, as well as establishing the **One Fret Less Award**, given in 2010 to **Clarksdale Moan**. **Delhi 2 Dublin** received the **Supernova Award**, and **The Musettes** were presented with the **Galaxie Rising Stars Award**.

The **Community Tent** was an opportunity for organizations to raise awareness among festival goers regarding various environmental and social initiatives. The following organizations participated: City of Ottawa Heritage Museums, University of Ottawa Heart Institute, OXFAM, Canadian Students for Sensible Drug Policy, Carp Ridge Ecowellness Centre, Spirit of Rasputin's, USC Canada, Bikes for Beats, Ottawa Centre NDP,

Ecology Ottawa, and the Guatemalan Stove Project.

The Community Tent provided space for a variety of community groups.

Friday, August 13

On the **CUPE Main Stage, Albert Dumont**, an Algonquin Aboriginal elder, hosted the opening ceremony. After **Ottawa Folklore Centre** owner **Arthur McGregor** played his customary acoustic ragtime version of "O Canada", **Folka Voca**, the Ottawa Folklore Centre's community choir led by Lee Hayes performed. The group of about 40 singers shared their love of folk music with a large crowd. The choir was followed by **Jon Brooks**, who delivered his brand of well-crafted protest songs reminiscent of Phil Ochs, Tom Paxton and Bob Dylan.

The Ottawa band **The Acorn** took to the stage next with its rural, rootsy sounds. **Rock Plaza Central**, a Toronto band that encompasses folk, rock and alt-country sounds performed before **Arrested Development** took to the stage. This much-lauded American group was formed in the 1990s as an alternative to gangsta rap and is a positive force to be reckoned with. The band wowed the opening night crowed with a powerful, high-energy performance packed with spellbinding lyrics.

In the **Galaxie Dance Tent** there was plenty of lively dancing, toe tapping and swaying to the accompaniment of groups with evocative names including **Bruce Peninsula**, the **Foggy Hogtown Boys**, and **Hoots & Hellmouth**. **Bruce Peninsula** showcased traditional world music, while the **Foggy Hogtown Boys** are a bluegrass band. **Hoots & Hellmouth**, on the other hand, fuse diverse influences including gospel, bluegrass and punk.

Saturday, August 14

The first session in the **Bowie Hall Stage** was **Strung Out**, featuring **Gareth Pearson, Christine Bougie, Kenny Pauze, Dan Whiteley** and **Kris Drevar**. **The Musettes** appeared in concert followed by **Poutine and a Pint** with **Galant, tu perds ton temps** and **LAU**. **The Woe Is Me** session showcased **Horse Feathers, Clarksdale Moan** and **Jenny Whiteley**.

Durham County Poets at the festival.

The entertainment on the **Hill Stage** began with a session titled **It's Indie Lovely** with **Horse Feathers, The Acorn, Bahamas** and **Aidan Knight**. The **Folk the 80s!** session featured **Bahamas, Krista Muir, Craig Cardiff, Peter Katz, Aidan Knight** and **Gareth Pearson**. **Jill Zmud** appeared in concert, and the day ended with the **Voices Carry** session showcasing **Arrested Development, Galant, Tu perds ton temps** and **Bruce Peninsula**.

On the **Point Stage**, the sassy **I Spit on Your Rave** session featured **LAU, Godknowswhat** and **Hoots & Hellmouth**. **Jon Brooks, Peter Katz, Lynn Miles, Frank Turner** and **Joel Gibb** participated in the **Political Affairs** session. **Clarksdale Moan** appeared in concert. The eclectic **A Place Called Home** session attracted a large crowd that turned out for sets by **The Acorn, Namgar, Tanya Tagaq, Kim Beggs** and **Calexico**.

Long-time sound man Dave O'Heare.

Audience members participated in the **Wake-Up! Yoga** session at the **PSAC Moon Stage**. The amusingly named **Wake Me Up Before You Blow Blow** session simply featured "horns and more". When **Chopper McKinnon**, host of the longstanding CKCU-FM folk music radio show *Canadian Spaces* could not attend the *Canadian Spaces* session due to illness, **Mike Regenstreif**, host of the Montreal radio show *Folk Roots/Folk Branches* stepped in to lead the session. A large crowd of "Space Cadets", fans of *Canadian Spaces*, turned out to hear **Lynn Miles, Chris McLean, Jon Brooks** and **Meredith Luce** perform. **Jim Bryson, Frank Turner, Carolyn Mark, Coco Love Alcorn** and **Chris McLean** appeared in the **Labour Pains** session.

A friendly greeter at the volunteer lunch.

In the **Ottawa Folklore Centre Tent**, **Rick McGrath** hosted the **Jam Etiquette** session, while **Arthur McGregor** led the **Jaw Harp** session. **Mary Gick** hosted the **Clawhammer Banjo** session. The **Tin Whistle** session was led by **Ross Davison**. A **Ukulele Crash Course** was hosted by **Mark McHale**. The last session of the day was the **Spirit of Rasputin's Open Stage**.

Participants could eat and drink while taking in the performances at the **Food Court Tent**, including a **Trad Singing Jam**, a **Celtic Jam**, a **Singable Songs Sing-A-Long** session, and the **Old Time Appalachian Jam**. Over at the **Trolley Station**, people gathered for a **Drumming Jam**, **Spirit of Rasputin's Open Jam**, a **Bluegrass Jam** and a **Ukulele Jam**.

In the **Kidzone**, children participated in the **Origami for Beginners** session with **Maya Papayasan**. The **Storytelling & Bird Feeder Making** session was hosted by **Dina** of **Barefoot Books**; **Yoga for Parents & Kids** was hosted by **Sheila Craig**. There was a **Percussion Instrument Making** session as well as a **Drum Circle** session with **Leo Brooks**. More sessions were also held with **Prof. Webfoot & Creatures from the River** as well as **Extreme Origami** with **Maya Papayasan**.

Festival goers rapt with attention.

On the **CUPE Main Stage,** the evening entertainment began with **Tone Cluster**, a tuneful choir with membership drawn mainly from Ottawa's gay, lesbian and transgender community. The five females comprising the francophone band **Galant, tu perds ton temps** performed traditional Québécois and Acadian tunes with great panache. The rootsy mood continued with **LAU**, a trio that features material rooted in Scottish folk traditions. **Carolyn Mark & the New Best Friends** left us laughing with satirical songs and imaginative patter, while Ottawa favourites **Jim Bryson** and **The Weakerthans** charmed the crowd with quirky yet brilliant selections. The evening ended with a lively performance from the eclectic seven-member Arizona band **Calexico**, which combines diverse musical influences including country, folk, Latin and jazz.

A magnificent sky was the backdrop for Saturday evening.

Sunday, August 15

On Sunday morning, a torrential downpour and high winds left the festival organizers no choice but to shut down all of its outdoor stages for safety reasons. Daytime concerts on Sunday were cancelled or moved inside. The **CUPE Main Stage** did not reopen. Since the **Ron Kolbus Lakeside Centre** had only one stage, there was no way to accommodate all of the programming. This resulted in many unscheduled collaborations between artists and plenty of unanticipated but interesting musical pairings. In fine festival tradition, the performers and audience rallied to the occasion and cheerfully went with the flow, making the best of a less than ideal situation.

Inuit songstress Tanya Tagaq entranced the audience with her emotive performance.

The **Galaxie Dance Tent** had the crowd hopping with an especially eclectic range of music. **Namgar**, a traditional Mongolian female musician and vocalist from Russia, gave a fascinating performance of music that is rarely witnessed in Canada. She and her band played traditional instruments such as the yatag, a zither-type instrument. English singer-songwriter **Frank Turner** turned in a solo performance tinged with punk influences. Inuit performer **Tanya Tagaq** provided an evocative and emotional performance that showcased her unique style of vocalization fusing contemporary styles with solo throat singing. Tanya was ably accompanied by fiddler **Jesse Zubot** and percussionist **Jean Martin**. The fun wound down with **The Hidden Cameras**, a nine-member band that combines complex and diverse musical influences.

Survey crew leader Robert Willson carrying on in the Sunday morning rain.

Pushing a car out of the mud in the parking area.

Mike Regenstreif hosted **A Conversation with Ramblin' Jack Elliott** in which Jack related fascinating stories drawn from his more than 50-year career in folk music.

Musicians slated to perform on Sunday included **Amy Millan, Carolyn Mark, Chris Eaton, Chris McLean, Coco Love Alcorn, Craig Cardiff, Dan Whiteley, Delhi 2 Dublin, Frank Turner, Galant, tu perds ton temps, Gareth Pearson, Jenny Whiteley, Joseph Edgar, Jill Zmud, LAU, Ladies of the Canyon, Ramblin' Jack Elliott, Jim Bryson, Jim Cuddy, Kim Beggs, Peter Katz, Robyn Dell'Unto, Terry Gillespie, The Musettes, The Mighty Popo, The Terry Penner Festival Choir** and **The Old Sod Band**.

Sessions scheduled to take place included **Hand Drumming** with **Dave Bossmin**, a **Ukelele Crash Course** with **Mark McHale**, **Nose Flute** with **Arthur McGregor**, and **Beginner Harmonica** with **Marc Seguin**. Jam sessions were also scheduled for shape note singing, storyteller story swaps, a ukulele orchestra and old-time Appalachian music.

Delhi 2 Dublin raised the roof of the Dance Tent.

By the evening the **Dance Tent** reopened, and many acts that were scheduled for the **CUPE Main Stage**, including the **Terry Penner Festival Choir** performed. Standout performances included one by the legendary **Ramblin' Jack Elliott**, who delivered original material developed over more than half a century. This "musician's musician" inspired both Bob Dylan and Arlo Guthrie, the son of his good friend Woody Guthrie. The high-energy, eclectic **Delhi 2 Dublin** got the crowd on its feet and dancing enthusiastically, setting the pace for the festival's electrifying final set by **The Jim Cuddy Band**, with featured performers **Luke Doucet** and **Melissa McClelland**.

The trolley station at the main gate also served as an impromptu jam site, where artists, volunteers and festival goers who had brought their instruments, or had just learned a few ukulele chords, joined in.

Veteran country folk performer Ramblin' Jack Elliott.

Anne Lindsay jamming with Jim Cuddy as part of The Jim Cuddy Band.

Luke Doucet and Melissa McClelland appeared with The Jim Cuddy Band.

Unknown to all, 2010 was the last year that the Ottawa Folk Festival would take place at much-loved **Britannia Park**, the festival's home for most of its history. The natural beauty of the park and beach afforded unforgettable scenes such as double rainbows, and gorgeous sunsets often followed by shooting stars, greatly enhancing the festival experience. The Ottawa River, whether sparkling like a million diamonds, calm or white-capped, was an amazing backdrop for the festival. The opportunity to stroll by the riverside between performances was wonderful, and greatly appreciated by festival goers.

This was not the first change of venue for the Ottawa Folk Festival. The first festival in 1994 was scheduled to take place at **Vincent Massey Park** and shifted six weeks before the event to **Victoria Island**. The festival began at **Britannia Park** in 1995. Although the festival would come under new management and relocate to **Hogs Back Park** in 2011, the location proved not as important as the spirit of the music and good will that permeates the Ottawa Folk Festival.

The Terry Gillespie Band with The Mighty Popo performed at the volunteer party at the Elmdale House Tavern.

Financial Support

The Ottawa Folk Festival thanks the following sponsors, partners and suppliers: OFC Music (The Ottawa Folklore Centre), Canadian Heritage, City of Ottawa, National Library of Canada, Human Resources Development Canada, Ontario Arts Council, The Ontario Trillium Foundation, Government of Canada, Public Service Alliance of Canada, Galaxie, Big Rock Brewery, Steve's Music Store, Crowne Plaza Hotels and Resorts, Pattison, Canadian Union of Public Employees, wall sound-lighting, Raven, Cameron, Ballantyne and Yazbeck, Metro, Yellow Tail, Birddog Design, McCrank's Cycles, Siren Bakery, HOPE Volleyball, SummerFest, Arbour, Carmello's, The Table, Dollco Printing, Event Water Solutions, Bowie Electrical Services, McKeen Metro, Diffusart.biz, Bridgehead, ECOGEN Energy Inc., Bagel Bagel, Ebam

Enterprises Ltd., B. goods, Ottawa Riverkeeper, Life Without Plastic, The Council of Canadians, and TD Friends of the Environment Foundation. Sincere thanks as well to all who donated to the Sustainability Fund to ensure the festival and its many community activities continue in the future.

Year 18 – 2011
Meet the Folkers! Major Moves and Changes

Audiences attending the 2011 Ottawa Folk Festival experienced many changes, along with a reassuring number of familiar elements. In the fall of 2010, the board of the Ottawa Folk Festival was faced with a high debt load accrued over several years exacerbated by the torrential rains of the final day of the 2010 festival. The board decided to gratefully accept an offer by Ottawa Bluesfest to take over management of the Ottawa Folk Festival under the supervision and guidance of Executive Producer **Mark Monahan**. A new general manager (**Mark Morrison**) was brought aboard, with continuity provided by core staff members, including sponsorship manager **Ana Miura**, volunteer manager **Emily Addison**, and office manager **Crystal Kirkpatrick**.

The second major change for the festival was its relocation to **Hogs Back Park** at Heron Road and Riverside Drive. The new location was chosen not only for its natural beauty but also for its more central location, readily accessible by bike and public transit, and with ample parking nearby.

The festival returned to a four-day format (Thursday and Friday nights; afternoons and evenings on Saturday and Sunday). Increased programming funds became available. The festival featured a number of "side projects" by major Canadian and international artists with wide reputations and followings from their bigger, more familiar bands or careers. The central location and advertising theme – "Meet the Folkers" – were aimed at attracting new and younger audiences. But also present were familiar elements of years past such as daytime workshops and the popular mixing and mingling of artists and styles; small stages where roots and acoustic acts drew intimate audiences; kid-friendly music and crafts; and the long-standing commitment to the environment and progressive educational and community activities.

Three major stages dominated the expansive site built along either side of the public bike path: the **CUPE-SCFP Main Stage** (with the **PSAC Moon Stage** alongside for "tweener" performances); the **Ravenlaw Stage** with its magnificent natural-bowl acoustics; and the **Falls Stage** with a larger than ever sprung-floor dance tent. Three smaller daytime stages (**Legacy**, **Heron** and **Slackwater**) and **Workshops on the Point** were programmed by the **Ottawa Folklore Centre**. Food vendors and artisan crafts, as well as **Arthur II**'s annual participatory mural project rounded out the site.

Except for a cooler final day, the warm weather brought out large audiences and was conducive to kicking back and enjoying the music well into the evenings. There was plenty of space in the vast lawn in front of the main stage for lawn-chair and standing/dancing crowds to coexist happily. Overall consensus: the changes were largely positive, and the essence of the Ottawa Folk Festival remained intact and healthy.

Thursday, August 25
On the **CUPE-SCFP Main Stage**, **Arthur McGregor** launched the weekend with the festival tradition of his unique acoustic version of our national anthem. This was followed by a tribute to recently deceased NDP leader **Jack Layton** by **PSAC Regional VP Larry Rousseau** and **CUPE National President Paul Moist**.

Hawksley Workman giving a leg up to folk music.

With the audience growing steadily larger over the warm evening, the main stage was opened by Ottawa's **Megan Jerome**, singer-songwriter-pianist and 2011 **Galaxie Rising Stars Award** winner. Next up was Canadian rocker-songwriter **Hawksley Workman** who performed a crowd-pleasing, dynamic set. The evening ended with American pianist and singer **Bruce Hornsby and the Noisemakers**, back in Ottawa after a 21-year absence. The set ranged widely across folk, jazz and bluegrass, delighting the audience all the way.

Festival Builders Hall of Fame members.

At the next break, **Gene Swimmer**, Ottawa Folk Festival Executive Director from 1996 to 2006, returned to the stage to receive the 2011 **Helen Verger Award**, presented by **Mark Monahan**.

One of the members of Bruce Hornsby & the Noisemakers on the CUPE-SCFP Main Stage.

Gene Swimmer received the Helen Verger Award for his many years of dedicated service to the festival.

Two award presentations took place on the **PSAC Moon Stage**. Board Vice-President **Penny Bertrand** presented the inaugural **Festival Builders Hall of Fame** awards to 18 people whose involvement in the first years of the festival gave it early momentum: **Karen Flanagan McCarthy, Rachel Hauraney, Roberta Huebener, Suzanne Lessard-Wynes, Joyce MacPhee, Rod McDowell, Chopper McKinnon, Arthur McGregor, Alan Marjerrison, Pam Marjerrison, Barry Pilon, Sheila Ross, Carol Silcoff, Gene Swimmer, Max Wallace, Chris White, Dean Verger** and **Peter Zanette**.

Drawing good crowds over on the **Ravenlaw Stage** were Ottawa roots-rocker **John Allaire**, gypsy folk band **Dry River Caravan**, and roots collective **Punch Brothers**, led by mandolin virtuoso **Chris Thile**.

In the dance tent at the **Falls Stage** people kicked up their heels to the country and western sounds of Ottawa's **Gerry Wall** band (featuring the festival's own **Ana Miura**) followed by improvisational singer-songwriter **Peter Himmelman**. A big crowd gathered to hear **Justin Townes Earle**, the son of Friday's headliner, **Steve Earle**.

A standup bass player performing in the Justin Townes Earl Band.

The drummer for Steve Earle and the Dukes ready to go.

Friday, August 26
All three stages were again active throughout the warm Friday evening. Leading things off on the **CUPE-SCFP Main Stage**, with their foot-stomping, old-time fiddling and songs were **The B-Flat Sisters** (**Kimberley Holmes** and **Sherryl Fitzpatrick**). In a change of pace from this rootsy start came singer **Dallas Green** (**City and Colour**) who attracted a large and enthusiastic audience. Closing out the evening to one of the weekend's largest crowds was New Orleans country, blues, and folk rock act **Steve Earle and the Dukes (& Duchesses)** featuring singer **Allison Moorer**. Between sets, **John Allaire** and **Jayme Stone** appeared on the **Moon Stage**.

The hillside in front of the **Ravenlaw Stage** also drew large, enthusiastic crowds. The evening's entertainment included creative drumming (on anything and everything!) from the Los Angeles ensemble **Street Drum Corps**. Veteran singer-songwriter **Garland Jeffreys** delivered a spirited performance of hits and new material. The U.S. festival-circuit favourites, upstate New York's **Gandalf Murphy & The Slambovian Circus of Dreams** also performed.

As an alternative to the big sounds on the main stage, the more intimate **Falls Stage** featured banjoist and world-music afficionado **Jayme Stone**, followed by the social commentary of deep-voiced American singer-songwriter **Vance Gilbert**.

Vance Gilbert appearing on the Falls Stage.

Bytown Ukelele Group (BUG) hosted a ukelele jam session on Saturday afternoon.

Saturday, August 27
Saturday Daytime Workshops

Afternoon workshops took place on the three smaller point stages on Saturday and Sunday. On the **Legacy Stage** the annual **Terry Penner Festival Choir** formed for two rehearsals Saturday and another Sunday, under the direction of **Lee Hayes**. Their final performance, originally slated for the **Slackwater Stage**, was moved to the Sunday 4:30 p.m. slot on the **CUPE-SCFP Main Stage** in keeping with the festival's tradition.

Ann Downey presented the Pass It Down: Banjo Basics session.

Also on the **Legacy Stage** a series of instrumental skills workshops were presented under the title **Pass It Down**. They included **Intro to Ukulele** with **The Little Stevies**, **Banjo Basics** with **Ann Downey**, **Don't You Put It In Your Mouth?** (tin whistle, nose flute, and kazoo with **Andy Daub**) and **I've Got Rhythm** with Ottawa drummer **Don Gibbons**.

On the **Heron Stage**, **Vance Gilbert** led the session **Judgement Day: Crash Course for Performers**. This was followed by the first part of a two-day **Music Olympics** featuring **Lynn Miles** and **Keith Glass**. **Old Traditions, New Songs** showcased **Rick Fines**, **Vance Gilbert** and **Jayme Stone**. An **Interview with Colin Hay** was led by **Joe Reilly**. **Song Maps** with **Orchid Ensemble & Kim Churchill** was the final session.

The intimate **Slackwater Stage** featured **Storytelling & Mythology** with **Anaïs Mitchell**, **Garland Jeffreys**, **Josiah** (of Gandalf Murphy and the Slambovian Circus); and two sessions of **Bluebird North** (presented by the **Songwriters Association of Canada**), the first featured **Lynn Miles**, **Jeremy Fisher** and **Dry River Caravan**; the second showcased **Rick Fines**, **Megan Jerome** and **Ana Miura**.

Late afternoon dancing.

Accompanied by all-day face-painting and crafts, programming at the **Kidzone** tent began with **Yoga for Big and Small** with **Sheila Craig**, delighting kids and adults with an imaginary camping trip to introduce yoga stretches and moves. An afternoon of rhythm activities began with the **Bang!** session with the **Street Drum Corps**, who made music on buckets and almost everything but actual drums. As well, **Leo Brooks** of Treefrog Percussion led a make-your-own drum workshop and rhythm jam session. Wabi-Sabi Textile artist **Carol Secord** led a create-your-own-art workshop, teaching the basics of felt making. The day ended with an imaginative, all-ages history of blues and jazz by **TJ Wheeler**.

A small tent near the community displays housed **Jam Sessions** open to anyone with a yen to join in on Saturday and Sunday afternoons. Saturday's lineup featured **Open Acoustic Folk Jam/Spirit of Rasputin's,** and a **Klezmer Extravaganza** led by **Don and Peter** of the **Sunday Ottawa Bagel Klezmer Jam**. **Arthur McGregor** of the **Ottawa Folklore Centre** hosted **Singable Songs** and **Ukulele Jam** with the **Bytown Ukulele Group** (BUG).

Again this year, **Arbour Environmental Shoppe's Sean Twomey** programmed an eclectic two days of **EnviroTent** lectures and workshops. Saturday's topics were **Go Solar and Make Money** with **Seanna and Steve Watson**; **Birth Options** with **Gillian Szolios** of **Ottawa Labour Support**; **Wild Edibles** with **Peggy Calder**; **Exploring Hogs Back Park** with the **Macoun Field Club**; and **Growing Gardeners: Gardening with Children** by **Geri Bilnick**.

Saturday Stages

The **CUPE-SCFP Main Stage** ran solidly from 2 p.m. until closing time. Veteran folk-blues finger-guitarist **Rick Fines** led things off, followed by singer-songwriter and master storyteller, **Steve Poltz**. Transitioning to the evening program, the **Street Drum Corps** got everyone on their feet with infectious beats. The audience grew steadily, attracted by indie-rock group **Rural Alberta Advantage**, followed by the hard-hitting political songs of **Tom Morello** (The Nightwatchman), and culminating with **Conor Oberst** and his roots-rock band **Bright Eyes** (joined for the final number by Tom Morello).

Between sets, the **Moon Stage** was the venue for **Spencer Scharf**, **TJ Wheeler**, **Kim Churchill** and **The Little Stevies**.

The **Ravenlaw Stage** operated steadily from 1:30 p.m. until 11:00 p.m., with offerings from around the world through sets by Memphis bluesman **TJ Wheeler**, Australia's **The Little Stevies**, New York duo **Chris Brown & Kate Fenner**, and Californian **Matt Costa**. By 7:30 p.m., the hillside bowl was packed for Polish-Canadian singer-songwriter **Basia Bulat** and on into the late evening with Australian musician **Colin Hay**, famous as the vocalist for the rock band **Men at Work**.

The **Falls Stage** dance tent started the day getting people up with an **Intro to Contra Dancing** featuring Ottawa's **Old Sod Band**. The dance-beat continued with Montreal's Havana-inspired **Doc Weiss** and band, Victoria, B.C. folk-rockers **Jon and Roy**, folk-country-rock band **The Wooden Sky**, the harmonies of **Madison Violet** (**Brenley MacEachern** and **Lisa MacIsaac** – this year's **Galaxie Supernova Award** winners), **JJ Grey & Mofro**, blending southern rock, blues and Florida swamp soul, and young guitar sensation **Kim Churchill**. The last act was **Lazybones** (East Coast duo **Matt Wells** and **Tim MacNeill** and their

The Steel Drum Corps banging out rhythms on the Ravenlaw Stage.

The audience applauds on Saturday afternoon.

hillbilly-reggae style kitchen party). **Lazybones** replaced the American performer **J. Mascis** who was prevented from attending the festival by hurricane-related travel difficulties.

Sunday, August 28
Sunday Daytime Workshops
The **Terry Penner Festival Choir** held its third rehearsal on the **Legacy Stage**, along with more of the **Pass it Down** series including **Intro to Harmonica** with **Catriona Sturton**, **Intro to Ukulele** with **The Little Stevies**, **Sea Shanty Singalong** with **Chris Ricketts**, **Accordian** with **Megan Jerome**, **I've Got Rhythm** with **Don Gibbons** and **Delta Blues Basics** with **Rick Fines**.

The **Heron Stage** was the scene of the second day of the **Music Olympics**. The events included an interview with Newfoundlander **Sean McCann** by **Joe Reilly**, and **The Write Way** workshop with Canadian singer-songwriters **Jimmy Rankin**, **Bruce Robison** and **Serena Ryder**. This was followed by another interview by **Joe Reilly,** this time with **Thurston Moore**.

The Envirodish crew hard at work.

The **Slackwater Stage** workshops began with **Cigar Box Guitar Jam-Along** with **TJ Wheeler**, **My Home Town** with **Nils Edenloff** of Rural Alberta Advantage and Halifax's **Steve Poltz**. The fun continued with **Sirens with Strings** with **Madison Violet** and **Basia Bulat**; **Southern Folk** with Ottawa's **Lynne Hanson**, **David Wax Museum** and Texans **Kelly Willis** and **Hayes Carll**; and **Together & Apart** with **The Little Stevies** and **Chris Brown & Kate Fenner**.

The **Kidzone** featured a workshop with American improvisational singer-songwriter **Peter Himmelman** where the participants wrote a song. **Sophie Latreille** of **Fire Weavers** led a **Poi Workshop** for kids of all ages to learn some moves with poi (Maori-inspired performance instruments) and to make poi to take home from recycled materials. After rehearsing a couple of lively tunes with **Brian Sanderson**, kids of all ages took to the site with the annual **Sunshine Parade** (accompanied by a tuba and a bass drum). Buffeted by strong winds, everyone hunkered down after the parade, and did origami and finger braiding in the shelter of the tent.

Jam Sessions included a **Storytellers Story Swap** led by **Ottawa Storytellers**; a **Celtic Session** with **Daev Clysdale**, **Paul Hawtin** and **Alexis MacIsaac**; a singalong session led by **Almonte Trad Sing**; and the open-to-everyone **Carleton Tavern Appalachian Jam Session**. Jam session participants also performed for the hard-working volunteers at the **EnviroDish** tent that afternoon. The **Klezmer** group entertained for the volunteers on Friday and the **Ukulele** group performed for them on Saturday night.

Sunday's **EnviroTent** workshops were **The Wisdom of Trees** with Algonquin elder **Albert Dumont**, **DIY Bike Repair** with **Mark Rehder**, **Climate Change** with **Helene Maynard (Climate Project Canada)**, **The Clean Energy Future** with

Volunteers attending to equipment for the CUPE-SCFP Main Stage.

The Levon Helm Band closed the festival with panache.

Adam Harris (**Ecology Ottawa**), and **Is Being Green a Moral Issue?** with **Kathryn Guindon** (**Green Sacred Spaces**).

Sunday Stages

With a sudden cool front and threats of rain, daytime audiences were somewhat sparse, although the evening's programming, especially the lure of headliner **Levon Helm**, brought larger crowds. Many sported ski jackets in the chill of the evening.

The **CUPE-SCFP Main Stage** ran steadily from 1 p.m., starting with **Lazybones**, continuing with Californian experimental band **Pepper Rabbit**, Canadian folk-pop troubadour **Jeremy Fisher**, and concluding with the annual performance of the **Terry Penner Festival Choir**. The evening lineup featured Newfoundlander **Sean McCann**, Texan singer-songwriter **Hayes Carll**, and American country-music duo **Kelly Willis & Bruce Robison**. The festival drew to a rollicking close with the eclectic **Levon Helm Band**. It was led by the legendary drummer and member of **The Band**. This group was renowned for being the backup band for Bob Dylan.

Between sets, the **Moon Stage** showcased Ottawa's **Anders Drerup**, and **Alex Boyd & Ian Sabourin** (from Ottawa band The Riot Police). A **Volunteer Recognition** presentation by Volunteer Manager **Emily Addison** awarded five-, ten-and fifteen-year volunteer pins. Singer **Rick Fines** did a set before the presentation of the **Galaxie Rising Stars Program Award** to **Madison Violet** (**Brenley MacEachern** and **Lisa MacIsaac**).

The **Ravenlaw Stage** lineup featured Ottawa's **The Riot Police**, Toronto singer-songwriter **Royal Wood**, and **Orchid Ensemble**, which blended ancient musical instruments and traditions from China and beyond. Boston-based quartet **David Wax Museum** led the crowd in a conga-line with their catchy Mexican-American rhythms.

JJ Grey & Mofro get down in the Falls Stage Dance Tent.

Also performing were songwriter and multi-instrumentalist **Joseph Arthur**, singer-songwriter **Joe Pug**, and east coast singer-songwriter **Jimmy Rankin** of the Rankin Family.

Starting mid-afternoon, the **Falls Stage** presented ways to keep people warm, starting with **Intro to Cajun Dance** featuring **Ball and Chain**, followed by a steady stream of talented singers who made the crowd forget about the cool weather. Also included were sets by locals **Lynne Hanson**, **Anders Drerup** and **Kelly Prescott**; Vermont-born, world-traveller **Anaïs Mitchell**; Canadians **Catherine MacLellan** and **Lynn Miles**; American alt-rocker, singer-guitarist **Thurston Moore**; and Ontario indie-star **Serena Ryder**.

Many plastic water bottles were saved thanks to the free filtered water.

Sophie Latreille of the Fire Weavers lit up the night.

A packed audience enjoys a performance in the Falls Stage Dance Tent.

The artisans remained a very popular aspect of the festival experience.

After a stormy day we were blessed with a beautiful sunset.

The final ParticiPaint mural for 2011.

Year 19 – 2012
Freewheelin' at Hogs Back Park!

For five freewheelin' days, folk fans flocked in record numbers to the 2012 Ottawa Folk Festival, in its second year at **Hogs Back Park**. Headliners included **Lindsey Buckingham**, **Bon Iver**, **Great Big Sea**, **Kathleen Edwards**, **Dan Mangan** and **Patrick Watson**.

Executive Director Mark Monahan addresses questions from the media.

Executive Director **Mark Monahan** was happy to report that the attendance had doubled from the previous year to between 25,000 and 30,000 visitors. This was the highest attendance for the festival, and did not include the workshop-centred free programming that attracted an additional 4,000 to 5,000 visitors. The weather ranged from cloudless skies to cloudbursts and from warm to cool temperatures, but the spirits were not dampened by inclement weather on Friday and Saturday.

"The combination of free programming plus the major acts we brought in resulted in a very successful year," said Monahan. "Fans really enjoyed the changes we made to the festival site, so we hope to continue to improve and to build on this success."

A new presenting sponsor, TELUS, came on board this year. "TELUS is pleased to have supported such a remarkable event – from the tremendous fan turn-out to the incredible performances of all the talented artists," said TELUS Vice-President **Michael Sangster**. "The Ottawa Folk Festival truly brought the community together in an unforgettable and enjoyable fashion. What a fantastic way to finish the summer."

Admission was free on the west side of the park, which was the location of the food vendors, beer garden, the Artisan Village and the info tent. The free area also included the ever-popular **Kidzone,** the funky **Dance Tent** and the **EnviroTent**, which hosted informative presentations about all things environmental and living green. Performance spaces for workshops and free concerts included the **PSAC-AFPC Stage**, the **Slackwater Stage**, the **Legacy Stage** and the **Workshops on the Point** area. The free workshops in this area were programmed by the Ottawa Folklore Centre.

Patrons became more used to electronic ticketing in its second year.

Tickets were needed for the east side, which included three large, well-equipped stages: the **CUPE-SCFP Main Stage**, the **Ravenlaw Stage** and the **Tartan Homes Stage**.

Sustainability remained an important aspect of the festival, with green features such as reusable dishes, compost and recycling services, and a policy excluding the sale of plastic water bottles. You could fill your own water bottle at one of many water stations. At the **EnviroTent**, there were a variety of earth-minded workshops on topics such as natural cosmetics, wild edibles, solar power, natural healing and more. In the first-ever **Envirocafe**, festival goers relaxed in bistro seating and enjoyed refreshments from vendors such as B. Goods Bakery.

A **Community Tent** gave people a chance to learn about public awareness campaigns and not-for-profit organizations working to inform and improve the Ottawa community.

At the **General Store**, festival goers could pick up Ottawa Folk Festival souvenirs, as well as CDs, T-shirts and posters from performing artists. The **Artisan Village** continued to play a vital role in the festival, enhancing the atmosphere and giving people a chance to bring home hand-crafted treasures such as groovy tie-dyed T-shirts and custom-made jewellery.

A raised deck was provided for those in wheelchairs and their companions.

The **Legacy Stage** hosted a variety of interesting hands-on workshops, including yodelling, breakdancing, beatboxing, and sessions on how to play the oud (a lute-type instrument used for Arabic music), mandolin and bouzouki. "Folk music isn't just people playing banjos," said Meredith Luce, coordinator of the workshop series at the festival during an interview in the *Ottawa Metro*. "Folk music is what grows out of community experience and the resources available."

The times they are a-changin' and the festival embraced the latest technology. Festival attendees shared their comments and pics in an online blog on the festival website. There's an app for that! You could download a free app to share photos and create calendars.

The *Ottawa Citizen* hosted The Digital Lounge, an online space that featured exclusive videos, interviews, reviews and live performances. On-site at the festival, you and your friends could have a photo taken at the Digital Lounge Booth and appear online as a daily front-page cover. What fun!

Many smartphones were raised high during the festival to record video and images as well. By comparison, at the first Ottawa Folk Festival mobile phones were bulky items about the size of a brick that had to be recharged constantly. And digital cameras were not yet widely available for consumers.

The Ottawa Folk Festival was grateful for the support of TELUS as well as two major sponsors, 14 official sponsors and suppliers, five hotel partners, an environmental partner and six government funders.

This year's sponsors included TELUS, CUPE-SCFP, PSAC-AFPC, Aerographics Creative Services, Auto Trim and Signs, BOB-FM, Carleton University, Carleton University Students Association (CUSA), Galaxie, Live 88.5 FM, MediaPlus, Mill Street Brewery, the *Ottawa Citizen*, Ottawa Folklore Centre (a founding sponsor), Ravenlaw, Steve's Music Store, and Tartan Homes. Our environmental partner was Arbour Environmental Shoppe and hotel partners included Albert at Bay Suites Hotel, ARC The Hotel, Best Western Plus Victoria Park Suites, Delta Ottawa City Centre, and Lord Elgin Hotel.

I was assisted in the information gathering for this year's festival history by my dedicated note takers: **Corinne Baumgarten**, **Elizabeth De Castro**,

Roberta Della Picca and **Mary McHale**. Thanks for helping out and hanging in there through the downpours and sunshine!

Thursday, Sept. 6

The festival opened on a beautiful sunny evening with a soft breeze that carried aloft the acoustic guitar strains of "O Canada" played by **Arthur McGregor** on the **Ravenlaw Stage**. Thanks to Arthur for opening the festival on various stringed instruments each year for the past 19 years!

Arthur McGregor opens the festival with an acoustic version of "O Canada".

On the **Ravenlaw Stage**, singer-songwriter **Danny Michel**, who attracted an enthusiastic crowd, sang and performed with his band and guest **Quique Escamilla**. Many audience members, ranging from a seven-year-old boy to a senior citizen, sang along on lively tunes such as "Feather, Fur & Fin".

Matt Mays & El Torpedo enthralled the audience gathered at the **CUPE-SCFP Main Stage** with a rock-infused performance. Mays is a recipient of multiple Juno Awards and East Coast Music Awards, and has been described as "a cross between Rod Stewart, Leonard Cohen and Mike Reno." The band included four guitarists, a drummer and a keyboard player. Maritimers in the audience were particularly appreciative when a song was dedicated to them!

Matthew Good performed solo for more than an hour, accompanying himself on a 12-string guitar. He was very well received by the youngish crowd, some of whom knew his music from the days of the Matthew Good Band. Several audience members waved their cigarette lighters high in the air during his performance.

The sole performer on the **Tartan Homes Stage** was **Mirel Wagner**, a twenty-something blues-folk singer born in Ethiopia and raised in Finland. Her angelic voice and poetic lyrics mesmerized the intimate crowd.

Missy Burgess was one of the Ottawa performers at the festival.

The setting for the **PSAC-AFPC Stage** was idyllic, being fringed with fir trees set against a cloudless blue sky. **Kelly Sloan**, the winner of the **Galaxie Rising Stars Award**, delivered a 45-minute set of jazzy folk/soft rock music. This award is presented to local, emerging Canadian performers. Past recipients include **Megan Jerome**, **The Musettes** and **Joe Grass**. Ottawa singer-songwriter **Missy Burgess** was in fine voice and was accompanied by **Todd Snelgrove** on acoustic guitar. She gave a splendid performance of her evocative tunes of love and life.

The beautiful evening ended with a spirited performance under starry skies by **Ben Harper** on the **CUPE-SCFP Main Stage**. The charismatic American singer-songwriter and activist attracted a crowd of about 10,000 who stayed to dance and sway to his blend of folk, blues, funk and reggae.

Lindsey Buckingham gave a thrilling performance that included Fleetwood Mac material.

Ben Harper closed the CUPE-SCFP Stage on Thursday night with a magical performance.

Friday, Sept. 7

The entertainment on the **CUPE-SCFP Main Stage** opened with popular Ottawa singer-songwriter **Kathleen Edwards**, clad in a striking orange dress. Her sweet, country-tinged vocals were complemented by her band, which included **Jim Bryson** on guitar and keyboards, **Julie Fader** on backup vocals and **Gord Tough** on guitar. A large and enthusiastic crowd assembled under overcast skies to listen to her personal and heartfelt songs that ranged from mellow to upbeat.

Fans of classic rock band Fleetwood Mac were thrilled with the performance of **Lindsey Buckingham**. The 62-year-old American musician appeared solo, and easily won the crowd over with his personal stories, original material and Fleetwood Mac numbers. Hearing Buckingham play hits like "Go Your Own Way" made it hard to believe that the Fleetwood Mac *Rumours* album came out in 1977! Buckingham's amazing guitar playing wowed the ever-growing crowd and his charismatic performance closed the evening on a high note.

Alberta Cross was first up on the **Ravenlaw Stage**. This Brooklyn-based band rocked out to an animated crowd. Then came the upbeat acoustic solo musician **Old Man Luedecke**, who charmed the toe-tapping crowd with homegrown banjo-led tunes like "I Quit My Job". Despite his stage name, this native of Chester, Nova Scotia is in his mid-thirties. This is Old Man Luedecke's third year at the Ottawa Folk Festival and hopefully will not be his last.

On the **Tartan Homes Stage**, solo performer **Joe Horowitz** opened. Although sound bleed interfered somewhat with his music, the New Yorker persevered with songs of love, politics and social commentary while accompanying himself on acoustic guitar. Canadian folkies **Timber Timbre** followed with an interesting set from a group whose music has been described as "beautifully restrained blues from an alternate universe, which creates an atmosphere that is cinematic and spooky."

The **Pat Moore Trio** opened the evening's musical entertainment on the **PSAC-AFPC Stage**. Singer-songwriter **Pat Moore** appeared with her band, including amazing guitarist **Pat McLaughlin**, fresh from a Gram Parsons tribute concert tour of Australia, and veteran bass player **Ann Downey**. Moore's music melds elements of folk, bluegrass and country. Her beautiful voice was showcased in original tunes such as the fast-paced "Wrong Train", and an inspired cover of the Warren Zevon song "Carmelita". The four-piece band

Groovin' in the rain on Saturday.

Pat Moore's beautiful voice was showcased in a set with her band, the Pat Moore Trio.

the **Kingmakers** next performed a rolicking rockabilly set that had everyone dancing in the rain. A trumpet player named Miko added pizzazz to some of the numbers. **Brock Zeman**, an Ottawa Valley alt-country performer from Carleton Place, appeared with a tuneful three-piece band. His set was punctuated with intriguing lyrics and great storytelling.

Saturday, Sept. 8
Saturday and Sunday featured four stages of free programming that attracted impressive crowds of 4,000 to 5,000 people over the weekend. That is a larger attendance than we had at the first Ottawa Folk Festival in 1994!

Saturday was a rainy day at **Hogs Back Park**, but the crowds still came and braved the wet weather, which ranged from a drizzle to a heavy, pelting downpour. Folk fans dancing in the rain were as common a sight as those taking shelter under the colourful umbrellas dotting the crowds.

There were many ways for the community to participate in free activities this year. **Workshops on the Point** were programmed by the **Ottawa Folklore Centre**. Anyone could participate in themed jam sessions, hosted by individuals or groups from the Ottawa music community.

The **Kidzone** returned as it had every year of the festival's history, to offer all-ages interactive workshops, and specialty programming for children and youth. A **musical petting zoo** gave kids of all ages a chance to try out more than 100 instruments, including ones most people don't have a chance to experience, such as dulcimers and autoharps. Another fun venue, the **Dance Tent**, allowed participants to free form dance to musical accompaniment or learn styles ranging from breakdancing to Bollywood during short demonstrations.

CUPE-SCFP Main Stage

First up was **Joe Horowitz** in his second appearance at the festival. This American singer-songwriter who is also a professional golfer, performed his bluesy, acoustic songs. One memorable number was "Daisy's Diner" a tune set in small town Louisiana. With the rain over, Albertan **Corb Lund** followed with a country-flavoured set. Lund, who was accompanied by his band, was happy to announce that his latest album, *Cabin Fever*, was
number one in Canada. His music drew an enthusiastic response from the huge crowd. Yee haw!

Wind and rain preceded a performance by the **Great Lake Swimmers**. The Toronto band drew a large crowd that didn't run for cover despite the weather. Their melodic rock charmed the onlookers, who enjoyed listening to material from the band's last two albums. The Great Lakes Swimmers were a prelude to a natural watery progression, the closing act of the night, **Great Big Sea**.

The rain had already stopped when the hugely popular Newfoundland band **Great Big Sea** was greeted by a great big audience of about 7,000 for their first Ottawa Folk Festival appearance. "We finally made it to the Ottawa Folk Festival," proclaimed lead singer **Alan Doyle**, as the band has performed to large crowds at many other venues in the nation's capital. Great Big Sea was in fine form and the audience danced and sang along to their interpretations of traditional East Coast music till the park closed for the night.

Bright lights, small city.

Ravenlaw Stage

The fun began with **Nudie and the Turks**. This P.E.I.-based band specializes in tunes with a classic country sound and a contemporary spin. The band is led by a fully-clothed guitar player and lead singer named Nudie, who spins amusing yarns between songs. The set included songs about small-town P.E.I., a yodelling tune and even a ditty about Ottawa. The pedal steel guitar was an especially appealing element of the music.

Also appearing was American **Kina Grannis** who is known for her sensitive lyrics and emotive vocals. Her straight-ahead folk was accompanied by a cello player. She amused the crowd by taking a video of the audience. Her closing number, "Message from the Heart," was sweet and philosophical. **Paul Langlois**, who is also a guitarist with **The Tragically Hip**, performed a rocking set with his band consisting of two guitarists and a drummer. A few of the songs, however, veered into folk territory.

There was a huge buzz before the festival about the artist known as **LP** (**Laura Pergolizzi**). She is a songwriter and recently turned performer who has penned material for Rihanna and the Backstreet Boys. At the festival she lived up to all the hullabaloo. A small woman with a mop of dark curly hair, this New Yorker who lives in L.A. was accompanied by a six-piece band as she sang and played a ukulele. LP easily won the audience over with her incredible voice and high-energy vibe as she worked her way through original material such as the monster hit "Into the Wild" and awesome covers from artists such as Roy Orbison and Beyonce.

Tartan Homes Stage

The day's festivities began in the mid-afternoon under heavy rain. Umbrellas were open across the audience as hardy festival goers hunkered down to hear Newfoundland band **The Once**. This popular Canadian trio includes a female vocalist and two musicians who play acoustic instruments (guitar, mandolin and violin). Their repertoire spanned traditional Maritime music, original tunes and inspired covers, and was warmly received by the audience.

Next up were the **Abrams Brothers**, two Canadian siblings who sang and played a variety of instruments. The duo included John on guitar, mandolin, keyboards and percussion, and James on violin. The crowd loved their mix of bluegrass, country and folk.

There were also blues-inspired sets that afternoon

from Texas performer **Guy Forsyth** and American singer-songwriter **Cassie Taylor**. Forsyth performed solo, and played a vintage guitar with internal amplification. He really shone with numbers that had a bluesy, gospel feel. Taylor is the striking, red-haired daughter of blues musician Otis Taylor. She played electric bass guitar and sang, performing with her band in an inspired rhythm-and-blues influenced set. For the finale number "Iko Iko", a traditional News Orleans song, Taylor and her band were joined by the **Abrams Brothers**, and members of the **Rag and Bone Puppet Theatre**.

In the evening, the music was rockier. **Hooded Fang** proved themselves to be masters of indie pop. The Toronto-based group energized the audience with a frenzied guitar-driven set. The alternative four-piece rock band **Yukon Blonde** drew a mostly young crowd that thoroughly enjoyed their high-octane performance. The set from this B.C. band was punctuated by soaring four-part harmonies.

Mari Wellman and Rosalie Reynolds took good care of the volunteers.

PSAC-AFPC Stage

TJ Wheeler & James Cohen, acoustic guitarists who combine influences spanning blues, jazz, flamenco and rock, were up first. They were followed by a set with influential English folk guitarist and singer **John Smith**.

Slackwater Stage

The performances included a set by **Sincerely Yours**. The **Guitar Hero** session was hosted by Ottawa blues musician **John Carroll**, who traded licks with an impressive group of guitar heroes: **Danny Michel**, **Michael Jerome Browne** and **Luke Doucet**. The group also shared stories about their musical adventures. The session **Somebody Else** included sets by **LP**, **Danny Michel** and **Brock Zeman**. The day wound down with a set from **Les Stroud**, a blues-influenced singer-songwriter and environmentalist, who is well known for his television show *Survivorman*.

Melissa McClelland, one-half of the duo Whitehorse along with Luke Doucet, performed at the festival.

Legacy Stage

On Saturday morning and afternoon there were live broadcasts of two long-standing CKCU-FM radio shows: *Canadian Spaces* and *The Back 40*. **Chopper McKinnon**, the creator and host of *Canadian Spaces*, hosted a live version of the longest-running folk show on Canadian community radio. His guests included Ottawa Folk Festival co-founder **Chris White** and **Mark Delorme**, a long-time production manager of the festival.

Chopper interviewed White about his exemplary contributions to Canadian folk music as White was receiving the **2012 Helen Verger Award**. White chatted about the origins of the folk festival and

Chris White receives the Helen Verger Award from Mark Monahan, Executive Director of the Ottawa Folk Festival.

the impact that three major influences, *Canadian Spaces*, Rasputin's and the Ottawa Folklore Centre, had on the local folk community.

In 1993, White co-founded the Ottawa Folk Festival with **Max Wallace** and was the festival's Artistic Director for 16 years. In a news release, White said he had "met an amazing number of talented and really nice people along the way, and I dedicate this award to them." Chris was involved in countless musical and community events in Ottawa, and in recent years served as the co-host of *Canadian Spaces*.

This was Chopper's last appearance at the Ottawa Folk Festival. Sadly, Chopper passed away in March 2013 after hosting *Canadian Spaces* for 33 years. Many people believe the Ottawa Folk Festival would not have come to fruition without his unfailing support and encouragement. Chopper hosted many live broadcasts of *Canadian Spaces* over the history of the festival. He co-hosted the evening main stage with **Karen Flanagan McCarthy** for 15 years and was well loved by folk festival audiences.

It was a testament to Chopper that he was able to continue with the show on a volunteer basis for over three decades. He hosted *Canadian Spaces* right up until his death in 2013 in what would have been the 33rd year of the show. Luckily the show lives on with host Chris White and guest hosts.

At noon, **The Back 40** live show was hosted by **Ron Moores**. The long-running show features traditional country, western and bluegrass music. Moores supplements the tunes with live performances and plenty of interviews, taped live in the studio or on location at musical venues across North America.

In the afternoon, people took part in participatory workshops including **Beatboxing Basics** with **Julia Dales**; **Rise Up Singing** (the title is taken from a popular book of singalong folk songs), led by **Arthur McGregor**; **Storytelling** with **Ruthanne Edward**; and **Harmonica 101** with **Catriona Sturton**.

Somebody's gotta do it and these volunteers took up the challenge.

Jam Sessions

The **Appalachian Jam** was cancelled due to rain, but there was a **Celtic Jam** and the **Terry Penner Festival Choir** came together for a rehearsal.

EnviroTent

In the **EnviroTent**, workshops were provided on topics including German New Medicine, The Otesha Project (a charity providing bicycle tours for young people), Wild Edibles, and Healing & Singing Folk Music.

Kidzone

Crafts, games, performances and workshops were available for kids of all ages.

Dance Tent

During the day, sessions were provided on two divergent art forms: breakdancing and stepdancing. **Saul Williams**, the American singer, musician, and hip-hop poet, was interviewed by journalist, musician and poet **Ian Keteku**, and performed some of his riveting poetry.

Gordie MacKeeman & His Rhythm Boys provided a stellar set in their second festival appearance. They were later presented with the **Galaxie Rising Stars Supernova Award** for outstanding live performance at the festival. This P.E.I. band of four seasoned performers combined bluegrass and country influences with excellent showmanship and lots of fun. This session, originally planned for the PSAC-AFPC Stage, was moved due to the rain.

The entertainment ended with a set from the American singer-songwriter and guitarist **Raúl Midón** whose music reflects jazz, blues, R&B and folk influences.

Sunday, Sept. 9
Sunday proved to be mostly overcast and cool but the crowds came in record numbers and enjoyed all the festival had to offer.

CUPE-SCFP Main Stage

The **Terry Penner Festival Choir** is named for the late Terry Penner, who co-founded of the **Ottawa Folklore Centre** with her husband **Arthur McGregor**. The choir is made up of volunteer participants who unite to celebrate the sheer joy of singing. This year's repertoire included "Wake Up" by Arcade Fire. The enthusiastic crowd loved the performance. The choir was sponsored by **Arthur McGregor** and **Hollis Morgan** who also provided acoustic accompaniment on guitar and dobro respectively.

Amy Helm, daughter of the late music legend Levon Helm, is an accomplished roots musician and vocalist in her own right. She performed a set infused with country and blues that included standards such as the Muddy Waters tune "The Life I Want" and original compositions like "I Lay Down". Helm's band, including members playing acoustic and electric guitars and drums, provided the perfect accompaniment for her gorgeous voice.

Double Juno Award-winning singer-songwriter **Dan Mangan**, who had recently returned from a tour in Europe, received a great response from the crowd. His band instrumentation included three electric guitars, an electric violin, drums, trumpet and

Scenes from the Terry Penner Festival Choir: instrumentalists Arthur McGregor, Alrick Huebener, Hollis Morgan; choir director Andy Rush; choir members Chipo Shambare, Missy Burgess & Lise Nickerson.

saxophone, while Mangan played acoustic guitar and sang. Mangan's set made it easy to see why he is becoming increasingly popular in Europe as well as in Canada.

The Galaxie Rising Stars Supernova Award was presented to **Gordie MacKeeman and His Rhythm Boys**. The four-member P.E.I. band was given a $1500 bursary, as well as potential airplay on the Galaxie music channels. "The competition for this award included some amazing talent," commented Ottawa musician and folk festival staffer Ana Miura. "Having seen Gordie MacKeeman and His Rhythm Boys at this year's Ottawa Folk Festival, I would say the jury got it right."

Singer-songwriter **Kelly Sloan** was presented with the **Galaxie Rising Stars Award,** which is presented annually to a local, emerging Canadian performer. Sloan is a classically trained singer with roots in the Ottawa Valley and has released two successful albums. Her music has been described as soul-infused folk, and country-roots rock. She is well-known for her expressive voice and riveting live performances.

Ravenlaw Stage

An electric violin punctuated the edgy country rock set of **Fiftymen**, adding to the band's sonic landscape of electric guitar, keyboards, banjo, drums and vocals. **Mark Michaud** was featured on electric guitar as the band performed catchy songs like "Let Me Not Be Forsaken".

Bombino, led by **Oram Moctar**, provided an upbeat world music sound. Moctar is a young, Tuareg guitarist born in Niger who was influenced by Saharan rock bands. To the delight of the audience, his band of three electric guitar players and a drummer (all dressed in traditional robes) really rocked out.

Said the Whale attracted a large, youngish audience that had a whale of a time. The Vancouver-based indie band entertained with a selection of memorable songs such as "Setting off Some Fire" and "Addicted to Technology".

The audience was treated to great vocals and spellbinding storytelling, demonstrating why the group won a Juno Award for Best Band in 2011.

Montreal singer-songwriter **Patrick Watson** performed with a large ensemble that included brass instruments, electric violin and keyboards, and exotic percussion instruments. The band's folky indie rock songs and Watson's appealing vocals were greatly appreciated by the large crowd who assembled to listen and dance along. Diverse elements included music from cowboy movies, choir boy-like backing vocals, Jimi Hendrix-style guitar riffs and classical violin!

Patrick Watson (centre) strikes a pose.

Tartan Stage

The first performers were **Gavin** and **Will** of the **Black Dogs**, two Ottawa lads who both sing and play stripped-down acoustic guitar. The songs were haunting, with shades of early Dylan and lovely arrangements. The audience included both of the performers' parents!

The world music set of **Haram** was heady Middle Eastern-jazz fusion music that attracted a large group of people who clapped to the rhythms and danced along. Soaring vocals were supported by an amazing array of instruments including doumbek (African drum), saxophone, trumpets, clarinet, fiddle, flute and lute.

Michael Jerome Browne opened with a wailing traditional Delta blues song that he co-wrote with his partner, **Bea Marcus**. Born in the U.S., Browne moved to Montreal with his parents and grew up immersed in the coffee house scene. He eventually mastered several instruments and attained an encyclopedic knowledge of American roots music. Browne's set encompassed original songs such as "Low Tide", written on Hornby Island, B.C., and traditional blues, jazz, Appalachian and Creole tunes.

Winnipeg singer-songwriter **John K. Samson** is a member of the folk-indie band **The Weakerthans**. In this solo outing, he appeared with a guitarist/backup vocalist. Many in the crowd were familiar with his material and enthusiastically sang along to tunes such as "I Hate Winnipeg".

Belle Starr featured three beautiful women fiddlers/vocalists who are "a whole lot country". Stepdancer, fiddler and singer **Stephanie Cadman** hails from Ottawa. The trio is rounded out by **Miranda Mulholland** (a member of **Great Lakes Swimmers**), and **Kendel Carson**, who also plays guitar. This incarnation of the band included two male instrumentalists. Belle Starr was the belle of the festival, entrancing the audience as the band members worked their way through a set that included original tunes and covers from artists such as Lynn Miles and Dolly Parton.

The highly anticipated indie folk act **Whitehorse** closed the evening on this stage. Whitehorse is husband and wife duo **Luke Doucet** and **Melissa McClelland**. They nimbly accompanied themselves on guitars, keyboards and percussion, frequently switching instruments. Quite a logistical and artistic feat! They delivered a lively and moving set of original tunes such as "Get Me Through December" and covers like "I'm on Fire" from Bruce Springsteen.

PSAC-AFPC Stage

Sessions on the **PSAC-AFPC Stage** included Ottawa alt rockers **Full Tipped Sleeve**, beat box specialist **Julia Dales**, and popular Ottawa Valley bluegrass band **Jan Purcell & Pine Road**.

The Kitchen Party session was a hoot, and showcased "down home" songs from bass player **Ann Downey**, harmonica whiz **Catriona Sturton**, folkie **Birdie Whyte** and her husband, blues singer-songwriter **John Carroll**.

The audience was thrilled to see the American folk supergroup **Red Horse** (**John Gorka, Eliza Gilkyson** and **Lucy Kaplansky**) perform.

It must be a folk festival!

Slackwater Stage

Musician **Jill Hennessy** is well known as an actress in *Law & Order, Crossing Jordan* and *Robocop 3*. In an interview session, Hennessy spoke about her early career in Edmonton where she was a busker, her recent projects, and her twin sister Robi who is also a musician. Hennessy's career has led her to live in the U.S. but she still enjoys working as a musician and performing in Canada when she can. "Music is a joy," said Hennessy who believes social media has opened up a whole new world for artists because they can receive immediate feedback from fans. She accompanied herself on acoustic guitar and performed songs such as "Ghosts in My Head", the title track of her 2010 CD.

Arthur McGregor, Nudie of **Nudie & the Turks**,

Eliza Gilkyson and **The Once** participated in **Any Way You String It**. The stringed instruments included guitars, banjos and mandolins. McGregor opened with an instrumental banjo tune and later played an acoustic version of the American national anthem. Nudie countered with a Sam Cooke folk/gospel number. Gilkyson asked **John Gorka** and **Lucy Kaplansky** to join her on "Death in Arkansas" and later played the title track from her album, "Roses at the End of Time". Three members of **The Once** demonstrated their mandolin and guitar skills and were joined by Nudie on "I'll Be Your Baby Tonight". The session wound down with Kaplansky leading a sing-along song, "Slouching Towards Bethlehem".

Hellos & Goodbyes was a session chronicling songs depicting beginnings and endings, and featured **Said the Whale**, **John Smith** and **Lucy Kaplansky**. Tunes included "I'll Be Saying Farewell" from Said the Whale, a Scottish folk song from Smith, and a Mother's Day ditty from Kaplansky.

Pat McLaughlin, on mandolin, joins others for the City Slickers, Country Songs session.

The City Slickers, **Country Songs** session was hosted by Ottawa's **Pat Moore**, who summed up things nicely when she said "Just because we live in the city, doesn't mean we don't have country in our blood." She was joined by city slickers **Gordie MacKeeman and His Rhythm Boys**, **Pat McLaughlin**, harmonica player **Catriona Sturton**, **Amy Helm** and **Don Littleton**. Highlights included Moore's "Take It to Heart", Helm's Woody Guthrie cover "I Ain't Got No Home" and a humorous ditty about the Wheel of Fortune television show by Sturton.

The **Wild Things** session featured the wild sounds of **Yukon Blonde**, **Black Dogs** and **Belle Starr**. According to workshop coordinator **Meredith Luce**, this session was overflowing with talent. It featured all three members of **Belle Starr**, a group of Ontario women who blend exquisite harmonies and pop sensibilities into their folk music, and the serene songs of Ottawa duo **Black Dogs**. They were joined by three members of Yukon Blonde, who performed acoustic versions of their raucous and danceable music.

Legacy Stage

In the **Guitar Masterclass**, host **John Carroll** and **Michael Jerome Browne** discussed blues and country music artists such as Robert Johnson, Leadbelly and Big Bill Broonzy. Carroll, Browne and guests showcased their guitar skills.

Jody Benjamin led the **Yodelling** session, discussing techniques and tricks, and encouraging the crowd to participate. Benjamin enlightened the curious crowd about the Jimmie Rodgers style of yodelling, cowboy yodelling and the "epiglottic click". People bravely yodelled along while Benjamin performed songs like "Country Sweetheart".

During the **Mandolin & Bouzouki** session, members of Newfoundland's **The Once** provided a thoughtful seminar on these two closely related instruments. The session combined instruction and information with demonstrative performances.

Jam Sessions

A **Bytown Ukulele** workshop was held in the early afternoon. The **Terry Penner Festival Choir** had its final rehearsal.

EnviroTent

In the **EnviroTent**, there were talks including Fair Trade Ottawa, Earth Quilt: Mother of Makers, Saving Ottawa's Ash Trees, Going Solar, and

Natural Cosmetics.

Kidzone

More crafts, games, performances and workshops were available for the little ones and their companions.

Dance Tent

People of all ages participated in the **Bollywood Dance** session led by **Kuljit Sodhi** of **Galitcha**. The session featured a rousing, hand-clapping, foot-stomping hour of fun set to Bollywood music sponsored by **Studio Mouvement** in Gatineau, Quebec. An **Elaborhythm Dance Session** was also held later in the afternoon.

An early detail from the festival mural.

Monday, Sept. 10
Ravenlaw Stage

The entertainment began in a big way with **The Low Anthem**, a six-piece indie folk ensemble from Providence, Rhode Island. It featured male and female vocals and an eclectic array of instruments including guitars, trumpets, unusual string and percussion instruments, and drums. The band opened with a slow ballad featuring New Orleans-style trumpet and progressed through a very interesting set of traditional and contemporary numbers, such as the eerie "Ghost Woman Blues".

The Big Dipper shone softly in the sky during the performance of **Hey Rosetta!**, a popular indie band from St. John's, Newfoundland. **The Lumineers** were scheduled to perform but had to cancel. Luckily, Hey Rosetta! was able to fill in on short notice. The band has a reputation for great songwriting, and layered instrumentation that includes keyboards and a variety of stringed instruments. This incarnation included three guitarists, a fiddler, cello player and drummer. The set inspired many moods via poetic lyrics and tunes ranging from dreamy to rocky. A colourful light show that would have been right at home in a stadium served as a backdrop. Confetti rather than rain showered down at the end of the concert!

CUPE-SCFP Main Stage

Anaïs Mitchell
It was refreshing to hear the deceptively sweet and simple music of **Anaïs Mitchell** who performed with a small ensemble. Her performance contrasted nicely with the large, mostly male bands performing the rest of the evening. In her early thirties, the American singer-songwriter has four successful albums and has been described as the queen of modern folk music. This was Mitchell's first date as the opening act for **Bon Iver**. The two groups also performed together in other venues over the following week.

Bon Iver was the band many of the festival goers were itching to see. By the time the American band hit the stage, the crowds swelled to become the festival's largest-ever audience, an impressive 12,000. Mysterious burlap-type material was draped in unusual shapes over tall columns on the stage, which created interesting patterns during the light show. Front man **Justin Vernon** created the first Bon Iver album by himself in an isolated Wisconsin cabin, but he soon found musical comrades to help him create a lush, layered sound. At the folk festival, Bon Iver gloried in instrumentation including brass, woodwinds, a variety of stringed instruments and percussion. The songs were interesting but not always easy to understand on first listening. Many in the crowd seemed familiar with the music and sang along however. The set concluded with a cut from Bon Iver's first album, *For Emma, Forever Ago*.

And so ended the most highly attended Ottawa Folk Festival ever!

www.ingramcontent.com/pod-product-compliance
Lightning Source LLC
Chambersburg PA
CBHW041036020526
44118CB00043BA/2997